ISAIAH'S PROPHECY
Light for All Mankind
VOLUME I

PUBLISHERS
Watchtower Bible and Tract Society of New York, Inc.
International Bible Students Association
Brooklyn, New York, U.S.A.

First Printing in English:
5,000,000 Copies

Unless otherwise indicated, Scripture quotations
are from the modern-language
New World Translation of the Holy Scriptures—With References

Isaiah's Prophecy—Light for All Mankind I
English (*ip-1-E*)

Made in the United States of America

CONTENTS

CHAPTER   PAGE

1 An Ancient Prophet With a Modern Message   5

2 A Father and His Rebellious Sons   11

3 "Let Us Set Matters Straight"   22

4 Jehovah's House Lifted Up   37

5 Jehovah Humiliates Self-Exalted Ones   49

6 Jehovah God Has Mercy on a Remnant   61

7 Woe to the Unfaithful Vineyard!   73

8 Jehovah God Is in His Holy Temple   87

9 Trust in Jehovah in the Face of Adversity   101

10 The Promise of a Prince of Peace   117

11 Woe to the Rebels!   133

12 Do Not Be Afraid of the Assyrian   144

13 Salvation and Rejoicing
Under the Messiah's Reign   157

14 Jehovah Humbles an Arrogant City   172

15 Jehovah's Counsel Against the Nations   189

CHAPTER	PAGE
16 Trust in Jehovah for Guidance and Protection	208
17 "Babylon Has Fallen!"	215
18 Lessons About Unfaithfulness	230
19 Jehovah Profanes the Pride of Tyre	244
20 Jehovah Is King	259
21 Jehovah's Hand Becomes High	271
22 Isaiah Foretells Jehovah's 'Strange Deed'	287
23 Keep in Expectation of Jehovah	302
24 No Help From This World	316
25 The King and His Princes	329
26 "No Resident Will Say: 'I Am Sick'"	342
27 Jehovah Pours Out Indignation Upon the Nations	356
28 Paradise Restored!	369
29 A King's Faith Is Rewarded	382
30 "Comfort My People"	398

CHAPTER ONE

An Ancient Prophet With a Modern Message

Isaiah 1:1

WHO today does not yearn for relief from the problems that face mankind? Yet, how often our longings go unfulfilled! We dream of peace, but we are plagued by war. We cherish law and order, but we cannot stem the rising tide of robbery, rape, and murder. We want to trust our neighbor, but we have to lock our doors for protection. We love our children and try to instill wholesome values in them, but all too often we watch helplessly as they succumb to the unwholesome influence of their peers.

2 We might well agree with Job, who stated that man's short life is "glutted with agitation." (Job 14:1) This seems especially so today, for society is deteriorating on a scale never before seen. One U.S. senator observed: "The Cold War is now over, but in a tragic sense, the world has now been made safer for ethnic, tribal, and religious vengeance and savagery. . . . We have watered down our moral standards to the point where many of our youth are confused, discouraged and in deep trouble. We are reaping the harvest of parental neglect, divorce, child abuse, teen pregnancy, school dropouts, illegal drugs, and streets full of violence. It's as if our house, having survived the great earthquake we call the Cold War, is now being eaten away by termites."

1, 2. (a) What sad state of affairs do we see in the world today? (b) How did one U.S. senator express his concern about the deterioration of society?

Who Was Isaiah?

MEANING OF NAME:
"Salvation of Jehovah"

FAMILY:
Married, with at least two sons

PLACE OF RESIDENCE:
Jerusalem

YEARS OF SERVICE:
No less than 46 years, from about 778 B.C.E. to sometime after 732 B.C.E.

CONTEMPORARY KINGS OF JUDAH:
Uzziah, Jotham, Ahaz, Hezekiah

CONTEMPORARY PROPHETS:
Micah, Hosea, Oded

3 However, we are not left without hope. Some 2,700 years ago, God inspired a man of the Middle East to utter a series of prophecies that have special meaning for our day. These messages are recorded in the Bible book bearing that prophet's name—Isaiah. Who was Isaiah, and why can we say that his prophecy, recorded almost three millenniums ago, provides light for all mankind today?

A Righteous Man in Turbulent Times

4 In the first verse of his book, Isaiah introduces himself as *"the son of Amoz,"** and he tells us that he served as God's prophet *"in the days of Uzziah, Jotham, Ahaz and Hezekiah, kings of Judah."* **(Isaiah 1:1)** This would mean that Isaiah continued as God's prophet to the nation of Judah for no less than 46 years, likely beginning at the end of Uzziah's reign—about the year 778 B.C.E.

---

* Isaiah's father, Amoz, is not to be confused with Amos who prophesied at the beginning of Uzziah's reign and who wrote the Bible book bearing his name.

---

3. What Bible book especially offers hope for the future?
4. Who was Isaiah, and when did he serve as Jehovah's prophet?

Isaiah and his wife made worship of God a family matter

5 Compared with what we know about some other prophets, we know little about the personal life of Isaiah. We do know that he was a married man and that he referred to his wife as "the prophetess." (Isaiah 8:3) According to McClintock and Strong's *Cyclopedia of Biblical, Theological, and Ecclesiastical Literature,* this designation indicates that Isaiah's married life "was not only consistent with his vocation, but that it was intimately interwoven with it." It may well be that, similar to some other godly women of ancient Israel, Isaiah's wife had her own prophetic assignment.—Judges 4:4; 2 Kings 22:14.

6 Isaiah and his wife had at least two sons, each given a name with prophetic significance. The firstborn, Shear-jashub, accompanied Isaiah when he delivered God's messages to wicked King Ahaz. (Isaiah 7:3) It is evident that Isaiah and his wife made worship of God a family matter—a fine example for married couples today!

7 Isaiah and his family lived during a turbulent period in Judah's history. Political unrest was common, bribery tainted the courts, and hypocrisy tore the religious fabric of society. The hilltops were covered with altars to false gods. Even some of the kings promoted pagan worship. Ahaz, for instance, not only tolerated idolatry among his subjects but personally engaged in it, making his own offspring "pass through the fire" in a ritual sacrifice to the Canaanite god Molech.* (2 Kings 16:3, 4; 2 Chronicles 28: 3, 4) And all of this took place among a people who were in a covenant relationship with Jehovah!—Exodus 19:5-8.

---

* Some say that to "pass through the fire" may simply indicate a purification ceremony. It seems, though, that in this context the phrase refers to a literal sacrifice. There is no question that child sacrifice was practiced by Canaanites and apostate Israelites.—Deuteronomy 12:31; Psalm 106:37, 38.

5, 6. What must have been true regarding Isaiah's family life, and why?
7. Describe conditions in Judah in Isaiah's day.

8 Commendably, some of Isaiah's contemporaries—including a few rulers—tried to promote true worship. Among them was King Uzziah, who did "what was upright in Jehovah's eyes." Still, during his reign the people were "sacrificing and making sacrificial smoke on the high places." (2 Kings 15:3, 4) King Jotham too "kept doing what was right in Jehovah's eyes." However, "the people were yet acting ruinously." (2 Chronicles 27:2) Yes, throughout much of Isaiah's prophetic ministry, the kingdom of Judah was in a deplorable spiritual and moral state. By and large, the people ignored any positive influence that came from their kings. Understandably, delivering God's messages to this stubborn people would not be an easy assignment. Nevertheless, when Jehovah posed the question, "Whom shall I send, and who will go for us?" Isaiah did not hesitate. He exclaimed: "Here I am! Send me."—Isaiah 6:8.

A Message of Salvation

9 Isaiah's name means "Salvation of Jehovah," and this could well be called the theme of his message. True, some of Isaiah's prophecies are of judgment. Still, the theme of salvation comes through loud and clear. Repeatedly, Isaiah related how in due time Jehovah would release the Israelites from captivity in Babylon, allowing a remnant to return to Zion and bring the land back to its former splendor. No doubt the privilege of speaking and writing prophecies concerning the restoration of his beloved Jerusalem gave Isaiah the greatest joy!

---

8. (a) What example did Kings Uzziah and Jotham set, and did the people follow their lead? (b) How did Isaiah show boldness in the midst of a rebellious people?

9. What is the meaning of Isaiah's name, and how does this relate to the theme of his book?

10 But what do these messages of judgment and salvation have to do with us? Happily, Isaiah does not prophesy simply for the benefit of the two-tribe kingdom of Judah. On the contrary, his messages have special significance for our day. Isaiah paints a glorious picture of how God's Kingdom will soon bring grand blessings to our earth. In this regard, a large portion of Isaiah's writings focuses on the foretold Messiah, who would rule as King of God's Kingdom. (Daniel 9:25; John 12:41) Surely it is no coincidence that the names Jesus and Isaiah express virtually the same thought, the name Jesus meaning "Jehovah Is Salvation."

11 Of course, Jesus was not born until some seven centuries after Isaiah's day. Yet, the Messianic prophecies contained in the book of Isaiah are so detailed and so accurate that they read like an eyewitness account of Jesus' life on earth. One source noted that in view of this, the book of Isaiah is sometimes called the "Fifth Gospel." Hence, it is hardly surprising that Isaiah was the Bible book most frequently quoted by Jesus and his apostles in order to make a clear identification of the Messiah.

12 Isaiah paints a glorious word picture of "new heavens and a new earth" wherein "a king will reign for righteousness itself" and princes will rule for justice. (Isaiah 32:1, 2; 65:17, 18; 2 Peter 3:13) Thus the book of Isaiah points to the heartwarming hope of God's Kingdom, under the Messiah Jesus Christ as enthroned King. What an encouragement for us to live each day in joyful expectation of "salvation by [Jehovah]"! (Isaiah 25:9; 40:28-31) Let us, then, eagerly examine the precious message in the book of Isaiah. As we do so, our confidence in God's promises will be greatly strengthened. Also, we will be helped to grow in our conviction that Jehovah is indeed the God of our salvation.

10, 11. (a) Why is the book of Isaiah of interest to us today? (b) How does the book of Isaiah direct attention to the Messiah?
12. Why do we eagerly embark on a study of the book of Isaiah?

CHAPTER TWO

A Father and His Rebellious Sons

HE PROVIDED well for his children, as would any loving parent. For many years he made sure that they were fed, clothed, and sheltered. When it was necessary, he disciplined them. But their punishment was never excessive; it was always administered "to the proper degree." (Jeremiah 30:11) We can only imagine, then, the pain that this loving father feels at having to make the statement: *"Sons I have brought up and raised, but they themselves have revolted against me."—Isaiah 1:2b.*

2 The rebellious sons referred to here are the people of Judah, and the aggrieved father is Jehovah God. How tragic! Jehovah has nourished the Judeans and raised them to an elevated position among the nations. "I went on to clothe you with an embroidered garment and to shoe you with sealskin and to wrap you in fine linen and to cover you with costly material," he later reminds them through the prophet Ezekiel. (Ezekiel 16:10) Yet, for the most part, the people of Judah do not appreciate what Jehovah has done for them. Instead, they rebel, or revolt.

3 With good reason, Jehovah prefaces these words regarding his rebellious sons with the statement: *"Hear, O heavens, and give ear, O earth, for Jehovah himself*

1, 2. Explain how Jehovah has come to have rebellious sons.
3. Why does Jehovah call upon the heavens and the earth to bear witness to Judah's revolt?

has spoken." (Isaiah 1:2a) Centuries earlier the heavens and the earth heard, as it were, the Israelites receive explicit warnings regarding the consequences of disobedience. Moses said: "I do take as witnesses against you today the heavens and the earth, that you will positively perish in a hurry from off the land to which you are crossing the Jordan to take possession of it." (Deuteronomy 4:26) Now in Isaiah's day, Jehovah calls upon the invisible heavens and the visible earth to bear witness to Judah's revolt.

4 The severity of the situation calls for a straightforward approach. Even in these dire circumstances, however, it is noteworthy—and heartwarming—that Jehovah presents himself to Judah as a loving parent rather than merely the owner who has purchased them. In effect, Jehovah is entreating his people to consider the matter from the standpoint of a father who is in anguish over his wayward sons. Perhaps some parents in Judah can even personally relate to such a predicament and are moved by the analogy. In any event, Jehovah is about to state his case against Judah.

Brute Beasts Know Better

5 Through Isaiah, Jehovah says: *"A bull well knows its buyer, and the ass the manger of its owner; Israel itself has not known, my own people have not behaved understand-*

---

4. How does Jehovah choose to present himself to Judah?
5. In contrast with Israel, in what way do the bull and the ass display a sense of faithfulness?

*ingly." (Isaiah 1:3)** The bull and the ass are draft animals familiar to those living in the Middle East. Indeed, the Judeans would not deny that even these lowly beasts display a sense of faithfulness, a keen awareness that they belong to a master. In this regard, consider what one Bible researcher witnessed at the close of the day in a Middle Eastern city: "No sooner had the drove got within the walls than it began to disperse. Every ox knew perfectly well his owner, and the way to his house, nor did it get bewildered for a moment in the mazes of the narrow and crooked alleys. As for the ass, he walked straight to the door, and up to 'his master's crib.'"

6 Since such scenes are no doubt common in Isaiah's day, the point of Jehovah's message is clear: If even a brute beast recognizes its master and its own manger, what excuse can the people of Judah offer for having left Jehovah? Truly, they have "not behaved understandingly." It is as if they have no consciousness of the fact that their prosperity and their very existence depend upon Jehovah. It is indeed an evidence of mercy that Jehovah still refers to the Judeans as "my own people"!

7 Never would we want to behave without understanding by failing to show appreciation for all that Jehovah has done for us! Instead, we should imitate the psalmist David, who said: "I will laud you, O Jehovah, with all my heart; I will declare all your wonderful works." (Psalm 9:1) Continually taking in knowledge of Jehovah will encourage us in this regard, for the Bible states that "the

---

* In this context, "Israel" refers to the two-tribe kingdom of Judah.

---

6. How have the people of Judah failed to act understandingly?
7. What are some ways in which we can show ourselves appreciative of Jehovah's provisions?

knowledge of the Most Holy One is what understanding
is." (Proverbs 9:10) Meditating daily on Jehovah's blessings will help us to be thankful and not take our heavenly Father for granted. (Colossians 3:15) "The one offering
thanksgiving as his sacrifice is the one that glorifies me,"
says Jehovah, "and as for the one keeping a set way, I will
cause him to see salvation by God."—Psalm 50:23.

A Shocking Affront to "the Holy One of Israel"

8 Isaiah continues his message with strong words for
the nation of Judah: *"Woe to the sinful nation, the people heavy with error, an evildoing seed, ruinous sons! They
have left Jehovah, they have treated the Holy One of Israel with disrespect, they have turned backwards." (Isaiah
1:4)* Wicked deeds can accumulate to the extent that they
become like a crushing weight. In Abraham's day Jehovah described the sins of Sodom and Gomorrah as "very
heavy." (Genesis 18:20) Something similar is now evident
in the people of Judah, for Isaiah says that they are "heavy
with error." In addition, he calls them "an evildoing seed,
ruinous sons." Yes, the Judeans are like delinquent children. They have "turned backwards," or as the *New Revised Standard Version* puts it, they are "utterly estranged"
from their Father.

9 By their wayward course, the people of Judah are showing gross disrespect for "the Holy One of Israel." What is
the significance of this phrase, which is found 25 times in
the book of Isaiah? To be holy means to be clean and pure.
Jehovah is holy to the superlative degree. (Revelation 4:8)
The Israelites are reminded of this fact every time they observe the words engraved on the shining gold plate on the

8. Why can the people of Judah be called "the sinful nation"?
9. What is the significance of the phrase "the Holy One of Israel"?

high priest's turban: "Holiness belongs to Jehovah." (Exodus 39:30) Hence, by referring to Jehovah as "the Holy One of Israel," Isaiah underscores the gravity of Judah's sin. Why, these rebels are directly violating the command given to their forefathers: "You must sanctify yourselves and you must prove yourselves holy, because I am holy"! —Leviticus 11:44.

10 Christians today must at all costs avoid following Judah's example of disrespecting "the Holy One of Israel." They must imitate Jehovah's holiness. (1 Peter 1:15, 16) And they need to "hate what is bad." (Psalm 97:10) Such unclean practices as sexual immorality, idolatry, thievery, and drunkenness can corrupt the Christian congregation. That is why those who refuse to stop practicing these things are disfellowshipped from the congregation. Ultimately, those who unrepentantly follow a course of uncleanness will be excluded from enjoying the blessings of God's Kingdom government. Really, all such wicked works constitute a shocking affront to "the Holy One of Israel." —Romans 1:26, 27; 1 Corinthians 5:6-11; 6:9, 10.

Sick From Head to Foot

11 Isaiah next strives to reason with the people of Judah by pointing out to them their sickly state. He says: *"Where else will you be struck still more, in that you add more revolt?"* In effect, Isaiah is asking them: 'Have you not suffered enough? Why bring further harm to yourselves by continuing to rebel?' Isaiah continues: *"The whole head is in a sick condition, and the whole heart is feeble. From the sole of the foot even to the head there is no sound spot in*

---

10. How can we avoid showing disrespect for "the Holy One of Israel"?

11, 12. (a) Describe Judah's bad condition. (b) Why should we not feel sorry for Judah?

it." (Isaiah 1:5, 6a) Judah is in a loathsome, diseased state—spiritually sick from head to foot. A grim diagnosis indeed!

12 Should we feel sorry for Judah? Hardly! Centuries earlier the entire nation of Israel was duly warned about the penalty for disobedience. In part, they were told: "Jehovah will strike you with a malignant boil upon both knees and both legs, from which you will not be able to be healed, from the sole of your foot to the crown of your head." (Deuteronomy 28:35) In a figurative sense, Judah is now suffering these very consequences of her stubborn course. And all of this could have been avoided if the people of Judah had simply obeyed Jehovah.

13 Isaiah continues to describe Judah's pitiable state: *"Wounds and bruises and fresh stripes—they have not been squeezed out or bound up, nor has there been a softening with oil." (Isaiah 1:6b)* Here the prophet refers to three types of injuries: wounds (cuts, such as those inflicted by a sword or a knife), bruises (welts resulting from beating), and fresh stripes (recent, open sores that seem beyond healing). The idea presented is that of a man who has been severely punished in every manner imaginable, with no part of his body escaping harm. Judah is truly in a broken-down state.

14 Does Judah's miserable condition move her to return to Jehovah? No! Judah is like the rebel described at Proverbs 29:1: "A man repeatedly reproved but making his neck hard will suddenly be broken, and that without healing." The nation seems beyond curing. As Isaiah puts it, her wounds "have not been squeezed out or bound up,

---

13, 14. (a) What injuries have been inflicted upon Judah? (b) Do Judah's sufferings cause her to reconsider her rebellious course?

nor has there been a softening with oil."* In a sense, Judah resembles an open, unbandaged, all-pervasive sore.

15 Taking a lesson from Judah, we must be on guard against spiritual sickness. Like physical illness, it can affect any one of us. After all, who of us is not susceptible to fleshly desires? Greed and a desire for excessive pleasure can take root in our hearts. Hence, we need to train ourselves to "abhor what is wicked" and "cling to what is good." (Romans 12:9) We also need to cultivate the fruits of God's spirit in our everyday lives. (Galatians 5:22, 23) By doing so, we will avoid the condition that plagued Judah—that of being spiritually sick from head to foot.

A Desolated Land

16 Isaiah now leaves his medical analogy and turns to the condition of Judah's terrain. As if he is gazing down on a battle-scarred plain, he says: *"Your land is a desolation, your cities are burned with fire; your ground—right in front of you strangers are eating it up, and the desolation is like an overthrow by strangers." (Isaiah 1:7)* Some scholars say that although these words are found early in Isaiah's book, they were probably uttered later in the prophet's career, perhaps during the reign of wicked King Ahaz. They assert that Uzziah's reign was too prosperous to justify such a bleak description. Granted, it cannot be stated with

---

* Isaiah's words reflect the medical practice of his day. Bible researcher E. H. Plumptre notes: "To 'close' or 'press' the festering wound was the process tried at first to get rid of the purulent discharge; then, as in Hezekiah's case (chap. xxxviii. 21), it was 'bound up,' with a poultice, then some stimulating oil or unguent, probably, as in Luke x. 34, oil and wine were used, to cleanse the ulcer."

---

15. In what ways can we protect ourselves from spiritual sickness?
16. (a) How does Isaiah describe the condition of Judah's terrain? (b) Why do some say that these words were likely uttered during the reign of Ahaz, but how might we understand them?

certainty whether Isaiah's book is compiled in chronological order. However, Isaiah's words about desolation are probably prophetic. In uttering the above statement, most likely Isaiah is employing a technique found elsewhere in the Bible—that of describing a future event as if it has already taken place, thus emphasizing the certainty of a prophecy's fulfillment.—Compare Revelation 11:15.

17 In any event, the prophetic description of the desolation of Judah should not come as a surprise to this stubborn and disobedient people. Centuries earlier Jehovah warned them of what would happen if they rebelled. He said: "I, for my part, will lay the land desolate, and your enemies who are dwelling in it will simply stare in amazement over it. And you I shall scatter among the nations, and I will unsheathe a sword after you; and your land must become a desolation, and your cities will become a desolate ruin."—Leviticus 26:32, 33; 1 Kings 9:6-8.

18 The words at Isaiah 1:7, 8 are apparently fulfilled during the invasions by Assyria that result in the destruction of Israel and widespread destruction and suffering in Judah. (2 Kings 17:5, 18; 18:11, 13; 2 Chronicles 29:8, 9) However, Judah is not totally wiped out. Isaiah says: *"The daughter of Zion has been left remaining like a booth in a vineyard, like a lookout hut in a field of cucumbers, like a blockaded city."—Isaiah 1:8.*

19 Amid all the devastation, "the daughter of Zion," Jerusalem, will be left standing. But she will look very vulnerable—like a shanty in a vineyard or a watchman's booth in a cucumber field. In a journey down the Nile, one 19th-century scholar was reminded of Isaiah's words when he

17. Why should the prophetic description of desolation not come as a surprise to the people of Judah?
18-20. When are the words of Isaiah 1:7, 8 fulfilled, and in what way does Jehovah 'leave a few remaining' at this time?

saw similar booths, which he describes as "little more than a fence against a north wind." In Judah when the harvest was over, these booths were allowed to fall apart and collapse. Still, as flimsy as Jerusalem might appear before the all-conquering Assyrian army, she will survive.

20 Isaiah concludes this prophetic statement: *"Unless Jehovah of armies himself had left remaining to us just a few survivors, we should have become just like Sodom, we should have resembled Gomorrah itself." (Isaiah 1:9)** Against the might of Assyria, Jehovah will finally come to Judah's aid. Unlike Sodom and Gomorrah, Judah will not be obliterated. It will live on.

---

* The *Commentary on the Old Testament,* by C. F. Keil and F. Delitzsch, says: "The prophet's address has here reached a resting-place. The fact that it is divided at this point into two separate sections, is indicated in the text by the space left between vers. 9 and 10. This mode of marking larger or smaller sections, either by leaving spaces or by breaking off the line, is older than the vowel points and accents, and rests upon a tradition of the highest antiquity."

21 More than 100 years later, Judah was again under threat. The people had not learned from the discipline inflicted through Assyria. "They were continually making jest at the messengers of the true God and despising his words and mocking at his prophets." As a result, "the rage of Jehovah came up against his people, until there was no healing." (2 Chronicles 36:16) The Babylonian monarch Nebuchadnezzar conquered Judah, and this time, there was nothing remaining "like a booth in a vineyard." Even Jerusalem was destroyed. (2 Chronicles 36:17-21) Still, Jehovah 'left a few remaining.' Even though Judah endured 70 years in exile, Jehovah ensured the continuance of the nation and especially of the Davidic line, which would produce the promised Messiah.

---

21. After Babylon destroyed Jerusalem, why did Jehovah 'leave a few remaining'?

Unlike Sodom and Gomorrah,
Judah will not be forever uninhabited

22 In the first century, Israel went through its final crisis as God's covenant people. When Jesus presented himself as the promised Messiah, the nation rejected him, and as a result, Jehovah rejected them. (Matthew 21:43; 23:37-39; John 1:11) Was this the end of Jehovah's having a special nation on earth? No. The apostle Paul showed that Isaiah 1:9 had yet another fulfillment. Quoting from the Septuagint version, he wrote: "Just as Isaiah had said aforetime: 'Unless Jehovah of armies had left a seed to us, we should have become just like Sodom, and we should have been made just like Gomorrah.'"—Romans 9:29.

23 This time the survivors were the anointed Christians, who put faith in Jesus Christ. These were, first of all, believing Jews. Later they were joined by believing Gentiles. Together they made up a new Israel, "the Israel of God." (Galatians 6:16; Romans 2:29) This "seed" survived the destruction of the Jewish system of things in 70 C.E. Indeed, "the Israel of God" is still with us today. It has now been joined by millions of believing individuals of the nations, who make up "a great crowd, which no man [is] able to number, out of all nations and tribes and peoples and tongues."—Revelation 7:9.

24 Soon this world will face the battle of Armageddon. (Revelation 16:14, 16) While this will be a crisis greater than either the Assyrian or the Babylonian invasion of Judah, greater even than the Roman devastation of Judea in 70 C.E., there will be survivors. (Revelation 7:14) How vital, then, that all consider carefully Isaiah's words to Judah! They meant survival for faithful ones back then. And they can mean survival for believing ones today.

22, 23. In the first century, why did Jehovah 'leave a few remaining'?
24. What should all take notice of if they wish to survive mankind's greatest crisis?

CHAPTER THREE

"Let Us Set Matters Straight"

THE inhabitants of Jerusalem may feel inclined to justify themselves after hearing the denunciation recorded at Isaiah 1:1-9. They no doubt would like to point proudly to all the sacrifices they offer to Jehovah. However, verses 10 through 15 give Jehovah's withering reply to such attitudes. It begins: *"Hear the word of Jehovah, you dictators of Sodom. Give ear to the law of our God, you people of Gomorrah."—Isaiah 1:10.*

2 Sodom and Gomorrah were destroyed not only for their perverted sex practices but also for their hardhearted, haughty attitudes. (Genesis 18:20, 21; 19:4, 5, 23-25; Ezekiel 16:49, 50) Isaiah's audience must be shocked to hear themselves being compared to the people of those accursed cities.* But Jehovah sees his people just as they are, and Isaiah does not soften God's message in order to 'tickle their ears.'—2 Timothy 4:3.

3 Notice how Jehovah feels about the formalistic worship

---

* According to ancient Jewish tradition, wicked King Manasseh had Isaiah executed, sawn asunder. (Compare Hebrews 11:37.) A source says that in order to bring on this death sentence, a false prophet used the following charge against Isaiah: "He has called Jerusalem Sodom, and the princes of Judah and Jerusalem he has declared (to be) the people of Gomorrah."

1, 2. To whom does Jehovah compare the rulers and the people of Jerusalem and Judah, and why is this valid?
3. What does Jehovah mean when he says that he has "had enough" of the people's sacrifices, and why is this the case?

of his people. " *'Of what benefit to me is the multitude of your sacrifices?' says Jehovah. 'I have had enough of whole burnt offerings of rams and the fat of well-fed animals; and in the blood of young bulls and male lambs and he-goats I have taken no delight.'* " (Isaiah 1:11) The people have forgotten that Jehovah does not *depend* upon their sacrifices. (Psalm 50:8-13) He does not *need* anything that humans may offer him. So if the people think that they are doing Jehovah a favor by presenting their halfhearted offerings, they are mistaken. Jehovah uses a powerful figure of speech. The expression "I have had enough" may also be rendered "I am satiated" or "I am glutted." Do you know the feeling of being so full of food that the very sight of more is repulsive? Jehovah felt similarly about those offerings—utterly repulsed!

4 Jehovah continues: *"When you people keep coming in to see my face, who is it that has required this from your hand, to trample my courtyards?"* (Isaiah 1:12) Is it not Jehovah's own law that requires the people to 'come in to see his face,' that is, to be in attendance at his temple in Jerusalem? (Exodus 34:23, 24) Yes, but they come there out of mere formalism, simply going through the motions of pure worship, without pure motives. To Jehovah, their numerous visits to his courtyards amount to mere 'trampling,' accomplishing nothing more than wearing away the floor.

5 No wonder that Jehovah now adopts even stronger language! *"Stop bringing in any more valueless grain offerings. Incense—it is something detestable to me. New moon and sabbath, the calling of a convention—I cannot put up with the use of uncanny power along with the solemn*

---

4. How does Isaiah 1:12 expose the emptiness of the people's attendance at the temple in Jerusalem?
5. What are some of the acts of worship performed by the Jews, and why have these become "a burden" to Jehovah?

assembly. Your new moons and your festal seasons my soul has hated. To me they have become a burden; I have become tired of bearing them." (Isaiah 1:13, 14) Grain offerings, incense, Sabbaths, and solemn assemblies are all part of God's Law to Israel. As to "new moons," the Law simply directs that these be observed, but wholesome traditions have gradually grown up around the observance. (Numbers 10:10; 28:11) The new moon is treated as a monthly sabbath, when the people would desist from work and even gather for instruction from the prophets and priests. (2 Kings 4:23; Ezekiel 46:3; Amos 8:5) Such observances are not wrong. The problem lies in doing them for mere show. Moreover, the Jews are resorting to "uncanny power," spiritistic practices, right along with their formal observance of God's Law.* Thus, their acts of worship to Jehovah are "a burden" to him.

6 How, though, could Jehovah feel "tired"? After all, he has an "abundance of dynamic energy . . . He does not tire out or grow weary." (Isaiah 40:26, 28) Jehovah is using a vivid figure of speech to enable us to understand his feelings. Have you ever borne a heavy burden for so long that you were weary to the very bone and just longed to throw it off? That is how Jehovah feels about his people's hypocritical acts of worship.

7 Jehovah now addresses the most intimate and personal of all acts of worship. *"When you spread out your palms, I hide my eyes from you. Even though you make many prayers, I am not listening; with bloodshed your very*

---

* The Hebrew word for "uncanny power" is also rendered "what is hurtful," "what is uncanny," and "erroneous." According to the *Theological Dictionary of the Old Testament,* Hebrew prophets used the word to denounce "evil caused by the misuse of power."

---

6. In what sense has Jehovah become "tired"?
7. Why has Jehovah stopped listening to the prayers of his people?

hands have become filled." **(Isaiah 1:15)** Spreading out the palms, holding the hands outstretched with palms upward, is a gesture of supplication. To Jehovah, this stance has become meaningless, for this people have hands full of bloodshed. Violence is rampant in the land. Oppression of the weak is commonplace. For such abusive, selfish people to pray to Jehovah and ask for blessings is obscene. No wonder Jehovah says, "I am not listening"!

8 In our day, Christendom has likewise failed to win God's favor with her ceaseless repetition of vain prayers and her other religious "works." (Matthew 7:21-23) It is of vital importance that we do not fall into the same trap. Occasionally, a Christian lapses into a practice of serious sin, then reasons that if he just hides what he is

---

8. What error does Christendom commit today, and how do some Christians fall into a similar trap?

doing and increases his activity in the Christian congregation, his deeds will somehow counterbalance his sin. Such formalistic works do not please Jehovah. There is only one cure for spiritual sickness, as the next verses of Isaiah show.

The Cure for Spiritual Sickness

9 Jehovah, the compassionate God, now shifts to a warmer, more appealing tone. *"Wash yourselves; make yourselves clean; remove the badness of your dealings from in front of my eyes; cease to do bad. Learn to do good; search for justice; set right the oppressor; render judgment for the fatherless boy; plead the cause of the widow."* (Isaiah 1: 16, 17) Here we find a string of nine imperatives, or commands. The first four are negative in the sense that they involve the removal of sin; the last five are positive actions that lead to receiving Jehovah's blessing.

10 Washing and cleanness have always been an important part of pure worship. (Exodus 19:10, 11; 30:20; 2 Corinthians 7:1) But Jehovah wants the cleansing to go deeper, into the very heart of his worshipers. Most important is moral and spiritual cleanliness, and this is what Jehovah refers to. The first two commands in verse 16 are not mere repetition. A Hebrew grammarian suggests that the first, "wash yourselves," refers to an initial act of cleansing, whereas the second, "make yourselves clean," refers to ongoing efforts to maintain that cleanness.

11 We can hide nothing from Jehovah. (Job 34:22; Proverbs 15:3; Hebrews 4:13) So his command, "Remove the badness of your dealings from in front of my eyes," can only mean one thing—to cease doing bad. That means not attempting to conceal serious sins, for doing so is a sin in

9, 10. How important is cleanness in our worship of Jehovah?
11. To combat sin, what should we do, and what should we never do?

itself. Proverbs 28:13 warns: "He that is covering over his transgressions will not succeed, but he that is confessing and leaving them will be shown mercy."

12 There is much to learn from the positive actions that Jehovah commands in verse 17 of Isaiah chapter 1. Notice that he does not merely say "do good" but *"learn* to do good." It takes personal study of God's Word to understand what is good in God's eyes and to want to do it. Further, Jehovah does not merely say "render justice" but *"search* for justice." Even experienced elders need to make a thorough search of God's Word in order to find the just course in some complex matters. Theirs too is the responsibility to "set right the oppressor," as Jehovah next commands. These directives are important to Christian shepherds today, for they want to protect the flock from "oppressive wolves."—Acts 20:28-30.

13 The final two commands involve some of the more vulnerable of God's people—orphans and widows. The world is all too ready to take advantage of such individuals; this must not be so among God's people. Loving elders "render judgment" for the fatherless boys and girls in the congregation, helping them to receive justice and protection in a world that wants to take advantage of them and corrupt them. Elders "plead the cause" of the widow or, as the Hebrew word can also mean, "strive" in her behalf. Really, all Christians want to be a source of refuge, comfort, and justice to the needy among us because they are precious to Jehovah.—Micah 6:8; James 1:27.

14 What a firm, positive message Jehovah conveys

---

12. (a) Why is it important to *"learn* to do good"? (b) How may elders in particular apply the directives to *"search* for justice" and "set right the oppressor"?
13. How might we today apply the commands regarding the fatherless boy and the widow?
14. What positive message is conveyed at Isaiah 1:16, 17?

through these nine commands! Sometimes those involved in sin convince themselves that it is simply beyond their power to do right. Such notions are discouraging. Moreover, they are wrong. Jehovah knows—and wants us to know—that with His help, any sinner can stop his sinful course, turn around, and do right instead.

A Compassionate, Just Plea

15 Jehovah's tone now takes on even greater warmth and compassion. *"'Come, now, you people, and let us set matters straight between us,' says Jehovah. 'Though the sins of you people should prove to be as scarlet, they will be made white just like snow; though they should be red like crimson cloth, they will become even like wool.'"* **(Isaiah 1:18)** The invitation that opens this beautiful verse is often misunderstood. For example, *The New English Bible* says, "Let us argue it out"—as if both sides must make concessions to reach an accord. Not so! Jehovah bears no fault, least of all in his dealings with this rebellious, hypocritical people. (Deuteronomy 32:4, 5) The verse speaks, not of a give-and-take discussion between equals, but of a forum to establish justice. It is as if Jehovah here challenges Israel to a court trial.

16 That may be a daunting notion, but Jehovah is the most merciful and compassionate Judge. His capacity for forgiveness is unparalleled. (Psalm 86:5) He alone can take Israel's sins that are "as scarlet" and cleanse them away, making them "white just like snow." No human effort, no formula of works, sacrifices, or prayers can remove the stain of sin. Only Jehovah's forgiveness can wash sin away. God grants such forgiveness on terms that he sets, which include genuine, heartfelt repentance.

---

15. How is the phrase "let us set matters straight between us" sometimes misunderstood, and what does it actually mean?
16, 17. How do we know that Jehovah is willing to forgive even serious sins?

17 So important is this truth that Jehovah repeats it in a poetic variation—"crimson" sins will become like new, undyed, white wool. Jehovah wants us to know that he truly is the Forgiver of sins, even very serious ones, as long as he finds us genuinely repentant. Those who find it hard to believe that this is true in their own case do well to consider such examples as Manasseh. He sinned horribly—for years. Yet, he repented and was forgiven. (2 Chronicles 33: 9-16) Jehovah wants all of us, including those who have committed serious sins, to know that it is not too late to "set matters straight" with him.

18 Jehovah reminds his people that they have a choice to make. *"If you people show willingness and do listen, the good of the land you will eat. But if you people refuse and are actually rebellious, with a sword you will be eaten up; for the very mouth of Jehovah has spoken it."* (*Isaiah 1:19, 20*) Here Jehovah emphasizes attitudes, and he uses another vivid figure of speech to drive his point home. Judah's choice is this: Eat or be eaten. If they have an attitude of willingness to listen to and obey Jehovah, they will eat the good produce of the land. However, if they persist in their rebellious attitude, they will be eaten—by the sword of their enemies! It seems almost unimaginable that a people would choose the sword of their enemies over the mercy and abundance of a forgiving God. Nevertheless, such is the case with Jerusalem, as the next verses of Isaiah show.

A Dirge Over the Beloved City

19 At Isaiah 1:21-23, we see the full extent of the wickedness of Jerusalem at this time. Isaiah now begins an

---

18. What choice does Jehovah put before his rebellious people?
19, 20. (a) How does Jehovah convey the sense of betrayal that he feels? (b) In what way has 'righteousness lodged in Jerusalem'?

inspired poem in the style of a dirge, or lament: *"O how the faithful town has become a prostitute! She was full of justice; righteousness itself used to lodge in her, but now murderers."—Isaiah 1:21.*

20 How the city, Jerusalem, has fallen! Once a faithful wife, she has now become a prostitute. What could more powerfully convey the sense of betrayal and disappointment that Jehovah feels? "Righteousness itself used to lodge in" this city. When? Well, even before Israel existed, back in Abraham's day, this city was called Salem. Over it ruled a man who was both king and priest. His name, Melchizedek, means "King of Righteousness," and it evidently suited him well. (Hebrews 7:2; Genesis 14:18-20) About 1,000 years after Melchizedek, Jerusalem reached a

peak, under the kingships of David and Solomon. "Righteousness itself used to lodge in her," especially when her kings set the example for the people by walking in Jehovah's ways. By Isaiah's day, though, such times are a distant memory.

21 It seems that the leaders among the people are a large part of the problem. Isaiah goes on with his lament: *"Your silver itself has become scummy dross. Your wheat beer is diluted with water. Your princes are stubborn and partners with thieves. Every one of them is a lover of a bribe and a chaser after gifts. For a fatherless boy they do not render judgment; and even the legal case of a widow does not get admittance to them."* (*Isaiah 1:22, 23*) Two vivid word pictures in quick succession set the tone for what must follow. The smith at his forge skims the scummy dross from the molten silver and throws it away. Israel's princes and judges are like the dross, not the silver. They need to be discarded. They have no more use than beer that has been diluted with water and lost its flavor. Such a beverage is fit only to be poured down the drain!

22 Verse 23 shows why the leaders deserve such a description. The Mosaic Law ennobled God's people, setting them apart from other nations. It did so, for example, by mandating the protection of orphans and widows. (Exodus 22:22-24) But in Isaiah's day, the fatherless boy has little hope of any favorable judgment. As for the widow, she cannot get anyone even to hear her case, let alone strive in her behalf. No, these judges and leaders are too busy looking after their own interests—seeking bribes, chasing gifts, and serving as partners to thieves, evidently protecting the criminals while allowing their victims to suffer. Worse

---

21, 22. What is signified by dross and diluted beer, and why do Judah's leaders merit such a description?

yet, they are "stubborn," or hardened, in their course of wrongdoing. What a sorry state of affairs!

Jehovah Will Refine His People

23 Jehovah will not tolerate such abuse of power forever. Isaiah continues: *"Therefore the utterance of the true Lord, Jehovah of armies, the Powerful One of Israel, is: 'Aha! I shall relieve myself of my adversaries, and I will avenge myself on my enemies.'"* (Isaiah 1:24) Jehovah is given three designations here, emphasizing his rightful lordship and his vast power. The exclamation "Aha!" likely signifies that Jehovah's pity is now mixed with determination to act upon his wrath. There is certainly reason for this.

24 Jehovah's own people have made themselves his enemies. They fully merit divine vengeance. Jehovah will "relieve," or rid, himself of them. Does this mean a complete, permanent obliteration of his name people? No, for Jehovah goes on to say: *"And I will turn back my hand upon you, and I shall smelt away your scummy dross as with lye, and I will remove all your waste products."* (Isaiah 1:25) Jehovah now uses the refining process as an illustration. A refiner in ancient times often added lye to help separate the dross from the precious metal. In a similar way, Jehovah, who does not see his people as completely wicked, will 'chastise them to the proper degree.' He will remove from them only the "waste products"—the stubborn, undesirable ones, who refuse to learn and obey.* (Jeremiah 46:28) With these words, Isaiah has the privilege of writing down history in advance.

---

* The expression "I will turn back my hand upon you" means that Jehovah will shift from supporting his people to chastising them.

---

23. What feelings toward his adversaries does Jehovah express?
24. What refining process does Jehovah purpose for his people?

25 Jehovah did indeed refine his people, removing the scummy dross of corrupt leaders and other rebels. In 607 B.C.E., long after Isaiah's time, Jerusalem was destroyed and its inhabitants led off for the 70-year exile in Babylon. This in some ways parallels an action God took much later. The prophecy at Malachi 3:1-5, written long after the Babylonian exile, showed that God would again do a refining work. It pointed to the time when Jehovah God would come to his spiritual temple accompanied by his "messenger of the covenant," Jesus Christ. This evidently happened at the end of World War I. Jehovah inspected all of those claiming to be Christians, sifting the true from the false. With what result?

26 Jehovah answers: *"I will bring back again judges for you as at the first, and counselors for you as at the start. After this you will be called City of Righteousness, Faithful Town. With justice Zion herself will be redeemed, and those returning of her, with righteousness."* (*Isaiah 1:26, 27*) Ancient Jerusalem experienced an initial fulfillment of this prophecy. After the exiles returned to their beloved city in 537 B.C.E., there were once again faithful judges and counselors like those of the past. The prophets Haggai and Zechariah, the priest Joshua, the scribe Ezra, and the governor Zerubbabel all served to guide and direct the faithful returning remnant to walk in God's paths. However, an even more important fulfillment occurred in the 20th century.

27 In 1919, Jehovah's modern-day people emerged from the period of testing. They were delivered from spiritual

---

25. (a) How did Jehovah refine his people in 607 B.C.E.? (b) When did Jehovah refine his people in modern times?
26-28. (a) What initial fulfillment did Isaiah 1:26 have? (b) How has this prophecy been fulfilled in our time? (c) How might this prophecy benefit elders today?

bondage to Babylon the Great, the world empire of false religion. The distinction between that faithful anointed remnant and the apostate clergy of Christendom became clear. God again blessed his people, 'bringing back for them judges and counselors'—faithful men who counsel God's people according to his Word and not according to the traditions of men. Today among the diminishing "little flock" and their increasing millions of "other sheep" companions, there are thousands of such men.—Luke 12: 32; John 10:16; Isaiah 32:1, 2; 60:17; 61:3, 4.

28 Elders keep in mind that they do, on occasion, act as "judges" in the congregation in order to keep it morally and spiritually clean and to correct wrongdoers. They are deeply concerned with doing things God's way, imitating his merciful, balanced sense of justice. In most matters, though, they serve as "counselors." This, of course, is a far cry from being princes or tyrants, and they make every effort never to give even the appearance of "lording it over those who are God's inheritance."—1 Peter 5:3.

29 What about the "dross" mentioned in the prophecy of Isaiah? What happens to those who refuse to benefit from God's refinement pro-

---

29, 30. (a) What does Jehovah pronounce for those who refuse to benefit from the refining process? (b) In what sense do the people become "ashamed" of their trees and gardens?

cess? Isaiah continues: ***"And the crash of revolters and that of sinful ones will be at the same time, and those leaving Jehovah will come to their finish. For they will be ashamed of the mighty trees that you people desired, and you will be abashed because of the gardens that you have chosen."*** (*Isaiah 1:28, 29*) Those who revolt and sin against Jehovah, ignoring the warning messages of his prophets until it is too late, do indeed "crash" and "come to their finish." This happens in 607 B.C.E. What, however, do these references to trees and gardens mean?

30 The Judeans have a persistent problem with idolatry. Trees, gardens, and groves often figure in their debased practices. For example, worshipers of Baal and his consort, Ashtoreth, believe that in the dry season, the two deities are dead and buried. To prompt them to awaken and mate, bringing fertility to the land, the idolaters gather to carry out perverted sexual acts under "sacred" trees in groves or in gardens. When rains and fertility come to the land, the false gods receive the credit; the idolaters feel confirmed in their superstitions. But when Jehovah brings the rebellious idolaters to their crashing finish, no idol-gods protect them. The rebels are "ashamed" of these impotent trees and gardens.

31 Idolatrous Judeans face something worse than shame, though. Shifting the illustration, Jehovah now likens the idolater himself to a tree. ***"You will become like a big tree the foliage of which is withering, and like a garden that has no water."*** (*Isaiah 1:30*) In the hot, dry climate of the Middle East, this illustration is apt. No tree or garden can last for long without a steady supply of water. Dried up, such vegetation is especially vulnerable to fire. Hence, the illustration in verse 31 follows naturally.

---

31. What do the idolaters face that is worse than shame?

³² *"The vigorous man will certainly become tow, and the product of his activity a spark; and both of them will certainly go up in flames at the same time, with no one to do the extinguishing." (Isaiah 1:31)* Who is this "vigorous man"? The Hebrew expression conveys the sense of strength and wealth. It likely refers to the prosperous, self-assured follower of false gods. In Isaiah's day, as in our own, there is no shortage of men who reject Jehovah and his pure worship. Some even seem successful. Yet, Jehovah warns that such men will be like "tow," coarse fibers of flax so frail and dry that they tear apart, as it were, at the very smell of fire. (Judges 16:8, 9) The product of the idolater's activity—whether his idol-gods, his wealth, or whatever he worships in place of Jehovah—will be like the igniting "spark." Both spark and tow will be consumed, wiped out, in a fire that no one can extinguish. No power in the universe can overturn Jehovah's perfect judgments.

³³ Is this final message compatible with the message of mercy and forgiveness in verse 18? By all means! Jehovah has such warnings written down and delivered by his servants *because* he is merciful. After all, "he does not desire any to be destroyed but desires all to attain to repentance." (2 Peter 3:9) It is the privilege of every true Christian today to proclaim God's warning messages to mankind so that repentant ones may benefit from his generous forgiveness and live forever. How kind it is on Jehovah's part to give mankind a chance to "set matters straight" with him before it is too late!

---

32. (a) Who is "the vigorous man" referred to in verse 31? (b) In what sense will he become "tow," what "spark" will ignite him, and with what result?

33. (a) How do God's warnings of coming judgment also indicate his mercy? (b) What opportunity is Jehovah now extending to mankind, and how does this affect each one of us?

CHAPTER FOUR

Jehovah's House Lifted Up

Isaiah 2:1-5

"THEY shall beat their swords into plowshares. And their spears into pruning hooks: nation shall not lift up sword against nation. Neither shall they learn war any more." These words are inscribed on a wall at the United Nations plaza in New York City. For decades the source of that quotation was not identified. Since the aim of the UN is to work toward global peace, it was easy to conclude that the quote originated with the founders of the UN, in 1945.

2 In 1975, however, the name Isaiah was chiseled into the wall below the quotation. It was then evident that the words were not of modern origin. They were, in fact, recorded as a prophecy over 2,700 years ago in what is now the 2nd chapter of the book of Isaiah. For millenniums lovers of peace have pondered over how and when the things Isaiah foretold would occur. There is no longer any need to wonder. Today we see before us the remarkable fulfillment of this ancient prophecy.

3 Who are the nations that beat their swords into plowshares? Surely, they are not the modern-day political nations and governments. Until now these nations have developed swords, or weapons, both to wage war and to preserve "peace" through strength. If anything, the tendency has always been for nations to beat

---

1, 2. What words are inscribed on a wall at the United Nations plaza, and what is their source?

3. Who are the nations that beat their swords into plowshares?

their plowshares into swords! Isaiah's prophecy finds fulfillment in *representatives* from all nations, people who worship Jehovah, "the God of peace."—Philippians 4:9.

The Nations That Stream to Pure Worship

4 Isaiah chapter 2 begins with these words: *"The thing that Isaiah the son of Amoz visioned concerning Judah and Jerusalem: And it must occur in the final part of the days that the mountain of the house of Jehovah will become firmly established above the top of the mountains, and it will certainly be lifted up above the hills; and to it all the nations must stream."—Isaiah 2:1, 2.*

5 Notice that what Isaiah foretells is not mere speculation. Isaiah is directed to record events that *"must* occur" —without fail. Whatever Jehovah purposes has "certain success." (Isaiah 55:11) Evidently to give emphasis to the reliability of his promise, God inspired the prophet Micah, a contemporary of Isaiah, to record in his book the same prophecy that is set out at Isaiah 2:2-4.—Micah 4:1-3.

6 When is Isaiah's prophecy to be fulfilled? "In the final part of the days." The *New International Version* reads: "In the last days." The Christian Greek Scriptures foretold features that would identify this period. Included among them are wars, earthquakes, pestilences, food shortages, and "critical times hard to deal with."* (2 Timothy 3:1-5; Luke 21:10, 11) The fulfillment of such prophecies gives abundant evidence that we are living "in the final part of the days," the last days of this present world system. Logi-

---

* See the book *Knowledge That Leads to Everlasting Life,* chapter 11, "These Are the Last Days!," published by the Watchtower Bible and Tract Society of New York, Inc.

4, 5. What do the opening verses of Isaiah chapter 2 foretell, and what underscores the reliability of those words?
6. When does Isaiah's prophecy find fulfillment?

cally, then, we would expect to see fulfilled in our time the things that Isaiah foretold.

A Mountain in Which to Worship

7 In a few words, Isaiah paints a vivid prophetic picture. We see a lofty mountain, crowned by a glorious house, the temple of Jehovah. This mountain towers above surrounding mountains and hills. Yet, it is not foreboding or intimidating; it is appealing. Peoples of all nations yearn to ascend to the mountain of the house of Jehovah; they *stream* to it. This is easy to visualize, but what does it mean?

8 In Isaiah's day hills and mountains are often associated with worship. For example, they serve as sites for idolatrous worship and for sanctuaries of false gods. (Deuteronomy 12:2; Jeremiah 3:6) However, the house, or temple, of Jehovah adorns the summit of Mount Moriah in Jerusalem. Faithful Israelites journey to Jerusalem three times a year and ascend Mount Moriah to worship the true God. (Deuteronomy 16:16) So the streaming of the nations to "the mountain of the house of Jehovah" pictures the gathering of many peoples to true worship.

9 Today, of course, God's people do not gather at a literal mountain with a temple of stone. Jehovah's temple in Jerusalem was destroyed by Roman armies in 70 C.E. Besides, the apostle Paul made it clear that the temple in Jerusalem and the tabernacle that preceded it were pictorial. They represented a greater, spiritual reality, "the true tent, which Jehovah put up, and not man." (Hebrews 8:2) That

---

7. What prophetic picture does Isaiah paint?
8. (a) With what are hills and mountains associated in Isaiah's day? (b) What does the streaming of the nations to "the mountain of the house of Jehovah" picture?
9. What does "the mountain of the house of Jehovah" represent?

spiritual tent is the arrangement for approaching Jehovah in worship based on the ransom sacrifice of Jesus Christ. (Hebrews 9:2-10, 23) In harmony with this, "the mountain of the house of Jehovah" mentioned at Isaiah 2:2 represents the exalted pure worship of Jehovah in our time. Those embracing pure worship do not gather at any geographic location; they gather in unity of worship.

The Elevating of Pure Worship

10 The prophet says that "the mountain of the house of Jehovah," or pure worship, would become "firmly es-

10, 11. In what sense has Jehovah's worship been elevated in our day?

tablished above the top of the mountains" and be "lifted up above the hills." Long before Isaiah's time, King David brought the ark of the covenant up to Mount Zion
in Jerusalem, which was located 2,500 feet above sea level. There the ark rested until it was transferred to the completed temple on Mount Moriah. (2 Samuel 5:7; 6:14-19;
2 Chronicles 3:1; 5:1-10) Thus, by Isaiah's day the sacred
ark had already been physically elevated and placed in the
temple, in a position higher than the many surrounding
hills used for false worship.

11 Of course, in a spiritual sense, Jehovah's worship has
always been superior to the religious practices of those
who serve false gods. During our day, however, Jehovah

has exalted his worship heaven high, above all forms of unclean worship, yes, far above all "the hills" and "the top of the mountains." How so? Largely through the gathering together of those who want to worship him "with spirit and truth."—John 4:23.

12 Christ Jesus referred to "a conclusion of a system of things" as a time of harvest when the angels would gather in "the sons of the kingdom"—those with the hope of ruling with Jesus in heavenly glory. (Matthew 13:36-43) Since 1919, Jehovah has empowered "the remaining ones" of these sons to share with the angels in the harvest work. (Revelation 12:17) Thus, to start with, "the sons of the kingdom," Jesus' anointed brothers, are the ones gathered. Then they share in a further gathering work.

13 During this time of harvest, Jehovah has progressively helped the anointed remnant to understand and apply his Word, the Bible. This too has contributed to the elevating of pure worship. Though 'darkness itself covers the earth, and thick gloom the national groups,' the anointed are "shining as illuminators" among humankind, having been cleansed and refined by Jehovah. (Isaiah 60:2; Philippians 2:15) "Filled with the accurate knowledge of his will in all wisdom and spiritual comprehension," these spirit-anointed ones "shine as brightly as the sun in the kingdom of their Father."—Colossians 1:9; Matthew 13:43.

14 Moreover, others have streamed to "the mountain of the house of Jehovah." Called by Jesus his "other sheep,"

---

12. Who are "the sons of the kingdom," and what gathering has taken place?

13. How has Jehovah blessed the anointed remnant?

14, 15. In addition to the gathering of "the sons of the kingdom," what ingathering has taken place, and how was this foretold by Haggai?

these have the hope of living forever on a paradise earth. (John 10:16; Revelation 21:3, 4) Starting in the 1930's, they appeared by the thousands, then by the hundreds of thousands, and now by the millions! In a vision given to the apostle John, they are described as "a great crowd, which no man was able to number, out of all nations and tribes and peoples and tongues."—Revelation 7:9.

15 The prophet Haggai foretold the appearance of this great crowd. He wrote: "This is what Jehovah of armies has said, 'Yet once—it is a little while—and I am rocking the heavens and the earth and the sea and the dry ground. And I will rock all the nations, and the desirable things of all the nations [those who join anointed Christians in pure worship] must come in; and I will fill this house with glory,' Jehovah of armies has said." (Haggai 2:6, 7) The existence of this still-growing "great crowd" and their anointed companions elevates, yes glorifies, pure worship in Jehovah's house. Never before have so many been recorded as united in the worship of the true God, and this brings glory to Jehovah and his enthroned King, Jesus Christ. King Solomon wrote: "In the multitude of people there is an adornment of a king."—Proverbs 14:28.

Worship Exalted in the Lives of People

16 Jehovah deserves all credit for the elevating of pure worship in our time. Still, those who approach him are privileged to share in this work. Just as it requires effort to climb a mountain, so, too, it requires effort to learn of and live according to God's righteous standards. Like Christians in the first century, God's servants today have left behind life-styles and practices that are

16-18. What changes have some made so as to worship Jehovah acceptably?

not compatible with true worship. Fornicators, idolaters, adulterers, thieves, greedy persons, drunkards, and others have changed their ways and been "washed clean" in God's sight.—1 Corinthians 6:9-11.

17 Typical is the experience of one young woman who wrote: "I once was lost with no hope. I lived a life of immorality and drunkenness. I had sexual diseases. I also sold drugs and just didn't care about anything." After studying the Bible, she made major changes in order to conform to God's standards. Now she says: "I enjoy peace of mind, self-respect, a hope for the future, a real family and, best of all, a relationship with our Father, Jehovah."

18 Even after coming to an approved standing before Jehovah, all must continue to elevate pure worship by giving it a place of prominence in their lives. Thousands of years ago, through Isaiah, Jehovah expressed his confidence that there would be multitudes today eager to make his worship the most important thing in their lives. Are you among them?

A People Taught Jehovah's Way

19 Isaiah tells us more about those who embrace pure worship today. He says: *"Many peoples will certainly go and say: 'Come, you people, and let us go up to the mountain of Jehovah, to the house of the God of Jacob; and he will instruct us about his ways, and we will walk in his paths.' For out of Zion law will go forth, and the word of Jehovah out of Jerusalem."*—Isaiah 2:3.

20 Jehovah does not let his people wander about like lost sheep. Through the Bible and Bible-based publications, he imparts to them his "law" and his "word" so that they

19, 20. What are God's people taught, and where?

learn his ways. This knowledge equips them to "walk in his paths." Out of hearts filled with appreciation and in harmony with divine direction, they speak to one another about the ways of Jehovah. They gather together at large conventions and in smaller groups—at Kingdom Halls and in private homes—so as to listen to and learn the ways of God. (Deuteronomy 31:12, 13) Thus they imitate the pattern of the early Christians, who met together to encourage and incite one another to abound in "love and fine works."—Hebrews 10:24, 25.

21 They invite others to "go up" to the exalted worship of Jehovah God. How well this harmonizes with the command Jesus gave to his disciples just before his ascension to heaven! He told them: "Go therefore and make disciples of people of all the nations, baptizing them in the name of the Father and of the Son and of the holy spirit, teaching them to observe all the things I have commanded you." (Matthew 28:19, 20) With divine backing, Jehovah's Witnesses obediently go throughout the earth, teaching and making disciples, baptizing them.

Swords Into Plowshares

22 Now we come to the next verse, part of which is inscribed on the wall at the UN plaza. Isaiah writes: *"He will certainly render judgment among the nations and set matters straight respecting many peoples. And they will have to beat their swords into plowshares and their spears into pruning shears. Nation will not lift up sword against nation, neither will they learn war anymore."*—Isaiah 2:4.

---

21. In what work do Jehovah's servants share?
22, 23. What does Isaiah 2:4 foretell, and what did one UN official say about it?

23 To achieve this would be no small accomplishment. Federico Mayor, director-general of the United Nations Educational, Scientific, and Cultural Organization, once said: "All the obscenities of war, brought home to us nowadays by audio-visual equipment, do not seem able to halt the advance of the huge war machine set up and maintained over many centuries. Present generations have the almost impossible, Biblical task of 'beating their swords into ploughshares' and making the transition from an instinct for war—developed since time immemorial—to a feeling for peace. To achieve this would be the best and most noble act that the 'global village' could accomplish, and the best legacy to our descendants."

24 The nations as a whole will never achieve this lofty goal. It is simply beyond their reach. Isaiah's words are fulfilled by individuals from many nations, who are united in pure worship. Jehovah has "set matters straight" among them. He has taught his people to live at peace with one another. Truly, in a divided and strife-ridden world, they have figuratively beaten their "swords into plowshares and their spears into pruning shears." How?

24, 25. In whom do Isaiah's words find fulfillment, and in what way?

25 For one thing, they do not take sides in the wars of the nations. Shortly before Jesus' death, armed men came to arrest him. When Peter lashed out with a sword to defend his Master, Jesus said to him: "Return your sword to its place, for all those who take the sword will perish by the sword." (Matthew 26:52) Since then, Jesus' footstep followers have beaten their swords into plowshares and have refrained from taking up weapons to kill their fellow man and from supporting war efforts in other ways. They "pursue peace with all people."—Hebrews 12:14.

Pursuing the Ways of Peace

26 The peace of God's people goes far beyond a refusal to engage in warfare. Though they are found in more than 230 lands and represent countless languages and cultures, they enjoy peace with one another. In them is found a modern fulfillment of the words of Jesus, who said to his disciples in the first century: "By this all will know that you are my disciples, if you have love among yourselves." (John 13:35) Christians today are "peacemakers." (Matthew 5:9, footnote) They "seek peace and pursue it." (1 Peter 3:11) Sustaining them is Jehovah, "the God who gives peace."—Romans 15:33.

27 There are dramatic examples of those who have learned to be peacemakers. A young man writes of his early life: "Hard experience taught me how to defend myself. It made me tough and angry about life. I would always end up in fights. Each day, I would fight a different kid in the neighborhood, sometimes with fists, sometimes with rocks or bottles. I grew up being very violent." Eventually, however, he responded to the invitation to go to "the

---

26, 27. How do God's people "seek peace and pursue it"? Give an example.

mountain of the house of Jehovah." He learned God's ways and became a peaceable servant of God.

28 Most of Jehovah's servants do not come from such a violent background. Still, even in relatively small things —acts of kindness, forgiveness, and empathy—they strive to promote peace with others. Although imperfect, they endeavor to apply the Bible's counsel to "continue putting up with one another and forgiving one another freely if anyone has a cause for complaint against another."—Colossians 3:13.

A Future of Peace

29 Jehovah has done a marvelous thing in this "the final part of the days." He has gathered from all nations people who want to serve him. He has taught them to walk in his ways, ways of peace. These are the ones who will survive the coming "great tribulation" and pass into a peaceful new world in which war will be abolished forever.—Revelation 7:14.

30 Swords—weaponry—will be no more. The psalmist wrote of that time: "Come, you people, behold the activities of Jehovah, how he has set astonishing events on the earth. He is making wars to cease to the extremity of the earth. The bow he breaks apart and does cut the spear in pieces; the wagons he burns in the fire." (Psalm 46:8, 9) In view of such a prospect, Isaiah's following exhortation is as appropriate today as it was when he wrote it: *"O men of the house of Jacob, come and let us walk in the light of Jehovah." (Isaiah 2:5)* Yes, let Jehovah's light illuminate our path now, and we will walk in his way for all eternity. —Micah 4:5.

---

28. What can Christians do to pursue peace?
29, 30. What prospect is there for the earth?

CHAPTER FIVE

Jehovah Humiliates Self-Exalted Ones

Isaiah 2:6–4:1

DISGUSTED with the condition of Jerusalem and Judah, the prophet Isaiah now turns to Jehovah God and declares: *"You have forsaken your people, the house of Jacob."* (*Isaiah 2:6a*) What has provoked God to reject the people whom he himself had chosen as his "special property"? —Deuteronomy 14:2.

2 Isaiah's denunciation of the Jews of his time is of great interest to us. Why? Because the condition of Christendom today is very similar to that of Isaiah's people, and so is the judgment that Jehovah pronounces. Paying attention to Isaiah's proclamation will give us a clear understanding of what God condemns and will help us to shun practices that he disapproves of. With keen anticipation, then, let us consider Jehovah's prophetic word as recorded at Isaiah 2:6–4:1.

In Pride They Bow Down

3 Confessing the error of his people, Isaiah says: *"They have become full of what is from the East, and they are practicers of magic like the Philistines, and with the children of foreigners they abound."* (*Isaiah 2:6b*) Some 800 years earlier, Jehovah had commanded his chosen people: "Do not make yourselves unclean by any of these things

---

1, 2. Why is the prophetic message of Isaiah to the Jews of his day of interest to us?

3. What error of his people does Isaiah confess?

Idols, riches, and military prowess do not save Jerusalem on the day of Jehovah's judgment

[by which] the nations whom I am sending out from before you have made themselves unclean." (Leviticus 18:24) Concerning those whom he had selected as his special property, Jehovah forced Balaam to say: "From the top of the rocks I see them, and from the hills I behold them. There as a people they keep tabernacling isolated, and among the nations they do not reckon themselves." (Numbers 23:9, 12) Yet, by Isaiah's day Jehovah's chosen ones have adopted the abominable practices of the surrounding nations and are "full of what is from the East." Rather than putting faith in Jehovah and his word, they are practicing "magic like the Philistines." Far from keeping separate from the nations, the land 'abounds' with "the children of foreigners"—doubtless, foreigners who introduce ungodly practices to God's people.

4 Noting the current economic prosperity and the military strength of Judah under King Uzziah, Isaiah states: *"Their land is filled with silver and gold, and there is no limit to their treasures. And their land is filled with horses, and there is no limit to their chariots." (Isaiah 2:7)* Do the people thank Jehovah for such wealth and military strength? (2 Chronicles 26:1, 6-15) Far from it! Instead, they put their trust in the wealth itself and turn away from its Source, Jehovah God. The result? *"Their land is filled with valueless gods. To the work of one's hands they bow down, to that which one's fingers have made. And earthling man*

---

4. Rather than causing them to thank Jehovah, how do riches and military strength affect the Jews?

bows down, and man becomes low, and you cannot possibly pardon them." **(Isaiah 2:8, 9)** They turn their faces away from the living God and bow down to lifeless idols.

5 Bowing down can be a sign of humility. But bowing down to lifeless things is futile, making the idol worshiper "low," degenerate. How can Jehovah pardon such a sin? What will these idolaters do when Jehovah calls them to account?

'Haughty Eyes Must Become Low'

6 Isaiah continues: *"Enter into the rock and hide yourself in the dust because of the dreadfulness of Jehovah, and from his splendid superiority."* **(Isaiah 2:10)** But no rock will be big enough to protect them, no cover thick enough to conceal them, from Jehovah, the Almighty. When he comes to execute his judgment, *"the haughty eyes of earthling man must become low, and the loftiness of men must bow down; and Jehovah alone must be put on high in that day."—Isaiah 2:11.*

7 *"The day belonging to Jehovah of armies"* is coming. It will be a time for God to express his anger *"upon all the cedars of Lebanon that are lofty and lifted up and upon all the massive trees of Bashan; and upon all the lofty mountains and upon all the hills that are lifted up; and upon every high tower and upon every fortified wall; and upon all the ships of Tarshish and upon all desirable boats."* **(Isaiah 2:12-16)** Yes, every organization raised up by man as a symbol of his pride and every ungodly individual will be given attention in the day of Jehovah's wrath. Thus, *"the haughtiness of the earthling man must bow down, and the*

---

5. Why is bowing down to idols not an act of humility?
6, 7. (a) What happens to self-exalted ones on the day of Jehovah's judgment? (b) Upon what and whom does Jehovah express his anger, and why?

loftiness of men must become low; and Jehovah alone must be put on high in that day."—Isaiah 2:17.

8 The foretold day of judgment comes upon the Jews in 607 B.C.E. when Babylonian King Nebuchadnezzar destroys Jerusalem. The inhabitants see their beloved city aflame, its proud buildings demolished, its mighty wall smashed. The temple of Jehovah is reduced to rubble. Neither their treasures nor their chariots amount to anything on "the day belonging to Jehovah of armies." And their idols? It happens just as Isaiah foretells: *"The value-less gods themselves will pass away completely."* (Isaiah 2: 18) The Jews—princes and mighty men included—are taken into exile to Babylon. Jerusalem is to lie desolate for 70 years.

9 How similar the condition of Christendom is to that of Jerusalem and Judah in Isaiah's day! Christendom has certainly cultivated a close relationship with the nations of this world. She is an enthusiastic supporter of the United Nations and has filled her house with idols and unscriptural practices. Her adherents are materialistic and put their confidence in military might. And do they not view their clergy as worthy of great distinction, attributing to them titles and honors? Christendom's self-exaltation will without fail be brought to nothing. But when?

The Impending "Day of Jehovah"

10 The Scriptures point to a "day of Jehovah" that will be of far greater significance than the day of judgment upon ancient Jerusalem and Judah. The apostle Paul, under inspiration, associated the coming "day of Jehovah" with the

8. How does the foretold day of judgment come upon Jerusalem in 607 B.C.E.?
9. In what way is the condition of Christendom similar to that of Jerusalem and Judah in Isaiah's day?
10. To what "day of Jehovah" do the apostles Paul and Peter point?

presence of the enthroned King Jesus Christ. (2 Thessalonians 2:1, 2) Peter spoke of that day in connection with the establishment of 'new heavens and a new earth in which righteousness is to dwell.' (2 Peter 3:10-13) It is the day on which Jehovah will execute his judgment upon the entire wicked system of things, including Christendom.

11 "Alas for the day," says the prophet Joel, "because the day of Jehovah is near, and like a despoiling from the Almighty One it will come!" In view of the imminence of that "day," should not security during that fear-inspiring time concern everyone? "Who can hold up under it?" asks Joel. He answers: "Jehovah will be a refuge for his people." (Joel 1:15; 2:11; 3:16) Will Jehovah God be a refuge for those who have a haughty spirit and who put their confidence in riches, military might, and man-made gods? Impossible! God abandoned even his chosen people when they acted in this way. How vital that all of God's servants "seek righteousness, seek meekness," and examine seriously the place of Jehovah's worship in their lives!—Zephaniah 2:2, 3.

"To the Shrewmice and to the Bats"

12 How will idol worshipers view their idols during Jehovah's great day? Isaiah answers: *"People will enter into the caves of the rocks and into the holes of the dust because of the dreadfulness of Jehovah and from his splendid superiority, when he rises up for the earth to suffer shocks. In that day the earthling man will throw his worthless gods of silver and his valueless gods of gold . . . to the shrewmice and to the bats, in order to enter into the holes in the rocks and*

---

11. (a) Who will "hold up under" the upcoming "day of Jehovah"?
(b) How can we make Jehovah our refuge?
12, 13. Why is it fitting for the idol worshipers to throw their gods "to the shrewmice and to the bats" on the day of Jehovah?

into the clefts of the crags, because of the dreadfulness of Jehovah and from his splendid superiority, when he rises up for the earth to suffer shocks. For your own sakes, hold off from the earthling man, whose breath is in his nostrils, for on what basis is he himself to be taken into account?"—Isaiah 2:19-22.

13 Shrewmice live in holes in the ground, and bats roost in dark and desolate caves. Moreover, where a large number of bats roost in one place, there is a repulsive smell and a buildup of thick layers of droppings. Casting idols into such places is fitting. A place of darkness and uncleanness is all that they deserve. As for the people, they will seek refuge in caves and clefts in the rock on the day of Jehovah's judgment. So the fate of the idols and their worshipers will be the same. True to Isaiah's prophecy, lifeless idols saved neither their worshipers nor Jerusalem from Nebuchadnezzar's hands in 607 B.C.E.

14 During the coming day of Jehovah's judgment upon Christendom and other segments of the world empire of false religion, what will people do? Faced with deteriorating conditions earth wide, most will likely come to realize that their idols are valueless. In place of these, they may well seek refuge and protection in nonspiritual, earthly organizations, perhaps including the United Nations, the "scarlet-colored wild beast" of Revelation chapter 17. It is "the ten horns" of that symbolic wild beast that will destroy Babylon the Great, the world empire of false religion, of which Christendom is a significant part.—Revelation 17: 3, 8-12, 16, 17.

---

14. During the upcoming day of Jehovah's judgment upon the world empire of false religion, what will worldly-minded men do?

On "the day of Jehovah,"
the world empire of false religion will be devastated

15 Although the devastating and burning of Babylon the Great may be the direct work of those symbolic ten horns, it is, in fact, the execution of Jehovah's judgment. Concerning Babylon the Great, Revelation 18:8 states: "That is why in one day her plagues will come, death and mourning and famine, and she will be completely burned with fire, because Jehovah God, who judged her, is strong." So to Jehovah God, the Almighty, goes the credit for liberating mankind from domination by false religion. As Isaiah states, "Jehovah alone must be put on high in that day. For it is the day belonging to Jehovah of armies."—Isaiah 2:11b, 12a.

'Leaders Are Causing You to Wander'

16 For a human society to be stable, it must have its "support and stay"—such necessities as food and water and, more important, trustworthy leaders who are able to guide the people and maintain social order. Concerning ancient Israel, though, Isaiah foretells: *"Look! the true Lord, Jehovah of armies, is removing from Jerusalem and from Judah support and stay, the whole support of bread and the whole support of water, mighty man and warrior, judge and prophet, and practicer of divination and elderly man, chief of fifty and highly respected man and counselor and expert in magical arts, and the skilled charmer."* (Isaiah 3:1-3) Mere boys will become princes and rule capriciously. Not only will the rulers oppress the people but *"the people will actually tyrannize one over the other . . . They will storm, the boy against the old man, and the lightly esteemed one against the one to be honored."* (Isaiah 3: 4, 5) Children "storm" against their elders, lacking respect for them. So low will be the condition of life that one will say to another who has no qualification for rulership: *"You*

---

15. How will Jehovah alone "be put on high" in his day of judgment?
16. (a) What constitute the "support and stay" of a human society? (b) How will Isaiah's people suffer from the removal of the "support and stay" of their society?

have a mantle. A dictator you ought to become to us, and this overthrown mass should be under your hand." (Isaiah 3:6) But the ones thus invited will refuse, insisting that they have neither the ability to heal the wounded land nor the wealth to handle the responsibility. They will say: *"I shall not become a wound dresser; and in my house there is neither bread nor a mantle. You men must not set me as dictator over the people."—Isaiah 3:7.*

17 Isaiah continues: *"Jerusalem has stumbled, and Judah itself has fallen, because their tongue and their dealings are against Jehovah, in behaving rebelliously in the eyes of his glory. The very expression of their faces actually testifies against them, and of their sin like that of Sodom they do tell. They have not hidden it. Woe to their soul! For they have dealt out to themselves calamity."* (Isaiah 3:8, 9) God's people have rebelled against the true God in words and deeds. Even the shameless and unrepentant expressions on their faces expose their sins, which are as disgusting as those of Sodom. They are in a covenant with Jehovah God, yet he will not change his standards for them. *"It will be well with the righteous one, for they will eat the very fruitage of their dealings. Woe to the wicked one!—Calamity; for the treatment rendered by his own hands will be rendered to him! As for my people, its task assigners are dealing severely, and mere women actually rule over it. O my people, those leading you on are causing you to wander, and the way of your paths they have confused."—Isaiah 3:10-12.*

18 To the elders and the princes in Judah, Jehovah 'passes sentence' and 'enters into judgment': *"You yourselves have*

---

17. (a) In what sense was the sin of Jerusalem and Judah "like that of Sodom"? (b) Whom does Isaiah blame for the condition of his people?
18. (a) What judgment does Jehovah pronounce upon the elders and the princes of Isaiah's day? (b) What lesson do we learn from Jehovah's judgment of the elders and the princes?

burned down the vineyard. What was taken by robbery from the afflicted one is in your houses. What do you men mean in that you crush my people, and that you grind the very faces of the afflicted ones?" (Isaiah 3:13-15) Instead of working for the welfare of the people, leaders engage in deceitful practices. They misuse their authority by enriching themselves and depriving the poor and needy. But these leaders must answer to Jehovah of armies for their oppression of the afflicted. What a warning this is to those in positions of responsibility today! May they be ever careful not to misuse their authority.

19 Christendom—particularly her clergy and principal ones—has fraudulently acquired much that should belong to the common people, whom she has oppressed and continues to oppress. She has also beaten, persecuted, and maltreated the people of God and has brought great reproach upon Jehovah's name. In his due time, Jehovah will certainly enter into judgment against her.

"A Brand Mark Instead of Prettiness"

20 After denouncing the wrongs of the leaders, Jehovah turns to the women of Zion, or Jerusalem. Apparently for reasons of fashion, "the daughters of Zion" wear "step chains"—chainlets fastened to their ankles—which make a melodious tinkling sound. The women restrict their stride and walk along *"with tripping steps,"* cultivating what might be considered a genteel feminine gait. What, if anything, is wrong with

---

19. Of what oppression and persecution has Christendom been guilty?
20. Why does Jehovah denounce "the daughters of Zion"?

this? It is the attitude of these women. Jehovah says: *"The daughters of Zion have become haughty and they walk with their throats stretched forth and ogling with their eyes." (Isaiah 3:16)* Such haughtiness does not escape retribution.

21 Hence, when Jehovah's judgment comes upon the land, these haughty "daughters of Zion" will lose everything—even the beauty of which they are so proud. Jehovah prophesies: *"Jehovah also will actually make the crown of the head of the daughters of Zion scabby, and Jehovah himself will lay their very forehead bare. In that day Jehovah will take away the beauty of the bangles and the headbands and the moon-shaped ornaments, the eardrops and the bracelets and the veils, the headdresses and the step chains and the breastbands and the 'houses of the soul'* [probably perfume receptacles] *and the ornamental humming shells* [or, charms], *the finger rings and the nose rings, the robes of state and the overtunics and the cloaks and the purses, and the hand mirrors and the undergarments and the turbans and the large veils." (Isaiah 3:17-23; see footnotes.)* What a tragic reversal!

22 The prophetic message goes on to say: *"Instead of balsam oil there will come to be merely a musty smell; and instead of a belt, a rope; and instead of an artistic hair arrangement, baldness; and instead of a rich garment, a girding of sackcloth; a brand mark instead of prettiness." (Isaiah 3:24)* In 607 B.C.E., the proud women of Jerusalem fall from wealth to poverty. They lose their freedom and receive "a brand mark" of slavery.

"She Will Certainly Be Cleaned Out"

23 Speaking now to the city of Jerusalem, Jehovah

---

21. How does Jehovah's judgment of Jerusalem affect the Jewish women?
22. Besides their ornaments, what else do the women of Jerusalem lose?
23. What does Jehovah proclaim concerning Jerusalem?

proclaims: *"By the sword your own men will fall, and your mightiness by war. And her entrances will have to mourn and express sorrow, and she will certainly be cleaned out. She will sit down on the very earth." (Isaiah 3:25, 26)* The men of Jerusalem, even her mighty ones, will be slain in battle. The city will be leveled to the ground. For "her entrances," it will be a time to "mourn and express sorrow." Jerusalem will be "cleaned out" and laid desolate.

24 The loss of men by the sword will have drastic consequences for the women of Jerusalem. Concluding this part of his prophetic book, Isaiah foretells: *"Seven women will actually grab hold of one man in that day, saying: 'We shall eat our own bread and wear our own mantles; only may we be called by your name to take away our reproach.'" (Isaiah 4:1)* The shortage of marriageable men will become so severe that several women will attach themselves to one man in order to be called by his name —that is, to be publicly known as his wives—and thus be free of the reproach of being without a husband. The Mosaic Law required that a husband provide sustenance and clothing for his wife. (Exodus 21:10) However, agreeing to 'eat their own bread and wear their own clothing,' these women are willing to release the man from his legal obligations. What a desperate situation for the once haughty "daughters of Zion"!

25 Jehovah humiliates self-exalted ones. In 607 B.C.E., he does indeed make the haughtiness of his chosen people "bow down" and cause their "loftiness" to become "low." May true Christians never forget that "God opposes the haughty ones, but he gives undeserved kindness to the humble ones."—James 4:6.

---

24. The loss of men by the sword has what drastic consequences for the women of Jerusalem?
25. What is in the offing for self-exalted ones?

CHAPTER SIX

Jehovah God Has Mercy on a Remnant

Isaiah 4:2-6

A VIOLENT storm descends upon a densely populated region. Strong winds, torrential rains, and heavy flooding cut a wide swath through the land, destroying homes, damaging crops, and claiming lives. But soon the storm passes, and in its aftermath a period of calm sets in. For those who have survived, it is a time for restoration and rebuilding.

2 The prophet Isaiah foretells something similar concerning Judah and Jerusalem. The storm clouds of divine judgment are moving ominously closer—and with good reason! The guilt of the nation is heavy. Both the rulers and the people have filled the land with injustice and bloodshed. Through Isaiah, Jehovah lays bare Judah's guilt and warns that He will execute judgment on that delinquent nation. (Isaiah 3:25) The land of Judah will be left completely desolate in the wake of this storm. That prospect must sadden Isaiah.

3 But there is good news! The storm of Jehovah's righteous judgment will pass, and a remnant will survive. Yes, Jehovah's judgment of Judah will be tempered with

---

1, 2. The prophet Isaiah foretells what concerning Judah and Jerusalem?

3. What good news does the inspired message at Isaiah 4:2-6 contain?

mercy! Isaiah's inspired message recorded at Isaiah 4:2-6 looks ahead to this blessed time. It is as if the sun breaks out from behind the clouds; the scene shifts from the sights and sounds of judgment—described at Isaiah 2:6 –4:1—to a beautifully renewed land and people.

4 Isaiah's prophecy regarding the restoration of a remnant and their subsequent security also finds a fulfillment in our time—"the final part of the days." (Isaiah 2:2-4) Let us discuss this timely message, for not only does it have prophetic significance but it also teaches us about Jehovah's mercy and how we as individuals might receive it.

'The Sprouting of Jehovah'

5 Isaiah's tone becomes warm as he looks beyond the coming tempest to a more peaceful time. He writes: *"In that day what Jehovah makes sprout* ["the sprouting (sprout) of Jehovah," footnote] *will come to be for decoration and for glory, and the fruitage of the land will be something to be proud of and something beautiful for those of Israel who have escaped."—Isaiah 4:2.*

6 Isaiah here speaks of restoration. The Hebrew noun rendered "sprout" refers to 'that which springs up, a shoot, a branch.' It is associated with prosperity, increase, and blessings from Jehovah. Isaiah thus paints a picture of hope—the approaching desolation will not last forever. With Jehovah's blessing, the once-prosperous

---

4. Why should we discuss Isaiah's prophecy of the restoration of a remnant?

5, 6. (a) How does Isaiah describe the peaceful time that follows the coming tempest? (b) What is the meaning of the term "sprout," and what does this indicate about the land of Judah?

A storm of divine judgment is coming upon Judah

land of Judah will again bring forth abundant fruitage.*
—Leviticus 26:3-5.

7 Isaiah uses vivid terms to describe the grandeur of the transformation that lies ahead. The sprouting of Jehovah will "be for decoration and for glory." The word "decoration" calls to mind the beauty of the Promised Land when Jehovah gave it to Israel centuries earlier. It was so beautiful that it was considered "the decoration ["jewel," *New*

---

* Some scholars suggest that the phrase 'sprout of Jehovah' is an allusion to the Messiah, who would not appear until after the restoration of Jerusalem. In the Aramaic Targums, the paraphrase of this expression reads: "The Messiah [Christ] of Jehovah." Interestingly, the same Hebrew noun (*tse'mach*) is later used by Jeremiah when he speaks of the Messiah as "a righteous sprout" raised up to David.—Jeremiah 23:5; 33:15.

---

7. In what way will the sprouting of Jehovah "be for decoration and for glory"?

American Bible] of all the lands." (Ezekiel 20:6) Isaiah's words thus assure the people that the land of Judah will be restored to its former glory and beauty. Indeed, it will be like a crowning jewel on the earth.

8 Who, though, will be on hand to enjoy the restored beauty of the land? "Those of Israel who have escaped," writes Isaiah. Yes, some will survive the humiliating destruction previously foretold. (Isaiah 3:25, 26) A remnant of the survivors will return to Judah and share in its restoration. For these returnees—"the escaped ones"—the abundant produce of their restored land will become "something to be proud of and something beautiful." (Isaiah 4:2; footnote) The humiliation of desolation will give way to a renewed sense of pride.

9 True to Isaiah's words, the storm of judgment arrived in 607 B.C.E. when the Babylonians destroyed Jerusalem and many Israelites perished. Some survived and were taken into exile in Babylon, but if it had not been for God's mercy, there would have been no survivors at all. (Nehemiah 9:31) Eventually, Judah was left completely desolate. (2 Chronicles 36:17-21) Then, in 537 B.C.E., the God of mercy allowed "escaped ones" to return to Judah in order to restore true worship.* (Ezra 1:1-4; 2:1) The heartfelt repentance of these returning exiles is beautifully expressed

---

* "The escaped ones" included some who had been born in exile. These could be considered to have "escaped," since they would never have been born if their ancestors had not survived the destruction. —Ezra 9:13-15; compare Hebrews 7:9, 10.

---

8. Who will be on hand to enjoy the restored beauty of the land, and how does Isaiah describe their feelings?

9. (a) In fulfillment of Isaiah's words, what happened in 537 B.C.E.? (b) Why may it be said that "the escaped ones" include some who have been born in exile? (See footnote.)

in Psalm 137, which was likely written during the captivity or shortly thereafter. Back in Judah they tilled the soil and sowed seed in the land. Think of how they must have felt when they saw that God was blessing their efforts, causing the land to sprout like the fruitful "garden of Eden"!—Ezekiel 36:34-36.

10 A similar restoration has taken place in our day. Early in the 20th century, the Bible Students, as Jehovah's Witnesses were then known, came into spiritual captivity to "Babylon the Great," the world empire of false religion. (Revelation 17:5) Although having rejected many false religious teachings, the Bible Students were still tainted by certain Babylonish ideas and practices. As a result of clergy-inspired opposition, some of them were literally imprisoned. Their spiritual land—their religious, or spiritual, estate—was left desolate.

11 But in the spring of 1919, Jehovah had mercy on this remnant of spiritual Israelites. (Galatians 6:16) He saw their repentance and their desire to worship him in truth, so he brought about their release from literal imprisonment and, more important, from spiritual captivity. These "escaped ones" were restored to their God-given spiritual estate, which he caused to sprout abundantly. This spiritual estate has presented an inviting, attractive appearance, which has drawn millions of other God-fearing people to join the remnant in true worship.

12 Isaiah's words here magnify the mercy that God has toward his people. Although the Israelites as a nation

----

10, 11. (a) In what way were the Bible Students in captivity to "Babylon the Great" early in the 20th century? (b) How did Jehovah bless the remnant of spiritual Israelites?

12. How do Isaiah's words magnify the mercy that Jehovah has toward his people?

turned against Jehovah, he had mercy on a repentant remnant. We can draw comfort from knowing that even those who err seriously can return to Jehovah with hope. Repentant ones need not feel that they are beyond Jehovah's mercy, for he does not reject a contrite heart. (Psalm 51:17) The Bible assures us: "Jehovah is merciful and gracious, slow to anger and abundant in loving-kindness. As a father shows mercy to his sons, Jehovah has shown mercy to those fearing him." (Psalm 103:8, 13) Surely, such a merciful God deserves all our praise!

A Remnant Becomes Holy to Jehovah

13 We have already been introduced to the remnant that would be shown mercy by Jehovah, but now Isaiah describes them in more detail. He writes: *"It must occur that the ones remaining in Zion and the ones left over in Jerusalem will be said to be holy to him, everyone written down for life in Jerusalem."—Isaiah 4:3.*

14 Who are "the ones remaining" and "the ones left over"? They are the escaped ones mentioned in the preceding verse—the Jewish exiles who will be permitted to return to Judah. Now Isaiah shows why Jehovah will have mercy on them—they will "be holy to him." Holiness means "religious cleanness or purity; sacredness." To be holy involves being clean, or pure, in word and action, to measure up to Jehovah's standard of what is right and proper. Yes, Jehovah will have mercy on those who are "holy to him," and he will allow them to return to "the holy city," Jerusalem.—Nehemiah 11:1.

---

13. As recorded at Isaiah 4:3, how does Isaiah describe the remnant that would be shown mercy by Jehovah?
14. Who are "the ones remaining" and "the ones left over," and why will Jehovah have mercy on them?

15 Will this faithful remnant remain there? They will be "written down for life in Jerusalem," promises Isaiah. This reminds us of the Jewish custom of keeping careful registers of Israel's families and tribes. (Nehemiah 7:5) To be written in a register meant to be alive, for when a person died, his name was removed. In other parts of the Bible, we read of a figurative register, or book, containing the names of those whom Jehovah rewards with life. But this book receives names conditionally, for Jehovah can 'wipe out' names. (Exodus 32:32, 33; Psalm 69:28) Isaiah's words, then, imply a sobering warning—the returnees may continue living in their restored land only if they *remain* holy in God's sight.

16 In 537 B.C.E., the remnant that returned to Jerusalem did so with a pure motive—to restore true worship. No one contaminated by pagan religious practices or by the unclean conduct that Isaiah had so forcefully warned against had a right to return. (Isaiah 1:15-17) Only those whom Jehovah viewed as holy could head back to Judah. (Isaiah 35:8) Similarly, since their release from spiritual captivity in 1919, the anointed remnant, now joined by millions of "other sheep"—those with the hope of everlasting life on earth—have made every effort to be holy in God's sight. (John 10:16) They have rid themselves of Babylonish teachings and practices. Individually, they strive to hold to God's high standards of morality. (1 Peter 1:14-16) Jehovah's mercy on them has not been in vain.

---

15. (a) The expression "written down for life in Jerusalem" reminds us of what Jewish custom? (b) What sobering warning do Isaiah's words imply?

16. (a) What did Jehovah require of those whom he permitted to head back to Judah in 537 B.C.E.? (b) Why can it be said that Jehovah's mercy on the anointed remnant and the "other sheep" has not been in vain?

17 Recall that Jehovah noted those in Israel who were holy and that he 'wrote down their names for life.' Today, too, Jehovah notices our endeavors to be clean in mind and body as we 'present our bodies a sacrifice living, holy, acceptable to God.' (Romans 12:1) And all who follow such a life course are recorded by God in his "book of life" —the figurative record containing the names of those who are in line to receive everlasting life, either in heaven or on earth. (Philippians 4:3; Malachi 3:16) Let us, then, do our utmost to remain holy in God's eyes, for then we may *keep* our names in that precious "book."—Revelation 3:5.

A Promise of Loving Care

18 Next Isaiah shows how the inhabitants of the restored land will come to be holy and what blessings await them. He says: *"When Jehovah will have washed away the excrement of the daughters of Zion and he will rinse away even the bloodshed of Jerusalem from within her by the spirit of judgment and by the spirit of burning down, Jehovah will also certainly create over every established place of Mount Zion and over her convention place a cloud by day and a smoke, and the brightness of a flaming fire by night; because over all the glory there will be a shelter."*
—Isaiah 4:4, 5.

19 Earlier Isaiah rebuked "the daughters of Zion," whose moral corruption was hidden beneath their showy ornaments. He also exposed the bloodguilt of the people generally, urging them to wash themselves. (Isaiah 1:15, 16; 3:16-23) Here, though, he looks ahead to the time when God himself will have "washed away the excrement," or

---

17. Whose names does Jehovah write in his "book of life," and what should we be determined to do?
18, 19. According to Isaiah 4:4, 5, what cleansing is to be effected by Jehovah, and how will it be accomplished?

moral filth, and 'cleansed the bloodstains.' (Isaiah 4:4, *New International Version*) How will this cleansing be effected? By "the spirit of judgment" and by "the spirit of burning down." The coming destruction of Jerusalem and the exile in Babylon will be blasts of God's judgment and burning anger on an unclean nation. The remnant that survives these calamities and returns home will have been humbled, refined. That is why they will be holy to Jehovah and receive mercy.—Compare Malachi 3:2, 3.

20 Jehovah, through Isaiah, promises that he will take this cleansed remnant into his loving care. The expressions "a cloud," "a smoke," and "a flaming fire" are reminiscent of how Jehovah cared for the Israelites after they

20. (a) Of what are the expressions "a cloud," "a smoke," and "a flaming fire" reminiscent? (b) Why will the purged exiles not need to fear?

left Egypt. A "pillar of fire and cloud" protected them from the pursuing Egyptians; it also led them in the wilderness. (Exodus 13:21, 22; 14:19, 20, 24) When Jehovah manifested himself at Mount Sinai, the mountain "smoked all over." (Exodus 19:18) The cleansed exiles, then, will not need to fear. Jehovah will be their Protector. He will be with them whether they gather in their own homes or meet together in holy conventions.

21 Isaiah concludes his description of divine protection by focusing on everyday life. He writes: *"There will come to be a booth for a shade by day from the dry heat, and for a refuge and for a hiding place from the rainstorm and from the precipitation." (Isaiah 4:6)* A booth, or hut, was often built in a vineyard or in a field to provide much-needed shelter from the burning sun of the dry season and from the cold and storms of the rainy season.—Compare Jonah 4:5.

22 When faced with the scorching heat of persecution and the storms of opposition, the cleansed remnant will find Jehovah to be their Source of protection, security, and refuge. (Psalm 91:1, 2; 121:5) A beautiful prospect is thus set before them: If they leave behind the unclean beliefs and practices of Babylon, submit to the cleansing of Jehovah's judgment, and endeavor to remain holy, they will remain safe, as if in "a booth" of divine protection.

23 Notice that first comes the cleansing, then the blessings. This has proved true in our day. Back in 1919 the anointed remnant humbly submitted to being refined, and Jehovah "washed away" their uncleanness. Since

---

21, 22. (a) A booth, or hut, was often built for what purpose? (b) What prospect is set before the cleansed remnant?
23. Why has Jehovah blessed the anointed remnant and their companions?

then, "a great crowd" of other sheep have also allowed themselves to be cleansed by Jehovah. (Revelation 7:9) Thus cleansed, the remnant and their companions have been blessed—Jehovah has taken them into his protective care. He does not miraculously prevent the heat of persecution or the storms of opposition from bearing down on them. But he does protect them, as if erecting over them 'a booth for shade and for a hiding place from the rainstorm.' How?

24 Consider this: Some of the most powerful governments in history have banned the preaching work of Jehovah's Witnesses or have tried to eliminate them completely. Yet, the Witnesses have remained firm and have continued to preach without letup! Why have mighty nations been unable to put a stop to the activity of this relatively small and seemingly defenseless group of people? Because Jehovah has placed his clean servants in "a booth" of protection that no human can tear down!

25 What about us as individuals? Having Jehovah as our Protector does not mean that we have a problem-free life in this system of things. Many faithful Christians face severe adversities, such as poverty, natural disasters, war, sickness, and death. When facing such distresses, let us never forget that our God is with us. He protects us spiritually, providing what we need—even "power beyond what is normal"—to endure trials faithfully. (2 Corinthians 4:7) Safe in his presence, we need not fear. After all, as long as we do our best to keep ourselves holy in his sight, nothing "will be able to separate us from God's love."—Romans 8:38, 39.

---

24. How is it evident that Jehovah has blessed his people as an organization?
25. What does having Jehovah as our Protector mean for us as individuals?

CHAPTER SEVEN

Woe to the Unfaithful Vineyard!

Isaiah 5:1-30

"FOR exquisite beauty of language and consummate skill in effective communication, this parable is virtually peerless." So said one Bible commentator referring to the opening verses of Isaiah chapter 5. More than simply a work of art, Isaiah's words paint a touching portrait of the loving care that Jehovah has for his people. At the same time, these words warn us against things that displease him.

2 Isaiah's parable begins: *"Let me sing, please, to my beloved one a song of my loved one concerning his vineyard. There was a vineyard that my beloved one came to have on a fruitful hillside. And he proceeded to dig it up and to rid it of stones and to plant it with a choice red vine, and to build a tower in the middle of it. And there was also a winepress that he hewed out in it. And he kept hoping for it to produce grapes, but it gradually produced wild grapes."—Isaiah 5:1, 2;* compare Mark 12:1.

The Care of the Vineyard

3 Whether Isaiah literally sings this parable to his listeners or not, it surely captures their attention. Most are

---

1, 2. What does the "beloved one" plant, but how does it prove disappointing?

3, 4. What loving care is expended on the vineyard?

probably familiar with the work of planting a vineyard, and Isaiah's description is vivid and realistic. Like
vine growers today, the vineyard owner plants, not grape
seeds, but a "choice," or rich, "red vine"—a cutting or
shoot from another vine. Appropriately, he plants this
vineyard "on a fruitful hillside," a place where a vineyard
will thrive.

4 It takes hard work to make a vineyard produce. Isaiah
describes the owner's 'digging the land and ridding it of
stones'—tedious, exhausting work! He likely uses the larger stones "to build a tower." In ancient times such towers
served as stations for watchmen who guarded the crops
against thieves and animals.* Also, he builds a stone wall
to line the vineyard terraces. (Isaiah 5:5) This was commonly done to prevent the washing away of vital topsoil.

5 Having worked so hard to protect his vineyard, the
owner has every right to expect that it will bear fruit. In
anticipation of this, he hews out a winepress. But does the
hoped-for harvest materialize? No, the vineyard produces
wild grapes.

The Vineyard and Its Owner

6 Who is the owner, and what is the vineyard? The vineyard owner points to the answers to these questions when
he himself speaks: *"Now, O you inhabitants of Jerusalem
and you men of Judah, please judge between me and my*

---

* Some scholars believe that cheaper temporary structures, such as
booths, or huts, were far more common than stone towers. (Isaiah
1:8) The presence of a tower would indicate that unusual efforts had
been put forth by the owner in behalf of his "vineyard."

---

5. What does the owner properly expect from his vineyard, but what
does he get?
6, 7. (a) Who is the owner of the vineyard, and what is the vineyard? (b) What judgment does the owner invite?

vineyard. What is there yet to do for my vineyard that I have not already done in it? Why is it that I hoped for it to produce grapes, but it gradually produced wild grapes? And now, please, may I make known to you men what I am doing to my vineyard: There will be a removing of its hedge, and it must be destined for burning down. There must be a breaking down of its stone wall, and it must be destined for a place of trampling."—Isaiah 5:3-5.*

7 Yes, Jehovah is the owner of the vineyard, and he has put himself, as it were, in a courtroom, asking for judgment to be rendered between him and his disappointing vineyard. What, then, is the vineyard? The owner explains: *"The vineyard of Jehovah of armies is the house of*

***Israel, and the men of Judah are the plantation of which
he was fond."—Isaiah 5:7a.***

8 Isaiah calls Jehovah, the owner of the vineyard, "my
loved one." (Isaiah 5:1) Isaiah can speak of God in such
an intimate way only because he has a close relationship
with Him. (Compare Job 29:4; Psalm 25:14.) However, the
prophet's love for God pales in comparison with the love
God has shown for his "vineyard"—the nation that he
'planted.'—Compare Exodus 15:17; Psalm 80:8, 9.

9 Jehovah "planted" his nation in the land of Canaan
and gave them his laws and regulations, which served
as a wall to protect them from being corrupted by other
nations. (Exodus 19:5, 6; Psalm 147:19, 20; Ephesians 2:
14) Furthermore, Jehovah gave them judges, priests, and
prophets to instruct them. (2 Kings 17:13; Malachi 2:7;
Acts 13:20) When Israel was threatened by military aggression, Jehovah raised up deliverers. (Hebrews 11:32,
33) With reason, Jehovah asks: "What is there yet to do
for my vineyard that I have not already done in it?"

Identifying God's Vineyard Today

10 Jesus may have had Isaiah's words in mind when he
gave the parable of the murderous cultivators: "There was
a man, a householder, who planted a vineyard and put a
fence around it and dug a winepress in it and erected a
tower, and let it out to cultivators, and traveled abroad."
Unhappily, the cultivators betrayed the vineyard owner,
even killing his son. Jesus went on to show that this parable involved more than just literal Israel when he said:

---

8. What is significant about Isaiah's calling Jehovah "my loved one"?
9. How has Jehovah treated his nation like a valued vineyard?
10. What parable involving a vineyard did Jesus give?

"The kingdom of God will be taken from you [fleshly Israel] and be given to a nation producing its fruits."—Matthew 21:33-41, 43.

11 That new "nation" proved to be "the Israel of God" —a spiritual nation of anointed Christians totaling 144,- 000. (Galatians 6:16; 1 Peter 2:9, 10; Revelation 7:3, 4) Jesus compared these disciples to "branches" on "the true vine," namely, himself. Naturally, these branches are expected to bear fruit. (John 15:1-5) They must manifest Christlike qualities and participate in the work of preaching "this good news of the Kingdom." (Matthew 24:14; Galatians 5:22, 23) But ever since the death of the twelve apostles, the great majority of those who claim to be branches of "the true vine" have proved to be counterfeits —producing wild grapes instead of good fruits.—Matthew 13:24-30, 38, 39.

12 Therefore, Isaiah's condemnation of Judah applies today to Christendom. A study of her history—her wars, her crusades, her Inquisitions—reveals just how sour her fruit has been! Nevertheless, the true vineyard of anointed Christians and their "great crowd" companions must heed Isaiah's words. (Revelation 7:9) If they are to please the vineyard's owner, they must, individually and as a group, produce fruits that please him.

"Wild Grapes"

13 Having gone to extraordinary lengths to nurture and cultivate his vineyard, Jehovah rightfully expects it

---

11. What spiritual vineyard existed in the first century, but what happened after the death of the apostles?
12. How do Isaiah's words condemn Christendom, and what lesson do they hold for true Christians?
13. What will Jehovah do to his vineyard because of its producing bad fruit?

to become "a vineyard of foaming wine!" (Isaiah 27:2) However, instead of producing usable fruit, it produces "wild grapes," literally "stinking things" or "putrid (rotten) berries." (Isaiah 5:2; footnote; Jeremiah 2:21) Therefore, Jehovah declares that he will remove his protective "hedge" from around the nation. The nation will be 'set as a thing destroyed' and will experience abandonment and drought. *(Read Isaiah 5:6.)* Moses had warned that they would undergo such things if they disobeyed God's Law.—Deuteronomy 11:17; 28:63, 64; 29:22, 23.

14 God expects the nation to produce good fruits. Isaiah's contemporary Micah declares: "What is Jehovah asking back from you but to exercise justice and to love kindness and to be modest in walking with your God?" (Micah 6:8; Zechariah 7:9) However, the nation fails to heed Jehovah's exhortation. *"[God] kept hoping for judgment, but, look! the breaking of law; for righteousness, but, look! an outcry." (Isaiah 5:7b)* Moses predicted that the unfaithful nation would produce poisonous grapes from "the vine of Sodom." (Deuteronomy 32:32) Likely, then, sexual immorality, including homosexuality, is part of their deviation from God's Law. (Leviticus 18:22) The expression "breaking of law" can also be rendered "outpouring of blood." Such brutal treatment has no doubt resulted in "an outcry" from mistreated ones—an outcry that has reached the ears of the Planter of the vineyard.—Compare Job 34:28.

15 Jehovah God is "a lover of righteousness and justice."

---

14. What fruitage does Jehovah expect of his nation, but what does it produce instead?

15, 16. How can true Christians avoid producing the bad fruits that Israel produced?

(Psalm 33:5) He commanded the Jews: "You people must not do injustice in the judgment. You must not treat the lowly with partiality, and you must not prefer the person of a great one. With justice you should judge your associate." (Leviticus 19:15) We must therefore shun partiality in our dealings with one another, never allowing such things as race, age, wealth, or poverty to color our judgment of people. (James 2:1-4) It is particularly important that those serving in positions of oversight 'do nothing according to a biased leaning,' always seeking to hear both sides of a matter before making judgment.—1 Timothy 5:21; Proverbs 18:13.

16 Further, it would be easy for Christians living in a lawless world to develop a negative or a rebellious attitude toward godly standards. But true Christians must be "ready to obey" God's laws. (James 3:17) Despite the sexual immorality and violence of "the present wicked system of things," they need to 'keep strict watch that how they walk is not as unwise but as wise persons.' (Galatians 1:4; Ephesians 5:15) They want to shun permissive views of sex, and when disagreements arise, they should settle these without "anger and wrath and screaming and abusive speech." (Ephesians 4:31) By cultivating righteousness, true Christians bring honor to God and gain his favor.

The Price of Greed

17 In verse 8, Isaiah is no longer quoting Jehovah's words. Condemning some of the "wild grapes" produced in Judah, he personally pronounces the first of six woes: ***"Woe to the ones joining house to house, and those who annex field to field until there is no more room and you***

---

17. What wicked conduct is condemned in Isaiah's first woe?

men have been made to dwell all by yourselves in the midst of the land! In my ears Jehovah of armies has sworn that many houses, though great and good, will become an outright object of astonishment, without an inhabitant. For even ten acres of vineyard will produce but one bath measure, and even a homer measure of seed will produce but an ephah measure."—Isaiah 5:8-10.

18 In ancient Israel all land ultimately belonged to Jehovah. Each family had a God-given inheritance, which they could rent or loan out but never sell "in perpetuity." (Leviticus 25:23) This law prevented abuses, such as real estate monopolies. It also protected families from sinking too far into poverty. Some in Judah, however, were greedily breaking God's laws regarding property. Micah wrote: "They have desired fields and have seized them; also houses, and have taken them; and they have defrauded an able-bodied man and his household, a man and his hereditary possession." (Micah 2:2) But Proverbs 20:21 warns: "An inheritance is being got by greed at first, but its own future will not be blessed."

19 Jehovah promises to strip these greedy ones of their ill-gotten gain. The houses they extort will be "without an inhabitant." The lands they covet will produce a mere fraction of their capacity. Exactly how and when this curse will be fulfilled is not stated. Likely it refers, at least in part, to the conditions brought on by the future Babylonian exile.—Isaiah 27:10.

20 Christians today must abhor insatiable greed like that manifested by some Israelites back then. (Proverbs 27:20)

18, 19. How do Isaiah's contemporaries ignore Jehovah's laws regarding property, and what will be the result for them?
20. How can Christians today avoid imitating the greedy attitude shown by some in Israel?

When material things take on exaggerated importance, it is easy to stoop to unscrupulous ways of getting money. One could easily become ensnared in shady business dealings or unrealistic get-rich-quick schemes. "He that is hastening to gain riches will not remain innocent." (Proverbs 28:20) How important it is, then, to be content with what we have!—1 Timothy 6:8.

The Snare of Questionable Entertainment

21 Next comes Isaiah's second woe: *"Woe to those who are getting up early in the morning that they may seek just intoxicating liquor, who are lingering till late in the evening darkness so that wine itself inflames them! And there must prove to be harp and stringed instrument, tambourine and flute, and wine at their feasts; but the activity of Jehovah they do not look at, and the work of his hands they have not seen."—Isaiah 5:11, 12.*

22 Jehovah is "the happy God" and does not begrudge his servants reasonable recreation. (1 Timothy 1:11) However, these pleasure-seekers go beyond all limits! "Those who get drunk are usually drunk at night," says the Bible. (1 Thessalonians 5:7) But the revelers of the prophecy begin their drunken sprees at daybreak and carry on drinking into the evening! They behave as if God did not exist, as if he would not hold them accountable for their actions. Isaiah predicts a dark future for such ones. *"My people will have to go into exile for lack of knowledge; and their glory will be famished men, and their crowd will be parched with thirst." (Isaiah 5:13)* Because of refusing to act according to true knowledge, God's covenant people

---

21. What sins are condemned in Isaiah's second woe?
22. What lack of restraint is manifest in Israel, and what will be the result for the nation?

—the high and the low—will go down into Sheol.—**Read Isaiah 5:14-17.**

23 "Revelries," or "wild parties," were also a problem among some Christians in the first century. (Galatians 5: 21; *Byington;* 2 Peter 2:13) So it is not surprising that some dedicated Christians today have shown poor judgment when it comes to social gatherings. Unrestrained use of alcoholic beverages has caused some to become loud and boisterous. (Proverbs 20:1) There have even been those who behaved immorally under the influence of excessive alcohol, and some gatherings have been allowed to go on virtually all night, interfering with Christian activities the next day.

24 Balanced Christians, however, produce godly fruit and exercise restraint and moderation in their choice of recreation. They heed Paul's advice found at Romans 13: 13: "As in the daytime let us walk decently, not in revelries and drunken bouts."

Hating Sin and Loving Truth

25 Hear now Isaiah's third and fourth woes: *"Woe to those drawing error with ropes of untruth, and as with wagon cords sin; those who are saying: 'Let his work hasten; do let it come quickly, in order that we may see it; and let the counsel of the Holy One of Israel draw near and come, that we may know it!' Woe to those who are saying that good is bad and bad is good, those who are putting darkness for light and light for darkness, those who are putting bitter for sweet and sweet for bitter!"—Isaiah 5:18-20.*

23, 24. What restraint and moderation are Christians called upon to show?
25, 26. What wicked thinking by the Israelites does Isaiah expose in his third and fourth woes?

26 What a vivid picture this paints of practicers of sin! They are attached to sin the way draft animals are tied to wagons. These sinners do not fear any coming day of judgment. Mockingly they say: "Let [God's work] come quickly!" Rather than submitting to God's Law, they twist things, declaring that "good is bad and bad is good." —Compare Jeremiah 6:15; 2 Peter 3:3-7.

27 Christians today must avoid such an attitude at all costs. For example, they refuse to embrace the world's view of fornication and homosexuality as acceptable. (Ephesians 4:18, 19) True, a Christian might 'take a false step' that could lead to committing a serious sin. (Galatians 6:1) The elders in the congregation are ready to

---

27. How can Christians today avoid an attitude like that of the Israelites?

A sinner is attached to sin like a draft animal to a wagon

help those who have fallen and need assistance. (James 5: 14, 15) With the aid of prayers and Bible-based counsel, spiritual recovery is possible. Otherwise, there is the danger of becoming "a slave of sin." (John 8:34) Rather than mocking God and losing awareness of the coming day of judgment, Christians strive to remain "spotless and unblemished" before Jehovah.—2 Peter 3:14; Galatians 6:7, 8.

28 Appropriately, Isaiah adds these final woes: *"Woe to those wise in their own eyes and discreet even in front of their own faces! Woe to those who are mighty in drinking wine, and to the men with vital energy for mixing intoxicating liquor, those who are pronouncing the wicked one righteous in consideration of a bribe, and who take away even the righteousness of the righteous one from him!"* (*Isaiah 5:21-23*) These words were evidently addressed to those serving as judges in the land. Congregation elders today avoid seeming "wise in their own eyes." They humbly accept counsel from fellow elders and adhere closely to organizational instructions. (Proverbs 1:5; 1 Corinthians 14:33) They are moderate in their use of alcoholic beverages, never indulging before carrying out congregation responsibilities. (Hosea 4:11) Elders also avoid giving even the appearance of showing favoritism. (James 2:9) How different from the clergy of Christendom! Many of these whitewash the influential and wealthy sinners in their midst, in direct contrast to the apostle Paul's warnings at Romans 1:18, 26, 27; 1 Corinthians 6:9, 10; and Ephesians 5:3-5.

29 Isaiah concludes this prophetic message by describing

---

28. What sins are condemned in Isaiah's final woes, and how can Christians today avoid such sins?
29. What calamitous end awaits Jehovah's Israelite vineyard?

a calamitous end for those who *"have rejected the law of Jehovah"* and have failed to bear righteous fruit. *(Isaiah 5: 24, 25;* Hosea 9:16; Malachi 4:1) He declares: *"[Jehovah] has raised up a signal to a great nation far away, and he has whistled to it at the extremity of the earth; and, look! in haste it will swiftly come in."—Isaiah 5:26;* Deuteronomy 28:49; Jeremiah 5:15.

30 In ancient times a pole on an elevated site could serve as "a signal," or rallying point, for people or armies. (Compare Isaiah 18:3; Jeremiah 51:27.) Now Jehovah himself will rally this unnamed "great nation" to execute his judgment.* He will 'whistle to it,' that is, draw its attention to his wayward people as an object worthy of conquest. The prophet next describes the swift and terrifying onslaught of these lionlike conquerers who will *"grab hold of the prey,"* that is, God's nation, *"and bring it safely away"* into captivity. *(Read Isaiah 5:27-30a.)* And what a sad result for the land of Jehovah's people! *"One will actually gaze at the land, and, look! there is distressing darkness; and even the light has grown dark because of the drops falling on it."—Isaiah 5:30b.*

31 Yes, the vineyard that God so lovingly planted proves itself to be barren—worthy only of destruction. What a powerful lesson Isaiah's words hold for all who would serve Jehovah today! May they strive to bear nothing but righteous fruit, to Jehovah's praise and to their own salvation!

---

* In other prophecies, Isaiah identifies Babylon as the nation that executes Jehovah's devastating judgment on Judah.

---

30. Who will rally "a great nation" against Jehovah's people, and with what outcome?
31. How can true Christians avoid suffering the punishment inflicted on Jehovah's Israelite vineyard?

CHAPTER EIGHT

Jehovah God Is in His Holy Temple

Isaiah 6:1-13

"IN THE year that King Uzziah died I, however, got to see Jehovah, sitting on a throne lofty and lifted up, and his skirts were filling the temple." (Isaiah 6:1) With these words of the prophet, the 6th chapter of the book of Isaiah begins. It is the year 778 B.C.E.

2 Uzziah's reign of 52 years as king of Judah was, for the most part, a brilliant success. Doing what "was right in Jehovah's eyes," he enjoyed God's backing in his military, building, and agricultural ventures. But his success also came to be his undoing. Eventually, his heart became haughty, "so that he acted unfaithfully against Jehovah his God and came into the temple of Jehovah to burn incense." Because of this presumptuous act and his rage against the priests who censured him, Uzziah died a leper. (2 Chronicles 26:3-22) It was about this time that Isaiah started his prophetic service.

3 We are not told where Isaiah is stationed when he sees the vision. But what he sees with his physical eyes is clearly a vision, not an actual sighting of the Almighty, as "no man has seen God at any time." (John 1: 18; Exodus 33:20) Still, to see the Creator, Jehovah, even

---

1, 2. (a) When does the prophet Isaiah receive his temple vision? (b) Why did King Uzziah lose Jehovah's favor?
3. (a) Does Isaiah actually see Jehovah? Explain. (b) What scene does Isaiah behold, and for what reason?

in vision, is an awesome sight. Sitting on a lofty throne, which symbolizes his role as everlasting King and Judge, is the Universal Ruler and Source of all rightful government! The skirts of his long, flowing robe fill the temple. Isaiah is being called to a prophetic service that will magnify Jehovah's sovereign power and justice. In preparation, he will be given a vision of God's holiness.

4 Isaiah provides no description of Jehovah's appearance in his vision—unlike the visions reported by Ezekiel, Daniel, and John. And those accounts all vary as to what is seen in heaven. (Ezekiel 1:26-28; Daniel 7:9, 10; Revelation 4:2, 3) However, the nature and purpose of these visions must be borne in mind. They are not literal descriptions of Jehovah's presence. The physical eye cannot see what is spiritual, nor can the finite human mind comprehend the spirit realm. Hence, the visions present in human terms the information that is to be conveyed. (Compare Revelation 1:1.) In Isaiah's vision a description of God's appearance is not necessary. The vision informs Isaiah that Jehovah is in his holy temple and that he is holy and his judgments are pure.

The Seraphs

5 Listen! Isaiah continues: *"Seraphs were standing above him. Each one had six wings. With two he kept his face covered, and with two he kept his feet covered, and with two he would fly about." (Isaiah 6:2)* Isaiah chapter 6 is the only place in the Bible where we find mention of seraphs. Obviously, they are angelic creatures in Jehovah's

---

4. (a) Why must descriptions of Jehovah seen in vision and recorded in the Bible be symbolic? (b) What is learned about Jehovah from Isaiah's vision?
5. (a) Who are the seraphs, and what does the term mean? (b) Why do the seraphs hide their faces and feet?

service who rank very highly in privileges and in honor, being stationed about Jehovah's heavenly throne. Unlike proud King Uzziah, they occupy their position in all humility and modesty. Because of being in the presence of the heavenly Sovereign, they cover their faces with one set of wings; and with reverence for the holy location, they cover their feet with another set. Close to the Universal Sovereign, the seraphs are all the more self-effacing, so as not to distract from God's personal glory. The term "seraphs," meaning "fiery ones" or "burning ones," suggests that they radiate brightness, yet they hide their faces from the greater brilliance and glory of Jehovah.

6 The seraphs use their third set of wings for flying and, no doubt, to hover, or 'stand,' in their places. (Compare Deuteronomy 31:15.) As to their position, Professor Franz Delitzsch comments: "The seraphim would not indeed tower above the head of Him that sat upon the throne, but they hovered above the robe belonging to Him with which the hall was filled." (*Commentary on the Old Testament*) This seems reasonable. They are "standing above," not as superior to Jehovah, but as waiting on him, obedient and ready to serve.

7 Listen, now, to those privileged seraphs! ***"This one called to that one and said: 'Holy, holy, holy is Jehovah of armies. The fullness of all the earth is his glory.'"* (*Isaiah 6:3*)** Their assignment is to see that Jehovah's holiness is declared and that his glory is acknowledged throughout the universe, of which the earth is a part. His glory is seen in all that he created and will soon be discerned by all earth's inhabitants. (Numbers 14:21; Psalm 19:1-3;

---

6. What is the position of the seraphs in relation to Jehovah?
7. (a) What assignment do the seraphs fulfill? (b) Why do the seraphs declare God's holiness three times?

Habakkuk 2:14) The threefold declaration, "holy, holy, holy," is no evidence of a Trinity. Rather, it is a threefold emphasizing of God's holiness. (Compare Revelation 4:8.) Jehovah is holy to the superlative degree.

8 Although the number of seraphs is not mentioned, there may be groups of seraphs stationed near the throne. In melodious song, they repeat one after another the declaration of God's holiness and glory. What result do we note? Listen again as Isaiah continues: *"The pivots of the thresholds began to quiver at the voice of the one calling, and the house itself gradually filled with smoke." (Isaiah 6:4)* In the Bible, smoke or a cloud often provides visible evidence of God's presence. (Exodus 19:18; 40:34, 35; 1 Kings 8:10, 11; Revelation 15:5-8) It denotes a glory to which we human creatures cannot approach.

Unworthy, Yet Cleansed

9 This vision of Jehovah's throne has a profound effect on Isaiah. He records: *"I proceeded to say: 'Woe to me! For I am as good as brought to silence, because a man unclean in lips I am, and in among a people unclean in lips I am dwelling; for my eyes have seen the King, Jehovah of armies, himself!'" (Isaiah 6:5)* What a stark contrast there is between Isaiah and King Uzziah! Uzziah usurped the position of the anointed priesthood and impiously invaded the Holy compartment of the temple. Although Uzziah saw the golden lampstands, the golden altar of incense, and the tables of "the bread of Presence," he did not see Jehovah's face of approval or receive any special commission from him. (1 Kings 7:48-50; footnote) On the

---

8. What results from the seraphs' declarations?
9. (a) What effect does the vision have on Isaiah? (b) What contrast is evident between Isaiah and King Uzziah?

other hand, the prophet Isaiah does not brush aside the priesthood or trespass on the temple. Yet, he sees a vision of Jehovah in his holy temple and is honored with a direct commission from God. While the seraphs do not presume to look upon the enthroned Lord of the temple, Isaiah is allowed, in vision, to look upon "the King, Jehovah of armies, himself!"

10 The contrast that Isaiah sees between God's holiness and his own sinfulness makes him feel most unclean. Filled with fear, he reasons that he will die. (Exodus 33: 20) He hears the seraphs praise God with clean lips, but his own lips are unclean and are further sullied by the uncleanness of the lips of the people among whom he dwells and whose speech he hears. Jehovah is holy, and his servants must reflect that quality. (1 Peter 1:15, 16) Although Isaiah has already been chosen as a spokesman for God, he is struck with the realization of his sinful

10. Why does Isaiah feel dread at seeing the vision?

condition and lacks the clean lips befitting a spokesman of the glorious and holy King. What will the heavenly response be?

11 Instead of banishing lowly Isaiah from before Jehovah's presence, the seraphs act to help him. The record states: *"At that, one of the seraphs flew to me, and in his hand there was a glowing coal that he had taken with*

11. (a) What does one of the seraphs do, and what does this action symbolize? (b) How can reflecting on what the seraph tells Isaiah help us when we feel unworthy as God's servants?

tongs off the altar. And he proceeded to touch my mouth and to say: 'Look! This has touched your lips, and your error has departed and your sin itself is atoned for.'" (Isaiah 6:6, 7) In a symbolic sense, fire has purifying power. When applying the glowing coal from the holy fire of the altar to Isaiah's lips, the seraph assures Isaiah that his sins have been atoned for to the extent necessary to enable him to receive God's favor and a commission. How reassuring this is to us! We too are sinful and unworthy to approach God. But we have been redeemed by the merit of Jesus' ransom sacrifice and can receive God's favor and approach him in prayer.—2 Corinthians 5:18, 21; 1 John 4:10.

12 Reminding us again that this is a vision is the mention of "the altar." (Compare Revelation 8:3; 9:13.) There were two altars at the temple in Jerusalem. Just before the curtain of the Most Holy was the small altar of incense, and in front of the entrance to the sanctuary was the large altar of sacrifice, where the fire was kept constantly burning. (Leviticus 6:12, 13; 16:12, 13) But these earthly altars were typical, representative of greater things. (Hebrews 8:5; 9:23; 10:5-10) It was fire from heaven that consumed the burnt offering upon the altar when the temple was inaugurated by King Solomon. (2 Chronicles 7:1-3) And now it is fire from the true, heavenly altar that removes the uncleanness of Isaiah's lips.

13 Let us listen with Isaiah. *"I began to hear the voice of Jehovah saying: 'Whom shall I send, and who will go for us?' And I proceeded to say: 'Here I am! Send me.'"* (Isaiah 6:8) The question propounded by Jehovah is clearly designed to elicit a response from Isaiah, as no other human prophet appears in the vision. It is unmistakably an

---

12. What altar does Isaiah see, and what is the effect of fire?
13. What question does Jehovah propound, and whom does he include when he says "us"?

"Here I am! Send me."

invitation for Isaiah to be Jehovah's messenger. But why does Jehovah ask, "Who will go for *us?*" By switching from the singular personal pronoun "I" to the plural pronoun "us," Jehovah now includes at least one other person with himself. Who? Was this not his only-begotten Son, who later became the man Jesus Christ? Indeed, it was this same Son to whom God said, "Let us make man in our image." (Genesis 1:26; Proverbs 8:30, 31) Yes, alongside Jehovah in the heavenly courts is his only-begotten Son.—John 1:14.

14 Isaiah does not hesitate to respond! Regardless of what the message might be, he immediately replies: "Here I

---

14. How does Isaiah respond to Jehovah's invitation, and what example does he set for us?

am! Send me." Neither does he ask what he might gain by accepting the assignment. His willing spirit is a fine example for all of God's servants today, who have the commission to preach the 'good news of the kingdom in all the inhabited earth.' (Matthew 24:14) Like Isaiah, they faithfully stick to their assignment and accomplish the "witness to all the nations," despite widespread unresponsiveness. And they go forward with confidence, as did Isaiah, knowing that their commission has the highest authorization.

Isaiah's Commission

15 Jehovah now outlines what Isaiah is to say and what the response will be: *"Go, and you must say to this people, 'Hear again and again, O men, but do not understand; and see again and again, but do not get any knowledge.' Make the heart of this people unreceptive, and make their very ears unresponsive, and paste their very eyes together, that they may not see with their eyes and with their ears they may not hear, and that their own heart may not understand and that they may not actually turn back and get healing for themselves." (Isaiah 6:9, 10)* Does this mean that Isaiah is to be blunt and tactless and repel the Jews, keeping them at odds with Jehovah? Absolutely not! These are Isaiah's own people for whom he feels an affinity. But Jehovah's words indicate how the people will respond to his message, no matter how faithfully Isaiah fulfills his task.

16 The fault lies with the people. Isaiah will speak to them "again and again," but they will not accept the message or gain understanding. The majority will be

---

15, 16. (a) What is Isaiah to say to "this people," and what will be their response? (b) Is the reaction of the people due to any fault on Isaiah's part? Explain.

stubborn and unresponsive, as if totally blind and deaf. By going to them repeatedly, Isaiah will let "this people" show that they do not want to understand. They will prove that they are shutting their minds and hearts to Isaiah's message—God's message—to them. How true this is of people today! So many of them refuse to listen to Jehovah's Witnesses as they preach the good news of the incoming Kingdom of God.

17 Isaiah is concerned: *"At this I said: 'How long, O Jehovah?' Then he said: 'Until the cities actually crash in ruins, to be without an inhabitant, and the houses be without earthling man, and the ground itself is ruined into a desolation; and Jehovah actually removes earthling men far away, and the deserted condition does become very extensive in the midst of the land.'"* (Isaiah 6:11, 12) By asking, "How long?" Isaiah is not asking how long he will have to continue preaching to an unresponsive people. Rather, he is concerned about the people and asks how long their bad spiritual state will continue and how long Jehovah's name will be dishonored on earth. (See Psalm 74:9-11.) So, then, how long will the senseless situation go on?

18 Alas, Jehovah's answer shows that the bad spiritual state of the people will continue until the full consequences of disobedience to God, as outlined in his covenant, are fulfilled. (Leviticus 26:21-33; Deuteronomy 28:49-68) The nation will come to ruin, the people will be deported, and the land will lie desolate. Isaiah will not live to see the destruction of Jerusalem and its temple by the Babylonian army in 607 B.C.E., although he will prophesy for over 40 years, continuing into the reign of

---

17. When Isaiah asks, "How long?" to what does he refer?
18. Until when will the bad spiritual state of the people continue, and will Isaiah live to see the prophecy's complete fulfillment?

King Uzziah's great-grandson Hezekiah. Still, Isaiah will keep faithfully at his commission until he dies, more than 100 years before that national disaster occurs.

19 Destruction that will leave Judah "ruined into a desolation" is bound to come, but the situation is not hopeless. (2 Kings 25:1-26) Jehovah assures Isaiah: *"There will still be in it a tenth, and it must again become something for burning down, like a big tree and like a massive tree in which, when there is a cutting down of them, there is a stump; a holy seed will be the stump of it." (Isaiah 6:13)* Yes, "a tenth, . . . a holy seed," will remain, just like the stump of a massive tree that is felled. This assurance, no doubt, comforts Isaiah—a holy remnant will be found within his people. Though the nation experiences

19. Although the nation will be felled like a tree, what assurance does God give Isaiah?

'Until the cities crash in ruins, to be without an inhabitant'

a repeated burning, like a big tree cut down for fuel, a vital stump of the symbolic tree of Israel will remain. It will be a seed, or offspring, that is holy to Jehovah. In time, it will sprout again, and the tree will regrow.—Compare Job 14:7-9; Daniel 4:26.

20 Did the words of the prophecy come true? Yes. Seventy years after the land of Judah had been desolated, a God-fearing remnant returned from exile in Babylon. They rebuilt the temple and the city, and they restored true worship to the land. This restoration of the Jews to their God-given homeland made possible a second fulfillment of this prophecy that Jehovah gave to Isaiah. What was that to be?—Ezra 1:1-4.

Other Fulfillments

21 Isaiah's prophetic task foreshadowed the work that the Messiah, Jesus Christ, would do some 800 years later.

---

20. How was the last part of Isaiah's prophecy initially fulfilled?
21-23. (a) With whom did Isaiah's prophecy find a first-century fulfillment, and how? (b) Who was the "holy seed" in the first century, and how was it preserved?

(Isaiah 8:18; 61:1, 2; Luke 4:16-21; Hebrews 2:13, 14) Although greater than Isaiah, Jesus was just as willing to be sent by his heavenly Father, saying: "Look! I am come to do your will."—Hebrews 10:5-9; Psalm 40:6-8.

22 Like Isaiah, Jesus faithfully carried out his assigned work and met with the same reaction. The Jews in Jesus' day were no more willing to accept the message than were those to whom the prophet Isaiah preached. (Isaiah 1:4) The use of illustrations was a feature of Jesus' ministry. This prompted his disciples to ask: "Why is it you speak to them by the use of illustrations?" Jesus replied: "To you it is granted to understand the sacred secrets of the kingdom of the heavens, but to those people it is not granted. This is why I speak to them by the use of illustrations, because, looking, they look in vain, and hearing, they hear in vain, neither do they get the sense of it; and toward them the prophecy of Isaiah is having fulfillment, which says, 'By hearing, you will hear but by no means get the sense of it; and, looking, you will look but by no means see. For the heart of this people has grown unreceptive, and with their ears they have heard without response, and they have shut their eyes; that they might never see with their eyes and hear with their ears and get the sense of it with their hearts and turn back, and I heal them.' "—Matthew 13:10, 11, 13-15; Mark 4:10-12; Luke 8:9, 10.

23 In quoting from Isaiah, Jesus was showing that the prophecy had a fulfillment in his day. The people as a whole had a heart attitude like that of the Jews in Isaiah's day. They made themselves blind and deaf to his message and likewise met with destruction. (Matthew 23:35-38; 24:1, 2) This occurred when the Roman forces under General Titus came against Jerusalem in 70 C.E. and

demolished the city and its temple. Yet, some had listened to Jesus and had become his disciples. Jesus pronounced these "happy." (Matthew 13:16-23, 51) He had informed them that when they saw "Jerusalem surrounded by encamped armies," they should "begin fleeing to the mountains." (Luke 21:20-22) Thus the "holy seed" that had exercised faith and that had been formed into a spiritual nation, "the Israel of God," was saved.*—Galatians 6:16.

24 About 60 C.E., the apostle Paul found himself under house arrest in Rome. There he arranged a meeting with "the principal men of the Jews" as well as others and gave them a "thorough witness concerning the kingdom of God." When many would not accept his message, Paul explained that this was in fulfillment of Isaiah's prophecy. (Acts 28:17-27; Isaiah 6:9, 10) So Jesus' disciples carried out a commission comparable to that of Isaiah.

25 Similarly, Jehovah's Witnesses today discern that Jehovah God is in his holy temple. (Malachi 3:1) Like Isaiah, they say: "Here I am! Send me." Zealously, they sound the warning message about the approaching end of this wicked system of things. But, as Jesus indicated, relatively few people open their eyes and ears to see and hear and be saved. (Matthew 7:13, 14.) Happy, indeed, are those who incline their hearts to listen and "get healing for themselves"!—Isaiah 6:8, 10.

---

* In 66 C.E., responding to a Jewish revolt, Roman forces under Cestius Gallus surrounded Jerusalem and penetrated the city as far as the temple walls. Then they withdrew, allowing Jesus' disciples to flee to the mountains of Perea before the Romans returned in 70 C.E.

---

24. What application did Paul make of Isaiah's prophecy, and what does this indicate?
25. What have modern-day Witnesses of God discerned, and how do they respond?

CHAPTER NINE

Trust in Jehovah in the Face of Adversity

Isaiah 7:1–8:18

ISAIAH chapters 7 and 8 are a study in contrasts. Isaiah and Ahaz both belonged to a nation dedicated to Jehovah; both had God-given assignments, one as a prophet, the other as a king of Judah; and both faced the same threat—the invasion of Judah by superior enemy forces. Isaiah, however, faced the threat with confidence in Jehovah, whereas Ahaz gave way to fear. Why the different reactions? Since Christians today are likewise surrounded by hostile forces, they do well to examine these two chapters of Isaiah to discover what lessons they contain.

Facing a Decision

2 Much like an artist who defines the outline of a new painting with a few sweeping strokes, Isaiah starts his account with a few broad statements that mark the beginning and the end of the events he is about to relate: *"It came about in the days of Ahaz the son of Jotham the son of Uzziah, the king of Judah, that Rezin the king of Syria and Pekah the son of Remaliah, the king of Israel, came up to Jerusalem for war against it, and he proved unable to war against it."—Isaiah 7:1.*

3 It is the eighth century B.C.E. Ahaz has succeeded his

---

1. Why will Christians today benefit by examining Isaiah chapters 7 and 8?
2, 3. What summary does Isaiah give in his opening words?

father, Jotham, as king over Judah. Rezin, the king of Syria, and Pekah, the king of the northern kingdom of Israel, invade Judah, and their armies hit hard. Eventually, they will besiege Jerusalem itself. However, the siege will fail. (2 Kings 16:5, 6; 2 Chronicles 28:5-8) Why? That we will learn later.

4 Earlier in the war, *"a report was made to the house of David, saying: 'Syria has leaned upon Ephraim.' And his heart and the heart of his people began to quiver, like the quivering of the trees of the forest because of a wind."* *(Isaiah 7:2)* Yes, it is frightening to Ahaz and his people to learn that the Syrians and the Israelites have teamed up and that their armies are at this very moment encamped on Ephraim's (Israel's) soil. They are merely a two- or three-day march from Jerusalem!

5 Jehovah tells Isaiah: *"Go out, please, to meet Ahaz, you and Shear-jashub your son, to the end of the conduit of the upper pool by the highway of the laundryman's field."* *(Isaiah 7:3)* Just think! At a time when the king should be looking for Jehovah's prophet and asking for guidance, the prophet has to go and find the king! Even so, Isaiah willingly obeys Jehovah. Similarly, God's people today readily go out to find people who are fearful because of the pressures of this world. (Matthew 24:6, 14) How satisfying that each year hundreds of thousands respond to the visits of these preachers of the good news and take hold of Jehovah's protective hand!

---

4. Why are the hearts of Ahaz and his people filled with fear?

5. In what way do God's people today resemble Isaiah?

Isaiah took Shear-jashub along
when he conveyed Jehovah's message to Ahaz

6 Isaiah finds Ahaz outside the walls of Jerusalem, where, in preparation for the expected siege, the king is inspecting the city's water supply. Isaiah gives him Jehovah's message: *"Watch yourself and keep undisturbed. Do not be afraid, and do not let your heart itself be timid because of the two tail ends of these smoking logs, because of the hot anger of Rezin and Syria and the son of Remaliah." (Isaiah 7:4)* When the attackers ravaged Judah earlier, their anger was as hot as flames. Now they are merely 'two tail ends of smoking logs.' Ahaz need not dread Syrian King Rezin or Israelite King Pekah, son of Remaliah. Today it is similar. For centuries, Christendom's leaders have subjected true Christians to fiery persecution. Now, though, Christendom resembles a log that is nearly burned up. Her days are numbered.

7 In Ahaz' day, not only Isaiah's message but also the meaning of Isaiah's name and that of his son give hope to those trusting in Jehovah. True, Judah is in danger, but the name Isaiah, meaning "Salvation of Jehovah," signals that Jehovah will provide deliverance. Jehovah tells Isaiah to take with him his son Shear-jashub, whose name means "A Mere Remnant Will Return." Even when the kingdom of Judah finally falls, God will mercifully bring a remnant back to the land.

More Than a War Between Nations

8 Jehovah, through Isaiah, reveals the strategy of Judah's enemies. Here is what they are planning: *"Let us go up against Judah and tear it apart and by breakthroughs take it for ourselves; and let us make another king reign in-*

6. (a) What heartening message does the prophet convey to King Ahaz? (b) What situation exists today?
7. Why do Isaiah's name and that of his son give reason for hope?
8. Why is the attack on Jerusalem more than a war between nations?

side it, the son of Tabeel." (Isaiah 7:5, 6) The Syro-Israelite league schemes to conquer Judah and replace Ahaz, a son of David, with *their* man. Clearly, the attack on Jerusalem is now more than a war between nations. It has become a struggle between Satan and Jehovah. Why? Because Jehovah God made a covenant with King David, thus assuring him that his sons would rule over Jehovah's people. (2 Samuel 7:11, 16) What a triumph for Satan if he could install some *other* royal dynasty on the throne in Jerusalem! He might even frustrate Jehovah's purpose for David's line to produce a permanent heir, the "Prince of Peace."—Isaiah 9:6, 7.

Jehovah's Loving Assurances

9 Will the scheme of Syria and Israel succeed? No. Jehovah declares: *"It will not stand, neither will it take place." (Isaiah 7:7)* Through Isaiah, Jehovah says that not only will the siege of Jerusalem fail but *"within just sixty-five years Ephraim will be shattered to pieces so as not to be a people." (Isaiah 7:8)* Yes, within 65 years Israel will no longer exist as a people.* This assurance, with its specific timetable, should give Ahaz courage. In the same way, God's people today are strengthened by knowing that the time left for Satan's world is running out.

10 Perhaps Ahaz' face registers disbelief, since Jehovah, through Isaiah, says: *"Unless you people have faith, you will in that case not be of long duration."* Jehovah, in his

---

* For further details about this prophecy's fulfillment, see *Insight on the Scriptures,* Volume 1, pages 62 and 758, published by the Watchtower Bible and Tract Society of New York, Inc.

9. What assurances should give courage to Ahaz as well as to Christians today?
10. (a) How can true Christians today imitate Jehovah? (b) What offer does Jehovah make to Ahaz?

patience, *"went on speaking some more to Ahaz."* **(Isaiah 7:9, 10)** What a fine example! Today, although many do not readily respond to the Kingdom message, we do well to imitate Jehovah by "speaking some more" as we visit again and again. Jehovah next tells Ahaz: *"Ask for yourself a sign from Jehovah your God, making it as deep as Sheol or making it high as the upper regions."* **(Isaiah 7:11)** Ahaz may ask for a sign, and Jehovah will perform it as a guarantee that he will protect the house of David.

11 Note that Jehovah says: 'Ask a sign from *your* God.' Jehovah is truly kind. Ahaz is already reportedly worshiping false gods and following disgusting pagan practices. (2 Kings 16:3, 4) Despite that and despite Ahaz' fearful attitude, Jehovah still calls himself the God of Ahaz. This assures us that Jehovah does not reject humans rashly. He is willing to reach out to those who err or whose faith has grown weak. Will this assurance of God's love move Ahaz to take hold of Jehovah's hand?

From Doubt to Disobedience

12 Ahaz replies defiantly: *"I shall not ask, neither shall I put Jehovah to the test."* **(Isaiah 7:12)** Ahaz is not here observing the words of the law: "You must not put Jehovah your God to the test." (Deuteronomy 6:16) Centuries later, Jesus quotes that same law when Satan tempts him. (Matthew 4:7) In Ahaz' case, though, Jehovah is inviting him to turn back to true worship and is offering to strengthen his faith by performing a sign. However, Ahaz prefers to seek protection elsewhere. It is possibly at this point that the king sends a large sum of money to Assyria, seeking help against his northern enemies. (2 Kings 16:

---

11. What assurance is found in Jehovah's expression *"your* God"?
12. (a) What haughty attitude does Ahaz adopt? (b) Instead of turning to Jehovah, to whom does Ahaz go for help?

7, 8) Meanwhile, the Syro-Israelite army encircles Jerusalem and the siege is on.

13 With the king's lack of faith on his mind, Isaiah says: *"Listen, please, O house of David. Is it such a little thing for you to tire out men, that you should also tire out my God?" (Isaiah 7:13)* Yes, Jehovah can get tired of constant defiance. Observe, too, that the prophet now says *"my* God," not *"your* God." An ominous change! When Ahaz rejects Jehovah and turns to Assyria, he loses a fine opportunity to restore his relationship with God. May we never sacrifice our relationship with God by compromising our Scriptural beliefs in order to gain temporary advantages.

The Sign of Immanuel

14 Jehovah remains faithful toward his covenant with David. A sign was offered, a sign will be given! Isaiah continues: *"Jehovah himself will give you men a sign: Look! The maiden herself will actually become pregnant, and she is giving birth to a son, and she will certainly call his name Immanuel. Butter and honey he will eat by the time that he knows how to reject the bad and choose the good. For before the boy will know how to reject the bad and choose the good, the ground of whose two kings you are feeling a sickening dread will be left entirely."—Isaiah 7:14-16.*

15 Here is good news for anyone fearing that the invaders will put an end to the Davidic line of kings. "Immanuel" means "With Us Is God." God is with Judah and will not allow his covenant with David to be nullified. In addition, Ahaz and his people are told not only what Jehovah will

13. What change do we notice in verse 13, signifying what?
14. How does Jehovah show his faithfulness to his covenant with David?
15. What two questions does the prophecy about Immanuel answer?

do but also when he will do it. Before the boy Immanuel is old enough to distinguish between good and bad, the enemy nations will be destroyed. And this proves true!

16 The Bible does not reveal whose child Immanuel is. But since the young Immanuel is to serve as a sign and Isaiah later states that he and his children "are as signs," Immanuel may be a son of the prophet. (Isaiah 8:18) Perhaps Jehovah leaves the identity of Immanuel in Ahaz' day uncertain so as not to distract later generations from the Greater Immanuel. Who is that?

17 Outside of the book of Isaiah, the name Immanuel occurs only once in the Bible, at Matthew 1:23. Jehovah inspired Matthew to apply the prophecy of Immanuel's birth to the birth of Jesus, the rightful Heir to the throne of David. (Matthew 1:18-23) The birth of the first Immanuel was a sign that God had not forsaken the house of David. Likewise, the birth of Jesus, the Greater Immanuel, was a sign that God had not forsaken mankind or his Kingdom covenant with David's house. (Luke 1:31-33) With Jehovah's chief representative now among mankind, Matthew could truly say, 'With us is God.' Today, Jesus rules as heavenly King and is with his congregation on earth. (Matthew 28:20) Surely, God's people have added reason to cry out boldly: "With us is God!"

More Consequences of Unfaithfulness

18 Comforting though his latest words are, Isaiah's next statement brings terror to his hearers: ***"Jehovah will bring***

---

16. Why may Jehovah have left the identity of Immanuel in Ahaz' day uncertain?
17. (a) Who is the Greater Immanuel, and what did his birth signify? (b) Why can God's people cry out today, "With us is God"?
18. (a) Why do Isaiah's next words bring terror to his listeners? (b) What turn of events is soon to take place?

against you and against your people and against the house of your father days such as have not come since the day of Ephraim's turning away from alongside Judah, namely, the king of Assyria." (Isaiah 7:17) Yes, disaster is coming, and at the hand of the king of Assyria. The prospect of domination by the notoriously cruel Assyrians must be the cause of many sleepless nights for Ahaz and his people. Ahaz has reasoned that befriending Assyria would relieve him of Israel and Syria. Indeed, Assyria's king will respond to Ahaz' plea by eventually attacking Israel and Syria. (2 Kings 16:9) This is likely why Pekah and Rezin will be forced to lift their siege of Jerusalem. Thus, the Syro-Israelite league will have proved unable to take Jerusalem. (Isaiah 7:1) Now, though, Isaiah tells his shocked audience that Assyria, their hoped-for protector, will become their oppressor!—Compare Proverbs 29:25.

19 For Christians today, this true historical account contains a warning. When under pressure we may be tempted to compromise Christian principles, thereby rejecting Jehovah's protection. This is shortsighted, even suicidal, as becomes evident from Isaiah's further words. The prophet goes on to describe what the Assyrian invasion will do to the land and its people.

20 Isaiah divides his pronouncements into four parts, each foretelling what will happen "in that day"—that is, the day when Assyria attacks Judah. *"It must occur in that day that Jehovah will whistle for the flies that are at the extremity of the Nile canals of Egypt and for the bees that are in the land of Assyria, and they will certainly come in and settle down, all of them, upon the precipitous torrent valleys and upon the clefts of the crags and upon all the*

---

19. What warning does this historical drama contain for Christians today?
20. Who are "the flies" and "the bees," and what will they do?

thorn thickets and upon all the watering places." (Isaiah 7:18, 19) The armies of Egypt and Assyria, like swarms of flies and bees, will have their attention directed to the Promised Land. This will not be a passing invasion. "The flies" and "the bees" will settle down, infesting every nook and cranny of the land.

21 Isaiah continues: *"In that day, by means of a hired razor in the region of the River, even by means of the king of Assyria, Jehovah will shave the head and the hair of the feet, and it will sweep away even the beard itself." (Isaiah 7:20)* Now only Assyria, the chief threat, is mentioned. Ahaz hires the Assyrian king to "shave" Syria and Israel. However, this "hired razor" from the Euphrates region will move against Judah's "head" and shave it clean, even removing the beard!

22 What will be the result? *"It must occur in that day that an individual will preserve alive a young cow of the herd and two sheep. And it must occur that, due to the abundance of the producing of milk, he will eat butter; because butter and honey are what everyone left remaining in the midst of the land will eat." (Isaiah 7:21, 22)* By the time the Assyrians have 'shaved' the land, so few people will be left that only a small number of animals will be needed to provide food. "Butter and honey" will be eaten—nothing else, no wine, no bread, no other staples. As if to stress the degree of desolation, Isaiah three times says that where there used to be valuable, productive land, there will now be thornbushes and weeds. Those venturing into the countryside will need *"arrows and the bow"* for protection against wild animals lurking in the thickets. Cleared fields will become trampling grounds for oxen

21. In what way will the Assyrian king be like a razor?
22. What examples does Isaiah use to show the consequences of Assyria's imminent invasion?

and sheep. *(Isaiah 7:23-25)* This prophecy begins to be fulfilled in Ahaz' own day.—2 Chronicles 28:20.

Precise Predictions

23 Isaiah now returns to the immediate situation. While Jerusalem is still under siege by the Syro-Israelite combine, Isaiah reports: *"Jehovah proceeded to say to me: 'Take for yourself a large tablet and write upon it with the stylus of mortal man, "Maher-shalal-hash-baz." And let*

---

23. (a) What is Isaiah now commanded to do? (b) How is the sign of the tablet confirmed?

*Why did Isaiah write
"Maher-shalal-hash-baz" on a large tablet?*

me have attestation for myself by faithful witnesses, Uriah the priest and Zechariah the son of Jeberechiah.' " *(Isaiah 8:1, 2)* The name Maher-shalal-hash-baz means "Hasten, O Spoil! He Has Come Quickly to the Plunder." Isaiah asks two respected men in the community to attest his writing this name on a large tablet, so that they can later confirm the authenticity of the document. This sign, though, is to be confirmed by a second sign.

24 Isaiah says: *"Then I went near to the prophetess, and she came to be pregnant and in time gave birth to a son. Jehovah now said to me: 'Call his name Maher-shalal-hash-baz, for before the boy will know how to call out, "My father!" and "My mother!" one will carry away the resources of Damascus and the spoil of Samaria before the king of Assyria.'* " *(Isaiah 8:3, 4)* Both the large tablet and the newborn boy will serve as signs that Assyria will soon plunder Judah's oppressors, Syria and Israel. How soon? Before the boy is able to say the first words that most babies learn—"Father" and "Mother." Such an exact prediction should build the people's confidence in Jehovah. Or it could cause some to ridicule Isaiah and his sons. Whatever the case, Isaiah's prophetic words come true. —2 Kings 17:1-6.

25 Christians can learn from Isaiah's repeated warnings. The apostle Paul revealed to us that in this historic drama, Isaiah portrayed Jesus Christ and Isaiah's sons foreshadowed Jesus' anointed disciples. (Hebrews 2:10-13) Jesus, through his anointed followers on earth, has been reminding true Christians of the need to "keep awake" in

24. What effect should the sign of Maher-shalal-hash-baz have on the people of Judah?
25. What similarities are there between the days of Isaiah and the present time?

these critical times. (Luke 21:34-36) At the same time, unrepentant opposers are warned of their coming destruction, although such warnings are often met with ridicule. (2 Peter 3:3, 4) The fulfillment of time-related prophecies in Isaiah's day is a guarantee that God's timetable for our day will also "without fail come true. It will not be late." —Habakkuk 2:3.

Devastating "Waters"

26 Isaiah continues his warnings: *"For the reason that this people has rejected the waters of the Shiloah that are going gently, and there is exultation over Rezin and the son of Remaliah; even therefore, look! Jehovah is bringing up against them the mighty and the many waters of the River, the king of Assyria and all his glory. And he will certainly come up over all his streambeds and go over all his banks and move on through Judah. He will actually flood and pass over. Up to the neck he will reach. And the outspreading of his wings must occur to fill the breadth of your land, O Immanuel!"—Isaiah 8:5-8.*

27 "This people," the northern kingdom of Israel, reject Jehovah's covenant with David. (2 Kings 17:16-18) To them, it looks as weak as the trickling waters of Shiloah, Jerusalem's water supply. They exult in their war against Judah. But this contempt will not go unpunished. Jehovah will allow the Assyrians to "flood," or overrun, Syria and Israel, much as Jehovah will soon allow the present political part of the world to flood the realm of false religion. (Revelation 17:16; compare Daniel 9:26.) Next, says Isaiah, the swelling "waters" will "move on through Judah," reaching right "up to the neck," up to Jerusalem,

---

26, 27. (a) What events does Isaiah foretell? (b) What do Isaiah's words indicate for Jehovah's servants today?

where Judah's head (king) rules.* In our time the political executioners of false religion will likewise close in on Jehovah's servants, surrounding them "up to the neck." (Ezekiel 38:2, 10-16) What will be the outcome? Well, what happens in Isaiah's time? Do the Assyrians surge across the city walls and sweep God's people away? No. God is with them.

Fear Not—"God Is With Us!"

28 Isaiah warns: ***"Be injurious, O you peoples*** [opposed to God's covenant people]*, **and be shattered to pieces; and give ear, all you in distant parts of the earth! Gird yourselves, and be shattered to pieces! Gird yourselves, and be shattered to pieces! Plan out a scheme, and it will be broken up! Speak any word, and it will not stand, for God is with us!" (Isaiah 8:9, 10)*** Some years later, during the reign of Ahaz' faithful son Hezekiah, these words come true. When the Assyrians threaten Jerusalem, Jehovah's angel strikes down 185,000 of them. Clearly, God is with his people and the royal line of David. (Isaiah 37:33-37) During the coming battle of Armageddon, Jehovah will likewise send the Greater Immanuel not only to dash His enemies to pieces but also to rescue all those who trust in Him.—Psalm 2:2, 9, 12.

29 Unlike Jews in Hezekiah's time, Ahaz' contemporaries lack faith in Jehovah's protection. They favor a confed-

---

* Assyria is also compared to a bird whose outspread wings "fill the breadth of your land." Thus, wherever the land extends, it will be covered by the Assyrian army.

28. Despite the strenuous efforts of their enemies, of what does Jehovah assure Judah?
29. (a) How do Jews in Ahaz' day differ from those in the days of Hezekiah? (b) Why do Jehovah's servants today refrain from making religious and political alliances?

eracy, or "conspiracy," with the Assyrians as a bulwark against the Syro-Israelite league. However, Jehovah's "hand" prods Isaiah to speak against "the way of this people," or the popular trend. He warns: *"The object of their fear you men must not fear, nor must you tremble at it. Jehovah of armies—he is the One whom you should treat as holy, and he should be the object of your fear, and he should be the One causing you to tremble." (Isaiah 8: 11-13)* With this in mind, Jehovah's servants today guard against conspiring with or putting their trust in religious councils and political leagues. Servants of Jehovah have full confidence in God's protective power. After all, if 'Jehovah is on our side, what can earthling man do to us?' —Psalm 118:6.

30 Isaiah goes on to reiterate that Jehovah will prove to be *"a sacred place,"* a protection, for those trusting in him. In contrast, those rejecting him *"will be certain to stumble and to fall and be broken, and to be snared and caught"*—five vivid verbs that leave no doubt about the fate of those not trusting in Jehovah. *(Isaiah 8:14, 15)* In the first century, those rejecting Jesus likewise stumbled and fell. (Luke 20:17, 18) A similar outcome awaits those today who fail to give allegiance to the enthroned heavenly King, Jesus.—Psalm 2:5-9.

31 In Isaiah's day, not all are stumbled. Isaiah says: *"Wrap up the attestation, put a seal about the law among my disciples! And I will keep in expectation of Jehovah, who is concealing his face from the house of Jacob, and I will hope in him." (Isaiah 8:16, 17)* Isaiah and those who heed his teaching will not abandon God's Law. They keep on

---

30. What will be the fate of those not trusting in Jehovah?
31. How can true Christians today follow the example of Isaiah and of those who listen to his teaching?

trusting in Jehovah, even though their delinquent com-
patriots refuse to and thus have Jehovah conceal his face
from them. May we follow the example of those trusting
in Jehovah and have the same determination to cling to
pure worship!—Daniel 12:4, 9; Matthew 24:45; compare
Hebrews 6:11, 12.

"Signs" and "Miracles"

32 Isaiah now proclaims: *"Look! I and the children whom
Jehovah has given me are as signs and as miracles in Israel from Jehovah of armies, who is residing in Mount Zion."
(Isaiah 8:18)* Yes, Isaiah, Shear-jashub, and Maher-shalal-
hash-baz are signs of Jehovah's purposes for Judah. Today,
Jesus and his anointed brothers similarly serve as signs.
(Hebrews 2:11-13) And they are joined in their work by
"a great crowd" of "other sheep." (Revelation 7:9, 14; John
10:16) Of course, a sign is valuable only if it stands out
from its surroundings. Likewise, Christians fulfill their
commission as signs only if they stand out as being different from this world, putting their full trust in Jehovah
and boldly proclaiming his purposes.

33 Let all, then, observe God's standards, not those of
this world. Continue to stand out fearlessly—as signs—carrying forward the commission given to the Greater Isaiah, Jesus Christ: "Proclaim the year of goodwill . . . and
the day of vengeance on the part of our God." (Isaiah 61:
1, 2; Luke 4:17-21) Indeed, when the Assyrian flood surges
across the earth—even if it reaches up to our necks—true
Christians will not be swept away. We will stand firm because "God is with us."

---

32. (a) Who today serve "as signs and as miracles"? (b) Why should
Christians stand out from the world?
33. (a) What are true Christians determined to do? (b) Why will true
Christians be able to stand firm?

CHAPTER TEN

The Promise of
a Prince of Peace

Isaiah 8:19–9:7

SOME six thousand years ago, the first human baby was born. His name was Cain, and his birth was very special. Neither his parents, nor the angels, nor even the Creator had seen a human baby before. This newborn infant could have brought hope to a condemned human race. How disappointing it was when, after he grew up, he became a murderer! (1 John 3:12) Since then mankind has witnessed countless other murders. Humans, inclined as they are to do bad, are not at peace with one another or with God.—Genesis 6:5; Isaiah 48:22.

2 Some four millenniums after the birth of Cain, another baby was born. His name was Jesus, and his birth too was very special. He was born of a virgin, by the power of holy spirit—the only such birth in history. At the time of his birth, a multitude of joyful angels sang praises to God, saying: "Glory in the heights above to God, and upon earth peace among men of goodwill." (Luke 2:13, 14) Far from being a murderer, Jesus opened the way for humans to be at peace with God and to gain everlasting life.—John 3:16; 1 Corinthians 15:55.

3 Isaiah prophesied that Jesus would be called "Prince of

___

1. What has mankind experienced since the time of Cain?
2, 3. What prospects were opened up by Jesus Christ, and what must we do to receive such blessings?

Peace." (Isaiah 9:6) He would offer his own life in behalf of mankind, thus making possible the forgiveness of sins. (Isaiah 53:11) Today, peace with God and the forgiveness of sins can be attained on the basis of faith in Jesus Christ. But such blessings are not automatic. (Colossians 1:21-23) Those who want them must learn to obey Jehovah God. (1 Peter 3:11; compare Hebrews 5:8, 9.) In Isaiah's day, Israel and Judah do exactly the opposite.

Turning to the Demons

4 Because of their disobedience, Isaiah's contemporaries are in a deplorable moral state, a veritable pit of spiritual darkness. Even the southern kingdom of Judah, the location of God's temple, has no peace. As a result of their unfaithfulness, the people of Judah are threatened with invasion by the Assyrians, and hard times lie ahead. To whom do they turn for help? Sadly, many turn to Satan, not to Jehovah. No, they do not invoke Satan by name. Rather, like King Saul of old, they engage in spiritism, looking for answers to their problems by trying to communicate with the dead.—1 Samuel 28:1-20.

5 Some are even promoting this practice. Isaiah points to such apostasy when he says: *"In case they should say to you people: 'Apply to the spiritistic mediums or to those having a spirit of prediction who are chirping and making utterances in low tones,' is it not to its God that any people should apply? Should there be application to dead persons in behalf of living persons?"* (*Isaiah 8:19*) Spirit mediums can trick people, "chirping and making utterances

---

4, 5. What is the state of affairs in Isaiah's day, and to whom do some turn?

The births of Cain and Jesus were both very special. Only that of Jesus had a happy outcome

in low tones." Such sound effects, attributed to the spirits of dead ones, can be worked through ventriloquism by a living medium. At times, though, the demons may get directly involved and impersonate the dead, as apparently happened when Saul inquired of the witch of Endor. —1 Samuel 28:8-19.

6 All of this is going on in Judah despite the fact that Jehovah has forbidden the practice of spiritism. Under the Mosaic Law, it is a capital offense. (Leviticus 19:31; 20:6, 27; Deuteronomy 18:9-12) Why do a people who are Jehovah's special possession commit such a grave transgression? Because they have turned their backs on Jehovah's Law and counsel and have become "hardened by the deceptive power of sin." (Hebrews 3:13) "Their heart has become unfeeling just like fat," and they have become alienated from their God.—Psalm 119:70.*

7 Likely they reason, 'Of what good is the Law of Jehovah when we are faced with an imminent attack by the Assyrians?' They want a quick and easy solution to their predicament and are not about to wait for Jehovah to work out his will. In our day too, many ignore Jehovah's law and search out spirit mediums, consult horoscopes, and resort to other forms of occultism to solve their problems. However, for the living to seek answers from the dead is just as ridiculous today as it was back then. The future of any who unrepentantly practice such things will be with the "murderers and fornicators and . . . idolaters and all the liars." They have no future prospects of life.—Revelation 21:8.

---

* Many believe that Psalm 119 was written by Hezekiah before he became king. If so, it was likely written while Isaiah was prophesying.

---

6. Why are the Israelites who have resorted to spiritism especially blameworthy?
7. How do many today imitate the Israelites of Isaiah's day, and what will be the future of such ones if they do not repent?

God's 'Law and Attestation'

8 Jehovah's law banning spiritism, together with his other commands, is not hidden in Judah. It is preserved in writing. Today his Word is available in its completed form in writing. It is the Bible, which includes not only a compilation of divine laws and regulations but also an account of God's dealings with his people. This Bible account of Jehovah's dealings forms an attestation, or testimony, teaching us about Jehovah's nature and qualities. Instead of consulting with the dead, where should the Israelites be going for direction? Isaiah answers: *"To the law and to the attestation!"* *(Isaiah 8:20a)* Yes, those seeking true enlightenment should go to God's written Word.

9 Some Israelites dabbling in spiritism may profess respect for the written Word of God. But such claims are empty and hypocritical. Isa-

There will be a famine far worse than a hunger for bread and a thirst for water

iah says: *"Surely they will keep saying what is according to this statement that will have no light of dawn."* *(Isaiah 8: 20b)* To what statement is Isaiah here referring? Perhaps to the statement: "To the law and to the attestation!" It may be that some apostate Israelites refer to the Word of God, just as apostates and others today may quote Scripture. But

8. What is "the law" and "the attestation" to which we today should be going for direction?
9. Is quoting the Bible from time to time of any value to unrepentant sinners?

these are mere words. Quoting Scripture will not lead to any "light of dawn," or enlightenment from Jehovah, if it is not accompanied by a doing of Jehovah's will and a shunning of unclean practices.*

---

* The phrase "this statement" at Isaiah 8:20 may refer to the statement regarding spiritism, quoted at Isaiah 8:19. If that is the case, Isaiah is saying that the promoters of spiritism in Judah will continue to urge others to apply to spirit mediums and thus will receive no enlightenment from Jehovah.

"A Famine, Not for Bread"

10 Disobedience to Jehovah results in mental darkness. (Ephesians 4:17, 18) In a spiritual sense, the people of Judah have become blind, without understanding. (1 Corinthians 2:14) Isaiah describes their condition: *"Each one will certainly pass through the land hard pressed and hungry." (Isaiah 8:21a)* Because of the nation's unfaithfulness —particularly during the reign of King Ahaz—the survival of Judah as an independent kingdom is threatened. The nation is surrounded by enemies. The Assyrian army assaults one Judean city after another. The enemy desolates the productive land, making food scarce. Many are "hard pressed and hungry." But another kind of hunger also afflicts the land. Some decades earlier Amos prophesied: " 'Look! There are days coming,' is the utterance of the Sovereign Lord Jehovah, 'and I will send a famine into the land, a famine, not for bread, and a thirst, not for water, but for hearing the words of Jehovah.' " (Amos 8:11) Judah is now in the throes of just such a spiritual famine!

11 Will Judah learn her lesson and return to Jehovah? Will her people turn away from spiritism and idolatry and return "to the law and to the attestation"? Jehovah foresees their reaction: *"It must occur that because he is hungry and has made himself feel indignant, he will actually call down evil upon his king and upon his God and will certainly peer upward." (Isaiah 8:21b)* Yes, many will blame their human king for leading them into this situation. Some will even foolishly blame Jehovah for their calamities! (Compare Jeremiah 44:15-18.) Today, many respond in a similar way, blaming God for tragedies caused by human wickedness.

---

10. How are the people of Judah suffering because of rejecting Jehovah?
11. Will Judah learn a lesson from the discipline she receives?

12 Will calling down evil upon God bring peace to the inhabitants of Judah? No. Isaiah foretells: *"To the earth he will look, and, lo! distress and darkness, obscurity, hard times and gloominess with no brightness."* (*Isaiah 8:22*) After raising their eyes to heaven to blame God, they look back to the earth, back to their hopeless prospects. Their turning away from God has led to calamity. (Proverbs 19:3) What, though, of the promises that God made to Abraham, Isaac, and Jacob? (Genesis 22:15-18; 28:14, 15) Will Jehovah default? Will the Assyrians or some other military power bring to an end the royal line promised to Judah and David? (Genesis 49:8-10; 2 Samuel 7:11-16) Will the Israelites be forever condemned to darkness?

A Land "Treated With Contempt"

13 Isaiah now alludes to one of the worst of the cataclysmic events that come upon the descendants of Abraham: *"The obscureness will not be as when the land had stress, as at the former time when one treated with contempt the land of Zebulun and the land of Naphtali and when at the later time one caused it to be honored—the way by the sea, in the region of the Jordan, Galilee of the nations."* (*Isaiah 9:1*) Galilee is a territory in the northern kingdom of Israel. In Isaiah's prophecy it includes "the land of Zebulun and the land of Naphtali" and also "the way by the sea," an ancient road that ran by the Sea of Galilee and led to the Mediterranean Sea. In Isaiah's day, the region is called "Galilee of the nations," likely because many of its cities are inhabited by non-Israelites.*

---

* Some have suggested that the 20 cities of Galilee that King Solomon offered to Hiram the king of Tyre were probably inhabited by non-Israelites.—1 Kings 9:10-13.

---

12. (a) To what has turning away from God led Judah? (b) What important questions are raised?
13. What is "Galilee of the nations," and how does it come to be "treated with contempt"?

How is this land "treated with contempt"? The pagan Assyrians conquer it, take the Israelites into exile, and resettle the whole region with pagans, who are not descendants of Abraham. Thus the ten-tribe northern kingdom disappears from history as a distinct nation!—2 Kings 17:5, 6, 18, 23, 24.

14 Judah too is under pressure from the Assyrians. Will it sink into a permanent "obscureness" as did the ten-tribe kingdom represented by Zebulun and Naphtali? No. At a "later time," Jehovah will bring blessings to the region of the southern kingdom of Judah and even to the land formerly ruled by the northern kingdom. How?

15 The apostle Matthew answers this question in his inspired record of the earthly ministry of Jesus. Describing the early days of that ministry, Matthew says: "After leaving Nazareth, [Jesus] came and took up residence in Capernaum beside the sea in the districts of Zebulun and Naphtali, that there might be fulfilled what was spoken through Isaiah the prophet, saying: 'O land of Zebulun and land of Naphtali, along the road of the sea, on the other side of the Jordan, Galilee of the nations! the people sitting in darkness saw a great light, and as for those sitting in a region of deathly shadow, light rose upon them.'"
—Matthew 4:13-16.

16 Yes, "the later time" foretold by Isaiah is the time of Christ's earthly ministry. Most of Jesus' earthly life was spent in Galilee. It was in the district of Galilee that he began his ministry and started to announce: "The kingdom of the heavens has drawn near." (Matthew 4:17) In

---

14. In what sense will Judah's "obscureness" be less than that of the ten-tribe kingdom?
15, 16. (a) At what "later time" will the situation change for "the districts of Zebulun and Naphtali"? (b) How does the land that was treated with contempt come to be honored?

Galilee, he delivered his famous Sermon on the Mount, chose his apostles, performed his first miracle, and appeared to some 500 followers after his resurrection. (Matthew 5:1–7:27; 28:16-20; Mark 3:13, 14; John 2:8-11; 1 Corinthians 15:6) In this way Jesus fulfilled Isaiah's prophesy by honoring "the land of Zebulun and the land of Naphtali." Of course, Jesus did not restrict his ministry to the people of Galilee. By preaching the good news throughout the land, Jesus 'caused to be honored' the entire nation of Israel, including Judah.

The "Great Light"

17 What, though, of Matthew's mention of "a great light" in Galilee? This too was a quotation from Isaiah's prophecy. Isaiah wrote: ***"The people that were walking in the darkness have seen a great light. As for those dwelling in the land of deep shadow, light itself has shone upon them." (Isaiah 9:2)*** By the first century C.E., the light of truth had been hidden by pagan falsehoods. Jewish religious leaders had compounded the problem by holding to their religious tradition with which they had "made the word of God invalid." (Matthew 15:6) Humble ones were oppressed and bewildered, following "blind guides." (Matthew 23:2-4, 16) When Jesus the Messiah appeared, the eyes of many humble people were opened in a wondrous way. (John 1:9, 12) Jesus' work while on earth and the blessings resulting from his sacrifice are aptly characterized in Isaiah's prophesy as "a great light."—John 8:12.

18 Those who responded to the light had much reason

---

17. How does "a great light" shine in Galilee?
18, 19. What reason did those who responded to the light have for great rejoicing?

Jesus was a light in the land

for rejoicing. Isaiah continued: *"You have made the na-tion populous; for it you have made the rejoicing great. They have rejoiced before you as with the rejoicing in the harvesttime, as those who are joyful when they divide up the spoil." (Isaiah 9:3)* As a result of the preaching ac-tivity of Jesus and his followers, honesthearted ones came forward, showing themselves desirous of worshiping Je-hovah with spirit and truth. (John 4:24) In less than four years, multitudes embraced Christianity. Three thousand were baptized on the day of Pentecost 33 C.E. Shortly af-terward, "the number of the men became about five thou-sand." (Acts 2:41; 4:4) As the disciples zealously reflected the light, "the number of the disciples kept multiplying in Jerusalem very much; and a great crowd of priests began to be obedient to the faith."—Acts 6:7.

19 Like those who rejoice in a bounteous harvest or who delight over the division of valuable spoil after a great mil-itary victory, Jesus' followers rejoiced over the increase. (Acts 2:46, 47) In time, Jehovah caused the light to shine among the nations. (Acts 14:27) So people of all races re-joiced that the way of approach to Jehovah had been opened to them.—Acts 13:48.

"As in the Day of Midian"

20 The effects of the activity of the Messiah are perma-nent, as we see from Isaiah's next words: *"The yoke of their load and the rod upon their shoulders, the staff of the one driving them to work, you have shattered to pieces as in the day of Midian." (Isaiah 9:4)* Centuries before Isa-iah's day, the Midianites conspired with the Moabites to

---

20. (a) In what ways did the Midianites prove to be enemies of Is-rael, and how did Jehovah bring an end to the threat they posed? (b) How on a future "day of Midian" will Jesus bring an end to the threat posed by enemies of God's people?

lure Israel into sin. (Numbers 25:1-9, 14-18; 31:15, 16) Later, Midianites terrorized the Israelites by raiding and plundering their villages and farms for seven years. (Judges 6: 1-6) But then Jehovah, through his servant Gideon, routed Midian's armies. After that "day of Midian," there is no evidence that Jehovah's people ever again suffered at the hands of the Midianites. (Judges 6:7-16; 8:28) In the near future, Jesus Christ, the greater Gideon, will deliver a deathblow to modern-day enemies of Jehovah's people. (Revelation 17:14; 19:11-21) Then, "as in the day of Midian," a complete and lasting victory will be gained, not by human prowess, but by Jehovah's power. (Judges 7:2-22) God's people will never again suffer under the yoke of oppression!

21 Displays of divine power are not a glorification of warfare. The resurrected Jesus is the Prince of Peace, and by annihilating his enemies, he will usher in eternal peace. Isaiah now speaks of military paraphernalia as being totally destroyed by fire: *"Every boot of the one tramping with tremors and the mantle rolled in blood have even come to be for burning as food for fire."* (*Isaiah 9:5*) The tremors caused by the tramping of the boots of marching soldiers will never again be felt. The bloody uniforms of combat-hardened warriors will no longer be seen. War will be no more!—Psalm 46:9.

"Wonderful Counselor"

22 At the time of his miraculous birth, the one born to be the Messiah received the name Jesus, meaning "Jehovah Is Salvation." But he has other names, prophetic names that outline his key role and his elevated position.

---

21. What does Isaiah's prophecy indicate as to the future of warfare?
22. What multiple prophetic name is Jesus given in the book of Isaiah?

One such name is Immanuel, meaning "With Us Is God." (Isaiah 7:14, footnote) Isaiah now describes another prophetic name: *"There has been a child born to us, there has been a son given to us; and the princely rule will come to be upon his shoulder. And his name will be called Wonderful Counselor, Mighty God, Eternal Father, Prince of Peace." (Isaiah 9:6)* Consider the rich meaning of this multiple prophetic name.

23 A counselor is one who gives counsel, or advice. When on earth Jesus Christ provided wonderful counsel. In the Bible we read that "crowds were astounded at his way of teaching." (Matthew 7:28) He is a wise and empathetic Counselor, with an extraordinary understanding of human nature. His counsel is not restricted to reprimands or chastisement. More often, it is in the form of instruction and loving advice. Jesus' counsel is wonderful because it is always wise, perfect, and infallible. When followed, it leads to everlasting life.—John 6:68.

24 Jesus' counsel is not simply the product of his brilliant mind. Rather, he says: "What I teach is not mine, but belongs to him that sent me." (John 7:16) As was the case with Solomon, Jehovah God is the Source of Jesus' wisdom. (1 Kings 3:7-14; Matthew 12:42) Jesus' example should motivate teachers and counselors in the Christian congregation always to base their instruction on God's Word.—Proverbs 21:30.

"Mighty God" and "Eternal Father"

25 Jesus is also "Mighty God" and "Eternal Father." This does not mean that he usurps the authority and position

---

23, 24. (a) In what way is Jesus a "Wonderful Counselor"? (b) How can Christian counselors today imitate Jesus' example?
25. What does the name "Mighty God" tell us about the heavenly Jesus?

of Jehovah, who is "God our Father." (2 Corinthians 1:2) "He [Jesus] . . . gave no consideration to a seizure, namely, that he should be equal to God." (Philippians 2:6) He is called Mighty God, not Almighty God. Jesus never thought of himself as God Almighty, for he spoke of his Father as "the only true God," that is, the only God who should be worshiped. (John 17:3; Revelation 4:11) In the Scriptures, the word "god" can mean "mighty one" or "strong one." (Exodus 12:12; Psalm 8:5; 2 Corinthians 4:4) Before Jesus came to earth, he was "a god," "existing in God's form." After his resurrection, he returned to an even higher position in the heavens. (John 1:1; Philippians 2: 6-11) Further, the designation "god" carries an additional implication. Judges in Israel were called "gods"—once by Jesus himself. (Psalm 82:6; John 10:35) Jesus is Jehovah's appointed Judge, "destined to judge the living and the dead." (2 Timothy 4:1; John 5:30) Clearly, he is well named Mighty God.

26 The title "Eternal Father" refers to the Messianic King's power and authority to give humans the prospect of eternal life on earth. (John 11:25, 26) The legacy of our first parent, Adam, was death. Jesus, the last Adam, "became a life-giving spirit." (1 Corinthians 15:22, 45; Romans 5: 12, 18) Just as Jesus, the Eternal Father, will live forever, so obedient mankind will enjoy the benefits of his fatherhood eternally.—Romans 6:9.

"Prince of Peace"

27 Besides everlasting life, man also needs peace, both with God and with his fellowman. Even today, those

---

26. Why can Jesus be called "Eternal Father"?
27, 28. What wonderful benefits come both now and in the future to subjects of the "Prince of Peace"?

subjecting themselves to the rule of the "Prince of Peace" have 'beaten their swords into plowshares and their spears into pruning shears.' (Isaiah 2:2-4) They do not nurse hatreds because of political, territorial, racial, or economic differences. They are united in the worship of the one true God, Jehovah, and they work to maintain peaceful relations with their neighbors, both inside and outside the congregation.—Galatians 6:10; Ephesians 4:2, 3; 2 Timothy 2:24.

28 In God's due time, Christ will establish on earth a peace that will be global, firmly established, permanent. (Acts 1:7) *"To the abundance of the princely rule and to peace there will be no end, upon the throne of David and upon his kingdom in order to establish it firmly and to sustain it by means of justice and by means of righteousness, from now on and to time indefinite." (Isaiah 9:7a)* In exercising his authority as the Prince of Peace, Jesus will not resort to tyrannical means. His subjects will not be stripped of their free will and subjugated by force. Rather, all that he will accomplish will be "by means of justice and by means of righteousness." What a refreshing change!

29 In view of the wonderful implications of Jesus' prophetic name, Isaiah's conclusion to this part of his prophecy is truly thrilling. He writes: *"The very zeal of Jehovah of armies will do this." (Isaiah 9:7b)* Yes, Jehovah acts with zeal. He does nothing in a halfhearted way. We can be sure that whatever he promises, he will fully accomplish. If anyone, then, longs to enjoy everlasting peace, let him serve Jehovah wholeheartedly. Like Jehovah God and Jesus, the Prince of Peace, may all servants of God be "zealous for fine works."—Titus 2:14.

---

29. What should we do if we wish to enjoy the blessing of everlasting peace?

CHAPTER ELEVEN

Woe to the Rebels!

Isaiah 9:8–10:4

WHEN Jehovah's covenant people were divided into two kingdoms, the northern ten-tribe kingdom came under the rulership of Jeroboam. The new king was an able, energetic ruler. But he lacked real faith in Jehovah. Because of this he made a terrible error that blighted the whole history of the northern kingdom. Under the Mosaic Law, the Israelites were commanded to travel three times a year up to the temple in Jerusalem, which was now in the southern kingdom of Judah. (Deuteronomy 16:16) Afraid that such regular journeys would make his subjects think about reunification with their southern brothers, Jeroboam "made two golden calves and said to the people: 'It is too much for you to go up to Jerusalem. Here is your God, O Israel, that brought you up out of the land of Egypt.' Then he placed the one in Bethel, and the other he put in Dan."—1 Kings 12:28, 29.

2 In the short term, Jeroboam's plan seemed to work. The people gradually left off going to Jerusalem and took up worshiping before the two calves. (1 Kings 12:30) However, this apostate religious practice corrupted the ten-tribe kingdom. In later years, even Jehu, who had shown such commendable zeal in clearing Baal worship out of Israel, continued to bow down to the golden calves. (2 Kings 10:28, 29) What else resulted from Jeroboam's tragically

---

1. What terrible error did Jeroboam make?
2, 3. What effects did Jeroboam's error have on Israel?

wrong decision? Political instability and suffering for the people.

3 Because Jeroboam had become apostate, Jehovah said that his seed would not reign over the land, and in the end the northern kingdom would suffer a terrible disaster. (1 Kings 14:14, 15) Jehovah's word proved true. Seven of Israel's kings ruled for two years or less—some for only a few days. One king committed suicide, and six were assassinated by ambitious men who usurped the throne. Especially after the reign of Jeroboam II, which ended about 804 B.C.E. while Uzziah was reigning in Judah, Israel was plagued with unrest, violence, and assassinations. It is against this backdrop that Jehovah through Isaiah sends a direct warning, or "word," to the northern kingdom. *"There was a word that Jehovah sent against Jacob, and it fell upon Israel."—Isaiah 9:8.*

Haughtiness and Insolence Earn God's Wrath

4 Jehovah's "word" will not be ignored. *"The people will certainly know it, even all of them, Ephraim and the inhabitant of Samaria, because of their haughtiness and because of their insolence of heart." (Isaiah 9:9)* "Jacob," "Israel," "Ephraim," and "Samaria" all refer to the northern kingdom of Israel, of which Ephraim is the predominant tribe and Samaria the capital. Jehovah's word against that kingdom is a strong judicial statement, for Ephraim has

---

* Isaiah 9:8–10:4 is made up of four strophes (sections of a rhythmic passage), each ending with the ominous refrain: "In view of all this his anger has not turned back, but his hand is stretched out still." (Isaiah 9:12, 17, 21; 10:4) This literary device has the effect of binding Isaiah 9:8–10:4 into one composite "word." (Isaiah 9:8) Note, too, that Jehovah's "hand is stretched out still," not to offer reconciliation, but to judge.—Isaiah 9:13.

4. What "word" does Jehovah send against Israel, and why?

become hardened in apostasy and is brazenly insolent toward Jehovah. God will not protect the people from the consequences of their wicked ways. They will be forced to hear, or pay attention to, God's word.—Galatians 6:7.

5 As conditions deteriorate, the people experience severe losses, including their homes—commonly made of mud bricks and inexpensive wood. Are their hearts softened as a result? Will they heed Jehovah's prophets and return to the true God?* Isaiah records the people's insolent response: *"Bricks are what have fallen, but with hewn stone we shall build. Sycamore trees are what have been cut down, but with cedars we shall make replacement." (Isaiah 9:10)* The Israelites defy Jehovah and spurn his prophets, who tell them why they are suffering such hardships. In effect, the people say: 'We may lose houses made of perishable mud bricks and inexpensive wood, but we will do more than make good for these losses by rebuilding with superior materials—hewn stone and cedar!' (Compare Job 4:19.) They leave Jehovah no choice but to discipline them further.—Compare Isaiah 48:22.

6 Isaiah continues: *"Jehovah will set the adversaries of Rezin on high against him." (Isaiah 9:11a)* King Pekah of Israel and King Rezin of Syria are allies. They are scheming to conquer the two-tribe kingdom of Judah and to place on Jehovah's throne in Jerusalem a puppet king—a certain "son of Tabeel." (Isaiah 7:6) But the conspiracy is doomed.

---

* Jehovah's prophets to the northern kingdom of Israel include Jehu (not the king), Elijah, Micaiah, Elisha, Jonah, Oded, Hosea, Amos, and Micah.

---

5. How do the Israelites show themselves unaffected by Jehovah's acts of judgment?
6. How does Jehovah undermine the Syro-Israelite scheme against Judah?

Rezin has powerful enemies, and Jehovah will 'set on high' these enemies against "him," Israel. The term 'set on high' means to allow them to wage effective warfare that will bring about the destruction of the alliance and its objectives.

7 The dissolving of this alliance begins when Assyria attacks Syria. "The king of Assyria went up to Damascus [the capital of Syria] and captured it and led its people into exile at Kir, and Rezin he put to death." (2 Kings 16:9) Having lost his powerful ally, Pekah finds that his designs on Judah are thwarted. In fact, shortly after Rezin's death, Pekah himself is assassinated by Hoshea, who thereafter usurps the throne of Samaria.—2 Kings 15:23-25, 30.

8 Syria, Israel's former ally, is now a vassal of Assyria, the dominant power in the region. Isaiah prophesies about how Jehovah will use this new political alignment: *"The enemies of that one [Israel] he [Jehovah] will goad on, Syria from the east and the Philistines from behind, and they will eat up Israel with open mouth. In view of all this his anger has not turned back, but his hand is stretched out still." (Isaiah 9:11b, 12)* Yes, Syria is now Israel's enemy, and Israel must prepare for attack from Assyria *and* Syria. The invasion succeeds. Assyria makes the usurper Hoshea his servant, exacting a hefty tribute. (A few decades earlier, Assyria received a large sum from King Menahem of Israel.) How true the prophet Hosea's words: "Strangers have eaten up his [Ephraim's] power"!—Hosea 7:9; 2 Kings 15: 19, 20; 17:1-3.

9 Does not Isaiah also say that the Philistines will invade "from behind"? Yes. Prior to the days of magnetic com-

---

7, 8. For Israel, what is the result of Assyria's conquest of Syria?
9. Why can we say that the Philistines attack "from behind"?

passes, the Hebrews indicated direction from the viewpoint of a person facing the sunrising. Thus, "the east" was the front, while the west, the coastal home of the Philistines, was "behind." The "Israel" mentioned at Isaiah 9:12 may include Judah in this instance because the Philistines invaded Judah during the reign of Pekah's contemporary, Ahaz, capturing and occupying a number of Judean cities and strongholds. Like Ephraim to the north, Judah deserves this discipline from Jehovah, for she too is riddled with apostasy.—2 Chronicles 28:1-4, 18, 19.

From 'Head to Tail'—A Nation of Rebels

10 In spite of all its suffering—and despite the strong pronouncements of Jehovah's prophets—the northern kingdom persists in rebellion against Jehovah. *"The people themselves have not returned to the One striking them, and Jehovah of armies they have not sought."* (*Isaiah 9:13*) Consequently, the prophet says: *"Jehovah will cut off from Israel head and tail, shoot and rush, in one day. The aged and highly respected one is the head, and the prophet giving false instruction is the tail. And those who are leading this people on prove to be the ones causing them to wander; and those of them who are being led on, the ones who are being confused."—Isaiah 9:14-16.*

11 The "head" and the "shoot" represent "the aged and highly respected one"—the leaders of the nation. The "tail" and the "rush" refer to false prophets who utter words pleasing to their leaders. A Bible scholar writes: "The false Prophets are called the tail, because they were morally the basest of the people, and because they

---

10, 11. What punishment will Jehovah bring against Israel because of their persistent rebellion?

were the servile adherents and supporters of wicked rulers." Professor Edward J. Young says of these false prophets: "No leaders were they but, following where the leaders led, they simply flattered and fawned, a wagging tail on a dog."—Compare 2 Timothy 4:3.

Even 'Widows and Fatherless Boys' Are Rebels

12 Jehovah is the Champion of widows and fatherless boys. (Exodus 22:22, 23) Yet, hear what Isaiah now says: *"Jehovah will not rejoice even over their young men, and upon their fatherless boys and upon their widows he will have no mercy; because all of them are apostates and evildoers and every mouth is speaking senselessness. In view of all this his anger has not turned back, but his hand is stretched out still." (Isaiah 9:17)* Apostasy has corrupted all levels of society, including the widows and fatherless boys! Jehovah patiently sends his prophets, hoping that the people will change their ways. For example, "Do come back, O Israel, to Jehovah your God, for you have stumbled in your error," pleads Hosea. (Hosea 14:1) How it must pain the Champion of widows and fatherless boys to have to execute judgment against even them!

13 Like Isaiah, we are living in critical times prior to Jehovah's day of judgment against the wicked. (2 Timothy 3: 1-5) How important, then, that true Christians, regardless of their situation in life, remain spiritually, morally, and mentally clean in order to retain God's favor. Let each one jealously guard his relationship with Jehovah. Let none who have escaped from "Babylon the Great" ever again "share with her in her sins."—Revelation 18:2, 4.

---

12. How deep into Israelite society has corruption penetrated?
13. What can we learn from the situation in Isaiah's day?

False Worship Breeds Violence

14 False worship is, in effect, the worship of demons. (1 Corinthians 10:20) As demonstrated before the Flood, demon influence leads to violence. (Genesis 6:11, 12) It is no surprise, then, that when Israel turns apostate and begins worshiping the demons, violence and wickedness fill the land.—Deuteronomy 32:17; Psalm 106:35-38.

15 In vivid word pictures, Isaiah describes the spread of wickedness and violence in Israel: *"Wickedness has become aflame just like a fire; thornbushes and weeds it will eat up. And it will catch fire in the thickets of the forest, and they will be borne aloft as the billowing of smoke. In*

14, 15. (a) What results from demon worship? (b) Isaiah prophesies that Israel will experience what ongoing suffering?

Wickedness and violence sweep through Israel like a forest fire

the fury of Jehovah of armies the land has been set afire,
and the people will become as food for the fire. No one
will show compassion even on his brother. And one will cut
down on the right and will certainly be hungry; and one
will eat on the left, and they will certainly not be satisfied.
They will each one eat the flesh of his own arm, Manasseh
Ephraim, and Ephraim Manasseh. Together they will be
against Judah. In view of all this his anger has not turned
back, but his hand is stretched out still."—Isaiah 9:18-21.

16 Like a flame that spreads from thornbush to thornbush, violence races out of control and quickly reaches "the thickets of the forest," creating a full-blown forest
fire of violence. Bible commentators Keil and Delitzsch describe the level of violence as being "the most inhuman
self-destruction during an anarchical civil war. Destitute of
any tender emotions, they devoured one another without
being satisfied." Likely, the tribes of Ephraim and Manasseh are singled out here because they are the main representatives of the northern kingdom and, as descendants
of Joseph's two sons, they are the most closely related of
the ten tribes. Despite this, however, they interrupt their
fratricidal violence only when they war against Judah to
the south.—2 Chronicles 28:1-8.

Corrupt Judges Meet Their Judge

17 Jehovah next focuses his judicial eye on Israel's corrupt judges and other officials. These abuse their power
by plundering the lowly and afflicted ones who come to

16. How are the words of Isaiah 9:18-21 fulfilled?
17, 18. What corruption exists in Israel's legal and administrative
system?

Jehovah will hold
to account those who prey on others

them seeking justice. Isaiah says: *"Woe to those who are enacting harmful regulations and those who, constantly writing, have written out sheer trouble, in order to push away the lowly ones from a legal case and to wrest away justice from the afflicted ones of my people, for the widows to become their spoil, and that they may plunder even the fatherless boys!"—Isaiah 10:1, 2.*

18 Jehovah's Law forbids all forms of injustice: "You people must not do injustice in the judgment. You must not treat the lowly with partiality, and you must not prefer the person of a great one." (Leviticus 19:15) Disregarding that law, these officials draw up their own "harmful regulations" so as to legitimize what amounts to outright theft of the cruelest kind—taking the scanty possessions of widows and fatherless boys. Israel's false gods are, of course, blind to this injustice, but Jehovah is not. Through Isaiah, Jehovah now focuses his attention on these wicked judges.

19 *"What will you men do at the day of being given attention and at the ruin, when it comes from far away? Toward whom will you flee for assistance, and where will you leave your glory, except it be that one must bow down under the prisoners and that people keep falling under those who have been killed?"* (Isaiah 10:3, 4a) The widows and fatherless boys have no honest judges to whom to appeal. How appropriate, then, that Jehovah now asks those corrupt Israelite judges whom they will turn to now that Jehovah is holding them to account. Yes, they are about to learn that "it is a fearful thing to fall into the hands of the living God."—Hebrews 10:31.

20 The "glory" of these wicked judges—the worldly prestige, honor, and power that come with their wealth and

19, 20. How will the situation of the corrupt Israelite judges be changed, and what will happen to their "glory"?

position—will be short-lived. Some will become prisoners of war, 'bowing down,' or crouching, among other prisoners, while the rest will be slain, their corpses covered with the war dead. Their "glory" also includes ill-gotten riches, which will be plundered by the enemy.

21 Isaiah concludes this final strophe with a grim warning: *"In view of all this* [all the woe that the nation has so far suffered] *his anger has not turned back, but his hand is stretched out still." (Isaiah 10:4b)* Yes, Jehovah has more to say to Israel. Jehovah's outstretched hand will not be drawn back until he delivers a final, devastating blow to the rebellious northern kingdom.

Never Fall Prey to Falsehood and Self-Interest

22 Jehovah's word through Isaiah fell heavily upon Israel and 'did not return to him without results.' (Isaiah 55:10, 11) History records the tragic end of the northern kingdom of Israel, and we can only imagine the suffering that its inhabitants had to endure. Just as surely, God's word will be fulfilled on the present system of things, especially on apostate Christendom. How important, then, that Christians give no ear to lying, anti-God propaganda! Thanks to God's Word, Satan's clever strategies have long been exposed, so that we need not be overreached by them as were the people of ancient Israel. (2 Corinthians 2:11) May all of us never cease to worship Jehovah "with spirit and truth." (John 4:24) In that case, his outstretched hand will not strike his worshipers as it did rebellious Ephraim; his arms will warmly embrace them, and he will help them along the road to everlasting life on a paradise earth.—James 4:8.

---

21. In view of the punishments that Israel has received, has Jehovah's anger against them ceased?
22. What lesson can we learn from what happened to Israel?

CHAPTER TWELVE

Do Not Be Afraid of the Assyrian

Isaiah 10:5-34

IN THE middle of the ninth century B.C.E., the Hebrew prophet Jonah, son of Amittai, ventured into Nineveh, the capital of the Assyrian Empire. He had a weighty message to deliver. Jehovah had told him: "Get up, go to Nineveh the great city, and proclaim against her that their badness has come up before me."—Jonah 1:2, 3.

2 When he first received his commission, Jonah ran off in the opposite direction, toward Tarshish. From a human standpoint, Jonah had reason to be reluctant. The Assyrians were a cruel people. Notice how one Assyrian monarch dealt with his enemies: "I cut off the limbs of the officers . . . Many captives from among them I burned with fire, and many I took as living captives. From some I cut off their hands and their fingers, and from others I cut off their noses." Still, when Jonah finally delivered Jehovah's message, the Ninevites repented of their sins and Jehovah spared the city at that time.—Jonah 3:3-10; Matthew 12:41.

Jehovah Takes Up "the Rod"

3 Do the Israelites, to whom Jonah also preached, re-

1, 2. (a) From a human standpoint, why did Jonah seem to have good reason to be reluctant to accept his commission to preach to the Assyrians? (b) How did the Ninevites react to Jonah's message?
3. How does the reaction of the Israelites to the warnings delivered by Jehovah's prophets differ from that of the Ninevites?

spond? (2 Kings 14:25) No. They turn their backs on pure worship. Indeed, they go so far as "to bow down to all the army of the heavens and to serve Baal." What is more, "they continued to make their sons and their daughters pass through the fire and to practice divination and to look for omens, and they kept selling themselves to do what was bad in the eyes of Jehovah, to offend him." (2 Kings 17:16, 17) Unlike the Ninevites, Israel does not respond when Jehovah sends prophets to warn them. So Jehovah determines to take stronger measures.

4 For some time after Jonah's visit to Nineveh, there is a decline in Assyrian aggression.* However, at the beginning of the eighth century B.C.E., Assyria reasserts itself as a military power, and Jehovah uses it in an astonishing way. The prophet Isaiah conveys a warning from Jehovah to the northern kingdom of Israel: *"Aha, the Assyrian, the rod for my anger, and the stick that is in their hand for my denunciation! Against an apostate nation I shall send him, and against the people of my fury I shall issue a command to him, to take much spoil and to take much plunder and to make it a trampling place like the clay of the streets."—Isaiah 10:5, 6.*

5 What a humiliation for the Israelites! God uses a pagan nation—"the Assyrian"—as a "rod" to punish them. In 742 B.C.E., Assyrian King Shalmaneser V lays siege to Samaria, capital of the apostate nation of Israel. From its strategic location on a hill some 300 feet high, Samaria wards off the enemy for almost three years. But no human strategy can block God's purpose. In 740 B.C.E., Samaria falls, trampled under Assyrian feet.—2 Kings 18:10.

---

* See *Insight on the Scriptures,* Volume 1, page 203.

4, 5. (a) What is meant by "the Assyrian," and how will Jehovah use him as a "rod"? (b) When does Samaria fall?

6 Although used by Jehovah to teach his people a lesson, the Assyrians themselves do not recognize Jehovah. That is why he goes on to say: *"Though [the Assyrian] may not be that way, he will feel inclined; though his heart may not be that way, he will scheme, because to annihilate is in his heart, and to cut off nations not a few." (Isaiah 10:7)* Jehovah means the Assyrian to be an instrument in the divine hand. But the Assyrian feels inclined to be something else. His heart urges him to scheme for something grander—conquest of the then-known world!

7 Many of the non-Israelite cities conquered by the Assyrian were previously ruled by kings. These former kings now have to submit to the king of Assyria as vassal princes, so he can truly boast: *"Are not my princes at the same time kings?" (Isaiah 10:8)* The false gods of prominent cities of the nations could not save their worshipers from destruction. The gods worshiped by the inhabitants of Samaria, such as Baal, Molech, and the golden calves, will not protect that city. Having forsaken Jehovah, Samaria has no right to expect him to intervene. Let any today who forsake Jehovah take notice of Samaria's fate! The Assyrian can well boast regarding Samaria and the other cities he has conquered: *"Is not Calno just like Carchemish? Is not Hamath just like Arpad? Is not Samaria just like Damascus?" (Isaiah 10:9)* They are all the same to the Assyrian—spoil for him to take.

8 However, the Assyrian goes too far in his boasting.

----

6. In what way does the Assyrian go beyond what Jehovah has in mind for him?

7. (a) Explain the expression "Are not my princes at the same time kings?" (b) Of what should those today who forsake Jehovah take note?

8, 9. Why is it that the Assyrian goes too far when he sets his sights on Jerusalem?

Sennacherib reasons that gathering the nations is as easy as gathering eggs from a nest

He says: **"Whenever my hand has reached the kingdoms of the valueless god whose graven images are more than those at Jerusalem and at Samaria, will it not be that just as I shall have done to Samaria and to her valueless gods, even so I shall do to Jerusalem and to her idols?"** (Isaiah 10:10, 11) The kingdoms already defeated by the Assyrian possessed far more idols than do Jerusalem or even Samaria. 'What,' he reasons, 'is to prevent me from doing to Jerusalem what I did to Samaria?'

9 The braggart! Jehovah will not allow him to take Jerusalem. True, Judah does not have a spotless record of supporting true worship. (2 Kings 16:7-9; 2 Chronicles 28:24) Jehovah has warned that because of her unfaithfulness, Judah will suffer much during the Assyrian invasion. But Jerusalem will survive. (Isaiah 1:7, 8) When the Assyrian invasion occurs, Hezekiah is king in Jerusalem. Hezekiah

is not like his father, Ahaz. Why, in the very first month of his reign, Hezekiah reopens the temple doors and restores pure worship!—2 Chronicles 29:3-5.

10 So Assyria's proposed attack on Jerusalem does not have Jehovah's approval. Jehovah promises an accounting with that insolent world power: *"It must occur that when Jehovah terminates all his work in Mount Zion and in Jerusalem, I shall make an accounting for the fruitage of the insolence of the heart of the king of Assyria and for the self-importance of his loftiness of eyes."—Isaiah 10:12.*

On to Judah and Jerusalem!

11 Eight years after the northern kingdom fell in 740 B.C.E., a new Assyrian monarch, Sennacherib, marches against Jerusalem. Isaiah poetically describes Sennacherib's prideful plan: *"I shall remove the boundaries of peoples, and their things stored up I shall certainly pillage, and I shall bring down the inhabitants just like a powerful one. And just as if a nest, my hand will reach the resources of the peoples; and just as when one gathers eggs that have been left, I myself will gather up even all the earth, and there will certainly be no one fluttering his wings or opening his mouth or chirping."* (Isaiah 10:13, 14) Sennacherib reasons that other cities have fallen and Samaria is no more, so Jerusalem will be easy prey! The city might put up a halfhearted fight, but with hardly a chirp, its inhabitants will be quickly subdued, their resources plucked up like eggs from an abandoned nest.

12 However, Sennacherib is forgetting something. Apos-

---

10. What does Jehovah promise regarding the Assyrian?
11. Why does the Assyrian think that Jerusalem will be easy prey?
12. What does Jehovah show to be the right way to view things with regard to the Assyrian's boasts?

tate Samaria deserved the punishment that it received. Under King Hezekiah, however, Jerusalem has once again become a bastion of pure worship. Anyone wanting to touch Jerusalem will have Jehovah to reckon with! Indignantly, Isaiah asks: *"Will the ax enhance itself over the one chopping with it, or the saw magnify itself over the one moving it back and forth, as though the staff moved back and forth the ones raising it on high, as though the rod raised on high the one who is not wood?"* **(Isaiah 10: 15)** The Assyrian Empire is a mere tool in Jehovah's hand, much as an ax, a saw, a staff, or a rod might be used by a woodsman, a sawyer, or a shepherd. How dare the rod now magnify itself over the one who uses it!

13 What will happen to the Assyrian? *"The true Lord, Jehovah of armies, will keep sending upon his fat ones a wasting disease, and under his glory a burning will keep burning away like the burning of a fire. And Israel's Light must become a fire, and his Holy One a flame; and it must blaze up and eat up his weeds and his thornbushes in one day. And the glory of his forest and of his orchard He will bring to an end, even from the soul clear to the flesh, and it must become like the melting away of one that is ailing. And the rest of the trees of his forest—they will become such a number that a mere boy will be able to write them down."* **(Isaiah 10:16-19)** Yes, Jehovah will whittle that Assyrian "rod" down to size! The "fat ones" of the Assyrian's army, his stout soldiers, will be struck with "a wasting disease." They will not look so strong! Like so many weeds and thornbushes, his ground troops will be burned by the Light of Israel, Jehovah God. And "the glory of his

---

13. Identify and tell what happens to (a) the "fat ones." (b) 'the weeds and thornbushes.' (c) "the glory of his forest."

forest," his military officers, will come to their end. After Jehovah finishes with the Assyrian, so few officers will remain that a mere boy will be able to number them on his fingers!—*See also Isaiah 10:33, 34.*

14 Still, the Jews living in Jerusalem in 732 B.C.E. must find it hard to believe that the Assyrian will be defeated. The vast Assyrian army is advancing relentlessly. Listen to the list of cities in Judah that have fallen: *"He has come upon Aiath . . . Migron . . . Michmash . . . Geba . . . Ramah . . . Gibeah of Saul . . . Gallim . . . Laishah . . . Anathoth . . . Madmenah . . . Gebim . . . Nob." (Isaiah 10:28-32a)** Finally the invaders reach Lachish, just 30 miles from Jerusalem. Soon a large Assyrian army is threatening the city. *"He waves his hand threateningly at the mountain of the daughter of Zion, the hill of Jerusalem." (Isaiah 10:32b)* What can stop the Assyrian?

15 In his palace in the city, King Hezekiah grows anxious. He rips his garments apart and covers himself with sackcloth. (Isaiah 37:1) He sends men to the prophet Isaiah to inquire of Jehovah on Judah's behalf. They soon return with Jehovah's answer: "Do not be afraid . . . I shall certainly defend this city." (Isaiah 37:6, 35) Still, the Assyrians are menacing and supremely confident.

16 Faith—that is what will carry King Hezekiah through this crisis. Faith is "the evident demonstration of realities though not beheld." (Hebrews 11:1) It involves look-

---

* For clarity, Isaiah 10:28-32 is discussed before Isaiah 10:20-27.

---

14. Describe the progress of the Assyrian on the soil of Judah by 732 B.C.E.

15, 16. (a) Why does King Hezekiah need strong faith? (b) What basis is there for Hezekiah's faith that Jehovah will come to his aid?

ing beyond the obvious. But faith is based on knowledge. Hezekiah likely remembers that ahead of time Jehovah spoke these comforting words: *"Do not be afraid, O my people who are dwelling in Zion, because of the Assyrian . . . For yet a very little while—and the denunciation will have come to an end, and my anger, in their wearing away. And Jehovah of armies will certainly brandish against him a whip as at the defeat of Midian by the rock Oreb; and his staff will be upon the sea, and he will certainly lift it up in the way that he did with Egypt." (Isaiah 10:24-26)** Yes, God's people have been in difficult situations before. Hezekiah's ancestors seemed hopelessly outclassed by the Egyptian army at the Red Sea. His forefather Gideon faced staggering odds when Midian and Amalek invaded Israel. Yet, Jehovah delivered his people on those two occasions.—Exodus 14:7-9, 13, 28; Judges 6: 33; 7:21, 22.

17 Will Jehovah do again what he did on those previous occasions? Yes. Jehovah promises: *"It must occur in that day that his load will depart from upon your shoulder, and his yoke from upon your neck, and the yoke will certainly be wrecked because of the oil." (Isaiah 10:27)* The Assyrian yoke will be lifted from the shoulder and the neck of God's covenant people. Indeed, the yoke will be "wrecked"—and wrecked it is! In one night, the angel of Jehovah kills 185,000 of the Assyrians. The threat is removed, and the Assyrians leave the soil of Judah forever. (2 Kings 19:35, 36) Why? "Because of the oil." This may refer to the oil used to anoint Hezekiah as king in the line

---

* For a discussion of Isaiah 10:20-23, see "Isaiah Looks Further Ahead," on page 155.

---

17. How is the Assyrian yoke "wrecked," and why?

of David. Thus, Jehovah fulfills his promise: "I shall certainly defend this city to save it for my own sake and for the sake of David my servant."—2 Kings 19:34.

18 The account of Isaiah discussed in this chapter has to do with events in Judah more than 2,700 years ago. But those events have the utmost relevance today. (Romans 15:4) Does this mean that the major players in this thrilling narrative—the inhabitants of Samaria and Jerusalem as well as the Assyrians—have modern-day counterparts? Yes, it does. Like idolatrous Samaria, Christendom claims to worship Jehovah, but she is apostate to the core. In *An Essay on the Development of Christian Doctrine,* Roman Catholic John Henry Cardinal Newman admits that items Christendom has used for centuries, such as incense, candles, holy water, priestly garb, and images, "are all of pagan origin." Jehovah is no more pleased with Christendom's paganized worship than he was with Samaria's idolatry.

19 For years, Jehovah's Witnesses have warned Christendom of Jehovah's displeasure. In 1955, for example, the public discourse entitled "Christendom or Christianity —Which One Is 'the Light of the World'?" was delivered worldwide. The talk graphically explained the way that Christendom had strayed from genuine Christian doctrine and practice. Thereafter, copies of this powerful lecture were mailed to clergymen in many countries. As an organization, Christendom has failed to heed the warning. She leaves Jehovah with no choice but to discipline her with a "rod."

---

18. (a) Does Isaiah's prophecy have more than one fulfillment? Explain. (b) What organization today is like ancient Samaria?
19. Of what has Christendom been warned, and by whom?

20 Whom will Jehovah use to discipline rebellious Christendom? We find the answer in the 17th chapter of Revelation. There we are introduced to a harlot, "Babylon the Great," representing all the world's false religions, including Christendom. The harlot is riding a scarlet-colored wild beast that has seven heads and ten horns. (Revelation 17:3, 5, 7-12) The wild beast represents the United Nations organization.* Just as the ancient Assyrian destroyed Samaria, the scarlet-colored wild beast "will hate the harlot and will make her devastated and naked, and will eat up her fleshy parts and will completely burn her with fire." (Revelation 17:16) Thus the modern-day Assyrian (nations associated with the UN) will deal Christendom a mighty blow and will crush her out of existence.

21 Will Jehovah's faithful Witnesses perish along with Babylon the Great? No. God is not displeased with them. Pure worship will survive. However, the wild beast that destroys Babylon the Great also casts a greedy eye in the direction of Jehovah's people. In doing so, the beast carries out, not God's thought, but the thought of someone else. Who? Satan the Devil.

22 Jehovah exposes Satan's prideful scheme: "It must occur in that day that things will come up into your [Satan's] heart, and you will certainly think up an injurious scheme; and you must say: 'I shall . . . come in upon those having no disturbance, dwelling in security, all of them

---

* Additional information regarding the identity of the harlot and the scarlet-colored wild beast is found in chapters 34 and 35 of the book *Revelation—Its Grand Climax At Hand!*, published by the Watchtower Bible and Tract Society of New York, Inc.

---

20. (a) What will serve as the modern-day Assyrian, and how will it be used as a rod? (b) To what extent will Christendom be disciplined?
21, 22. Who will motivate the wild beast to attack God's people?

dwelling without [a protective] wall . . .' It will be to get a big spoil and to do much plundering." (Ezekiel 38:10-12) Satan will reason, 'Yes, why not incite the nations to attack Jehovah's Witnesses? They are vulnerable, unprotected, without political influence. They will offer no resistance. How easy it will be to pluck them like eggs from an unprotected nest!'

23 But watch out, nations! Be advised that if you touch Jehovah's people, you will have to reckon with God himself! Jehovah loves his people, and he will fight for them just as surely as he fought for Jerusalem in the days of Hezekiah. When the modern-day Assyrian tries to annihilate Jehovah's servants, he will really be battling Jehovah God and the Lamb, Jesus Christ. That is a battle that the Assyrian cannot win. "The Lamb will conquer them," the Bible says, "because he is Lord of lords and King of kings." (Revelation 17:14; compare Matthew 25:40.) Like the Assyrian of old, the scarlet-colored wild beast will 'go off into destruction.' It will be feared no more.—Revelation 17:11.

24 True Christians can face the future without fear if they keep their relationship with Jehovah strong and if they make the doing of his will their primary concern in life. (Matthew 6:33) Then they need "fear nothing bad." (Psalm 23:4) With their eyes of faith, they will see God's mighty arm raised high, not to punish them, but to shield them from his enemies. And their ears will hear these reassuring words: "Do not be afraid."—Isaiah 10:24.

---

23. Why will the modern-day Assyrian be unable to do to God's people what he does to Christendom?
24. (a) What are true Christians determined to do to prepare for the future? (b) How does Isaiah look further ahead? (See box on page 155.)

ISAIAH LOOKS FURTHER AHEAD

Isaiah 10:20-23

The 10th chapter of Isaiah focuses primarily on the way that Jehovah will use the Assyrian invasion to execute judgment upon Israel and on his promise to defend Jerusalem. Since verses 20 to 23 are located in the middle of this prophecy, they can be viewed as having a general fulfillment during the same period. (Compare Isaiah 1: 7-9.) However, the wording indicates that these verses apply more specifically to later periods when Jerusalem too would have to answer for the sins of her inhabitants.

King Ahaz tries to gain security by turning to Assyria for help. The prophet Isaiah foretells that at a future time, the survivors of the house of Israel will never again pursue such a senseless course. Isaiah 10:20 says that they will "support themselves upon Jehovah, the Holy One of Israel, in trueness." Verse 21 shows, however, that only a small number will do so: "A mere remnant will return." This reminds us of Isaiah's son Shear-jashub, who is a sign in Israel and whose name means "A Mere Remnant Will Return." (Isaiah 7:3) Verse 22 of chapter 10 warns of a coming "extermination" that has been decided on. Such an extermination will be righteous because it is a just punishment on a rebellious people. As a result, from a thickly populated nation that is "like the grains of sand of the sea," only a remnant will return. Verse 23 warns that this coming extermination will affect the whole land. Jerusalem will not be spared this time.

These verses well describe what happened in 607 B.C.E. when Jehovah used the Babylonian Empire as his "rod." The whole land, including Jerusalem, fell to the invader.

The Jews were taken captive to Babylon for 70 years. After that, though, some—even if only "a mere remnant"—returned to reestablish true worship in Jerusalem.

The prophecy at Isaiah 10:20-23 had a further fulfillment in the first century, as shown at Romans 9:27, 28. (Compare Isaiah 1:9; Romans 9:29.) Paul explains that in a spiritual sense, a "remnant" of Jews 'returned' to Jehovah in the first century C.E., inasmuch as a small number of faithful Jews became followers of Jesus Christ and began worshiping Jehovah "with spirit and truth." (John 4:24) These were later joined by believing Gentiles, making up a spiritual nation, "the Israel of God." (Galatians 6:16) On this occasion the words of Isaiah 10:20 were fulfilled: "Never again" did a nation dedicated to Jehovah turn away from him to human sources for support.

CHAPTER THIRTEEN

Salvation and Rejoicing Under the Messiah's Reign

IN THE days of Isaiah, the spiritual condition of God's covenant people was bad. Even under the rule of faithful kings, such as Uzziah and Jotham, many of the people worshiped at the high places. (2 Kings 15:1-4, 34, 35; 2 Chronicles 26:1, 4) When Hezekiah became king, he had to remove the appendages of Baal worship from the land. (2 Chronicles 31:1) No wonder that Jehovah urged his people to return to him and warned of discipline to come!

2 Still, not all were out-and-out rebels. Jehovah had faithful prophets, and likely there were some Jews who listened to them. Jehovah had comforting words for these ones. After describing the terrible depredations that Judah would experience during the Assyrian invasion, the prophet Isaiah was inspired to pen one of the most beautiful passages in the whole Bible, a description of the blessings to come under the reign of the Messiah.* Some aspects of these blessings turned out to have a small-scale

---

* "Messiah" is derived from the Hebrew word *ma·shi'ach,* meaning "Anointed One." The Greek equivalent is *Khri·stos',* or "Christ."—Matthew 2:4, footnote.

---

1. Describe the spiritual condition of God's covenant people in the days of Isaiah.
2, 3. What encouragement does Jehovah supply for those who desire to serve him despite widespread unfaithfulness?

fulfillment when the Jews returned from captivity in Babylon. But the prophecy as a whole has a major fulfillment today. True, Isaiah and other faithful Jews of his time did not live to see these blessings. But they looked forward to them in faith and will see a fulfillment of Isaiah's words after the resurrection.—Hebrews 11:35.

3 Jehovah's modern-day people also need encouragement. Rapidly decaying moral values in the world, vicious opposition to the Kingdom message, and personal weaknesses challenge all of them. Isaiah's wonderful words about the Messiah and his reign can strengthen and help God's people to meet these challenges.

The Messiah is "a twig" out of Jesse, through King David

Messiah—A Capable Leader

4 Centuries before Isaiah's time, other Hebrew Bible writers pointed to the coming of the Messiah, the true Leader, whom Jehovah would send to Israel. (Genesis 49:10; Deuteronomy 18:18; Psalm 118:22, 26) Now through Isaiah, Jehovah adds further details. Isaiah writes: *"There must go forth a twig out of the stump of Jesse; and out of his roots a sprout will be fruitful." (Isaiah 11:1;* compare Psalm 132:11.) "Twig" and "sprout" both indicate that the Messiah will be the *descendant* of Jesse through his son David, who was anointed with oil as king of Israel. (1 Samuel 16:13; Jeremiah 23:5; Revelation 22:16) When the true Messiah arrives, this "sprout," from the house of David, is to produce good fruit.

5 The promised Messiah is Jesus. The gospel writer Matthew alluded to the words of Isaiah 11:1 when he said that Jesus' being called "a Nazarene" fulfilled the words of the prophets. Because he was brought up in the town of Nazareth, Jesus was called a Nazarene, a name apparently related to the Hebrew word used in Isaiah 11:1 for "sprout."*
—Matthew 2:23, footnote; Luke 2:39, 40.

6 What kind of ruler will the Messiah be? Will he be like the cruel, self-willed Assyrian who destroys the ten-tribe northern kingdom of Israel? Of course not. Of the Messiah, Isaiah says: *"Upon him the spirit of Jehovah must settle down, the spirit of wisdom and of understanding, the spirit of counsel and of mightiness, the spirit of knowledge and of the fear of Jehovah; and there will be enjoyment by*

---

* The Hebrew word for "sprout" is *ne'tser,* and for "Nazarene" is *Nots-ri'.*

4, 5. What did Isaiah prophesy regarding the coming of the Messiah, and what application of Isaiah's words did Matthew apparently make?

6. What kind of ruler is the Messiah prophesied to be?

him in the fear of Jehovah." (Isaiah 11:2, 3a) The Messiah is anointed, not with oil, but with God's holy spirit. This happens at Jesus' baptism, when John the Baptizer sees God's holy spirit descending on Jesus in the form of a dove. (Luke 3:22) Jehovah's spirit 'settles down upon' Jesus, and he gives evidence of this when he acts with wisdom, understanding, counsel, mightiness, and knowledge. What excellent qualities for a ruler!

7 Jesus' followers too can receive holy spirit. In one of his discourses, Jesus declared: "If you, although being wicked, know how to give good gifts to your children, how much more so will the Father in heaven give holy spirit to those asking him!" (Luke 11:13) Hence, we should never hesitate to ask God for holy spirit, nor should we cease to cultivate its wholesome fruitage—"love, joy, peace, long-suffering, kindness, goodness, faith, mildness, self-control." (Galatians 5:22, 23) Jehovah promises to answer the request of Jesus' followers for "wisdom from above" to help them deal successfully with the challenges of life. —James 1:5; 3:17.

8 What is the fear of Jehovah that the Messiah displays? Jesus certainly is not terrified by God, fearful of his condemnation. Rather, the Messiah has a respectful awe of God, a loving reverence for him. A God-fearing person desires always to "do the things pleasing to him," as Jesus does. (John 8:29) By word and example, Jesus teaches that there is no greater joy than walking every day in the wholesome fear of Jehovah.

A Righteous and Merciful Judge

9 Isaiah foretells more of the Messiah's characteristics: **"He**

---

7. What promise did Jesus make to his faithful followers?
8. How does Jesus find enjoyment in the fear of Jehovah?
9. What example does Jesus give to those called upon to judge matters in the Christian congregation?

will not judge by any mere appearance to his eyes, nor reprove simply according to the thing heard by his ears." (Isaiah 11:3b) If you had to stand before a court of law, would you not be grateful for a judge like that? In his capacity as Judge of all mankind, the Messiah is not swayed by false arguments, clever courtroom tactics, rumors, or superficial factors, such as wealth. He sees through deception and looks beyond unflattering outward appearances, discerning "the secret person of the heart," "the hidden man." (1 Peter 3:4, footnote) Jesus' superlative example serves as the model for all who are called upon to judge matters in the Christian congregation.—1 Corinthians 6:1-4.

10 How will the Messiah's superlative qualities influence his judicial decisions? Isaiah explains: *"With righteousness he must judge the lowly ones, and with uprightness he must give reproof in behalf of the meek ones of the earth. And he must strike the earth with the rod of his mouth; and with the spirit of his lips he will put the wicked one to death. And righteousness must prove to be the belt of his hips, and faithfulness the belt of his loins."—Isaiah 11:4, 5.*

11 When his followers need correction, Jesus delivers it in the way that benefits them most—an excellent example for Christian elders. On the other hand, those who practice wickedness can expect judgment of a severe sort. When God calls this system of things to account, the Messiah will "strike the earth" with his authoritative voice, issuing a judgment of destruction for all the wicked. (Psalm 2:9; compare Revelation 19:15.) Eventually, there will be no wicked people left to disturb the peace of mankind. (Psalm 37:10, 11) Jesus, with his hips and loins girded with righteousness and faithfulness, has the power to accomplish this.—Psalm 45:3-7.

10, 11. (a) In what way does Jesus correct his followers? (b) What judgment does Jesus render to the wicked?

Changed Conditions on Earth

12 Picture an Israelite who has just learned of Cyrus' decree that the Jews return to Jerusalem and rebuild the temple. Will he leave the security of Babylon to make the long trip home? During Israel's 70-year absence, the deserted fields have become overgrown with weeds. Wolves, leopards, lions, and bears now freely prowl those fields. Cobras too make their home there. The returning Jews will have to depend on domestic animals for survival—flocks and herds will provide milk, wool, and meat, and oxen will pull the plow. Will these fall victim to predators? Will small children be bitten by snakes? What about the danger of being ambushed on the journey?

13 Isaiah now paints a heartwarming picture of the conditions that God will bring about in the land. He says: *"The wolf will actually reside for a while with the male lamb, and with the kid the leopard itself will lie down, and the calf and the maned young lion and the well-fed animal all together; and a mere little boy will be leader over them. And the cow and the bear themselves will feed; together their young ones will lie down. And even the lion will eat straw just like the bull. And the sucking child will certainly play upon the hole of the cobra; and upon the light aperture of a poisonous snake will a weaned child actually put his own hand. They will not do any harm or cause any ruin in all my holy mountain; because the earth will certainly be filled with the knowledge of Jehovah as the waters are covering the very sea."* (Isaiah 11: 6-9) Do these words not touch the heart? Notice that the

---

12. What concerns might a Jew have when he contemplates returning from Babylon to the Promised Land?
13. (a) What heartwarming picture does Isaiah paint? (b) How do we know that the peace Isaiah describes involves more than safety from wild animals?

peace described here results from the knowledge of Jehovah. Hence, more is involved than mere safety from wild animals. The knowledge of Jehovah will not change animals, but it will affect people. Neither on the way home nor in their restored land will the Israelites need to fear wild beasts or beastlike men.—Ezra 8:21, 22; Isaiah 35:8-10; 65:25.

14 This prophecy, however, has a larger fulfillment. In 1914, Jesus, the Messiah, was enthroned on heavenly Mount Zion. In 1919 the remaining ones of "the Israel of God" experienced release from Babylonish captivity and shared in the restoration of true worship. (Galatians 6:16) As a result, the way was opened for a modern-day fulfillment of Isaiah's Paradise prophecy. "Accurate knowledge," the knowledge of Jehovah, has changed personalities. (Colossians 3:9, 10) Formerly violent people have become peaceable. (Romans 12:2; Ephesians 4:17-24) These developments have now affected millions because Isaiah's prophecy has come to include a rapidly increasing number of Christians with an earthly hope. (Psalm 37:29; Isaiah 60:22) These have learned to look to the time when the whole earth will be restored as a secure, peaceful paradise, according to God's original purpose.—Matthew 6:9, 10; 2 Peter 3:13.

15 In that restored Paradise, will Isaiah's prophecy have a further, perhaps more literal, fulfillment? It seems reasonable to think so. The prophecy gives to all who will live under the Messiah's rule the same assurance that it gave to the returning Israelites; they and their children will not feel threatened by harm from any source—human or animal. Under the Messiah's Kingdom rule, all earth's inhab-

---

14. What is the larger fulfillment of Isaiah 11:6-9?
15. Can we reasonably expect Isaiah's words to have a literal fulfillment in the new world? Explain.

itants will enjoy peaceful conditions like those that Adam and Eve enjoyed in Eden. Of course, the Scriptures do not reveal every detail of what life was like in Eden—or of what it will be like in Paradise. We can be confident, though, that under the wise and loving rule of the King Jesus Christ, everything will be just as it should be.

Pure Worship Restored Through the Messiah

16 Pure worship first came under attack in Eden when Satan successfully influenced Adam and Eve to disobey Jehovah. To this day, Satan has not given up his goal of turning as many as possible away from God. But Jehovah will never permit pure worship to vanish from the earth. His name is involved, and he cares about those who serve him. Hence, through Isaiah he makes a striking promise: *"It must occur in that day that there will be the root of Jesse that will be standing up as a signal for the peoples. To him even the nations will turn inquiringly, and his resting-place must become glorious." (Isaiah 11:10)* Back in 537 B.C.E., Jerusalem, the city that David had made the national capital, served as a signal, calling a faithful remnant of the dispersed Jewish people to return and rebuild the temple.

17 However, the prophecy points to more than that. As already seen, it points to the rule of the Messiah, the one true Leader for people of all nations. The apostle Paul quoted Isaiah 11:10 to show that in his day people of the nations would have a place in the Christian congregation. Quoting the *Septuagint* rendering of this verse, he wrote: "Isaiah says: 'There will be the root of Jesse, and there will be one arising to rule nations; on him nations will rest their hope.'" (Romans 15:12) Moreover, the prophecy reaches even further—down to our day when people of

---

16. What stood as a signal for God's people in 537 B.C.E.?
17. How did Jesus 'arise to rule nations' in the first century and in our day?

the nations show their love for Jehovah by supporting the anointed brothers of the Messiah.—Isaiah 61:5-9; Matthew 25:31-40.

18 In the modern-day fulfillment, "that day" referred to by Isaiah began when the Messiah was enthroned as King of God's heavenly Kingdom in 1914. (Luke 21:10; 2 Timothy 3:1-5; Revelation 12:10) Since then, Jesus Christ has been a clear signal, a rallying point, for spiritual Israel and for people of all nations who long for righteous government. Under the Messiah's direction, the good news of the Kingdom has been carried to all the nations, as Jesus foretold. (Matthew 24:14, Mark 13:10) This good news has a powerful effect. "A great crowd, which no man [is] able to number, out of all nations" is submitting to the Messiah by joining the anointed remnant in pure worship. (Revelation 7:9) As many new ones continue to come into association with the remnant in Jehovah's spiritual "house of prayer," they add to the glory of the Messiah's "resting-place," God's great spiritual temple.—Isaiah 56:7; Haggai 2:7.

A United People Serve Jehovah

19 Isaiah next reminds the Israelites that Jehovah once before provided salvation for them when the nation faced oppression by a powerful enemy. That part of Israel's history—Jehovah's liberation of the nation from captivity in Egypt—is dear to the hearts of all faithful Jews. Isaiah writes: *"It must occur in that day that Jehovah will again offer his hand, a second time, to acquire the remnant of his people who will remain over from Assyria and from Egypt and from Pathros and from Cush and from Elam and from*

18. In our day, how has Jesus been a rallying point?
19. On what two occasions does Jehovah restore a remnant of his people scattered throughout the earth?

Shinar and from Hamath and from the islands of the sea. And he will certainly raise up a signal for the nations and gather the dispersed ones of Israel; and the scattered ones of Judah he will collect together from the four extremities of the earth." **(Isaiah 11:11, 12)** As if taking them by the hand, Jehovah will lead a faithful remnant of both Israel and Judah out from the nations to which they have been scattered and will bring them safely home. In a minor way, this happens in 537 B.C.E. How much more glorious, though, is the major fulfillment! In 1914, Jehovah raised the enthroned Jesus Christ as "a signal for the nations." Starting in 1919 the remaining ones of "the Israel of God" began to flock to this signal, eager to share in pure worship under God's Kingdom. This unique spiritual nation comes "out of every tribe and tongue and people and nation."—Revelation 5:9.

20 Isaiah now describes the unity of the restored nation. Referring to the northern kingdom as Ephraim and to the southern kingdom as Judah, he says: *"The jealousy of Ephraim must depart, and even those showing hostility to Judah will be cut off. Ephraim itself will not be jealous of Judah, nor will Judah show hostility toward Ephraim. And they must fly at the shoulder of the Philistines to the west; together they will plunder the sons of the East. Edom and Moab will be those upon whom they will thrust out their hand, and the sons of Ammon will be their subjects."* **(Isaiah 11:13, 14)** When the Jews return from Babylon, they will no longer be divided into two nations. Members from all tribes of Israel will return unitedly to their land. (Ezra 6: 17) No longer will they show resentment and hostility toward one another. As a united people, they will take a triumphant stand against their enemies in the surrounding nations.

---

20. What unity will God's people enjoy upon their return from Babylon?

21 Still more impressive is the unity of "the Israel of God." The 12 symbolic tribes of spiritual Israel have for almost 2,000 years enjoyed a unity based on love for God and for their spiritual brothers and sisters. (Colossians 3: 14; Revelation 7:4-8) Today, Jehovah's people—both spiritual Israelites and those with an earthly hope—enjoy peace and worldwide unity under the Messiah's rule, conditions unknown in the churches of Christendom. Jehovah's Witnesses present a united spiritual front against Satan's efforts to interfere with their worship. As one people, they carry out Jesus' commission to preach and teach the good news of the Messiah's Kingdom in all the nations.—Matthew 28:19, 20.

Barriers Will Be Overcome

22 There are many barriers, both literal and figurative, to hinder the Israelites' return from exile. How will they be overcome? Isaiah says: *"Jehovah will certainly cut off the tongue of the Egyptian sea, and wave his hand at the River in the glow of his spirit. And he must strike it in its seven torrents, and he will actually cause people to walk in their sandals." (Isaiah 11:15)* It is Jehovah who will remove all impediments to his people's return. Even a barrier as formidable as a tongue of the Red Sea (such as the Gulf of Suez) or as impassable as the mighty Euphrates River will be dried up, as it were, so that a person can cross without having to take off his sandals!

23 In Moses' day, Jehovah prepared a way for Israel to escape from Egypt and march to the Promised Land. He will do something similar now: *"There must come to be a highway out of Assyria for the remnant of his people who will*

---

21. How is the unity of God's people today truly outstanding?
22. How will Jehovah "cut off the tongue of the Egyptian sea" and "wave his hand at the River"?
23. In what way will there "come to be a highway out of Assyria"?

remain over, just as there came to be one for Israel in the day of his coming up out of the land of Egypt." (*Isaiah 11:16*) Jehovah will lead returning exiles as if they were walking along a highway from their place of exile to their homeland. Opposers will attempt to stop them, but their God, Jehovah, will be with them. Anointed Christians and their companions today likewise come under vicious attack, but they go forward courageously! They have come out of modern Assyria, Satan's world, and they help others to do the same. They know that pure worship will succeed and flourish. It is not man's work, but God's.

Endless Rejoicing for the Subjects of the Messiah!

24 In joyful language Isaiah now describes the exultation of Jehovah's people over the fulfillment of His word: *"In that day you will be sure to say: 'I shall thank you, O Jehovah, for although you got incensed at me, your anger gradually turned back, and you proceeded to comfort me.'"* (*Isaiah 12:1*) Jehovah's discipline of his wayward people is severe. But it accomplishes its purpose of healing the nation's relationship with him and of restoring pure worship. Jehovah reassures his faithful worshipers that ultimately he will save them. No wonder they express appreciation!

25 The restored Israelites have their confidence in Jehovah completely confirmed, and they cry out: *"'Look! God is my salvation. I shall trust and be in no dread; for Jah Jehovah is my strength and my might, and he came to be the salvation of me.' With exultation you people will be certain to draw water out of the springs of salvation."* (*Isaiah 12: 2, 3*) The Hebrew word translated "might" in verse 2

24, 25. With what expressions of praise and gratitude will Jehovah's people cry out?

appears as "praise" in the Septuagint version. Worshipers break out in songs of praise over salvation from "Jah Jehovah." As an abbreviated form of the name Jehovah, "Jah" is used in the Bible to convey heightened feelings of praise and gratitude. Using the expression "Jah Jehovah"—doubling the divine name—raises the intensity of praise to God to an even higher level.

26 Genuine worshipers of Jehovah cannot keep their joy

---

26. Who today make God's dealings known among the nations?

Isaiah 12:4, 5, as it appears in the Dead Sea Scrolls (Occurrences of God's name are highlighted) to themselves. Isaiah foretells: ***"In that day you will certainly say: 'Give thanks to Jehovah, you people! Call upon his name. Make known among the peoples his dealings. Make mention that his name is put on high. Make melody to Jehovah, for he has done surpassingly. This is made known in all the earth.'"*** (*Isaiah 12:4, 5*) Since 1919, anointed Christians—later with the help of their "other sheep" companions—have 'declared abroad the excellencies of the one that called them out of darkness into his wonderful light.' They are "a chosen race, . . . a holy nation" set apart for this purpose. (John 10:16; 1 Peter 2:9) Anointed ones declare that Jehovah's holy name is put on high and share in making it known in all the earth. They lead all of Jehovah's worshipers in rejoicing in his provision for their salvation. It is just as Isaiah exclaims: ***"Cry out shrilly and shout for joy, O you inhabitress of Zion, for great in the midst of you is the Holy One of Israel"!*** (*Isaiah 12:6*) The Holy One of Israel is Jehovah God himself.

Look to the Future With Confidence!

27 Today millions have flocked to the "signal for the peoples"—Jesus Christ enthroned in God's Kingdom. They rejoice to be subject to that Kingdom and are thrilled to know Jehovah God and his Son. (John 17:3) They find great happiness in their united Christian fellowship and strive hard to preserve the peace that is the mark of Jehovah's true servants. (Isaiah 54:13) Convinced that Jah Jehovah is a God who fulfills his promises, they are confident in their hope and find great delight in sharing it with others. May each worshiper of Jehovah continue to use all his strength to serve God and to help others do likewise. Let all take Isaiah's words to heart and rejoice in salvation through Jehovah's Messiah!

---

27. While awaiting the realization of their hope, in what are Christians confident?

CHAPTER FOURTEEN

Jehovah Humbles an Arrogant City

THE prophetic book of Isaiah was written in the eighth century B.C.E. against the background of the Assyrian invasion of the Promised Land. As has been seen in previous chapters of his book, Isaiah foretells with remarkable accuracy the course that events will take. However, the book looks beyond the time of Assyrian ascendancy. It foretells the return of Jehovah's covenant people from exile in many lands, including Shinar, the location of Babylon. (Isaiah 11:11) In Isaiah chapter 13, we find a remarkable prophecy that upon fulfillment will open the way for such a return. This prophecy is introduced with these words: *"The pronouncement against Babylon that Isaiah the son of Amoz saw in vision."—Isaiah 13:1.*

'Haughtiness I Shall Abase'

2 Judah becomes involved with Babylon during Isaiah's lifetime. King Hezekiah falls seriously ill and then recovers. Ambassadors from Babylon come to congratulate him on his recovery, likely with the secret purpose of enlisting Hezekiah as an ally in their war against Assyria. Unwisely, King Hezekiah shows them all his treasures. As a result, Isaiah tells Hezekiah that after the king's death, all that

---

1. How far ahead does the book of Isaiah now look?
2. (a) How does Hezekiah get involved with Babylon? (b) What is the "signal" that will be raised up?

wealth will be carried off to Babylon. (Isaiah 39:1-7) This is fulfilled in 607 B.C.E. when Jerusalem is destroyed and the nation is taken into exile. However, God's chosen people will not stay in Babylon forever. Jehovah foretells how he will open the way for their return home. He begins: *"Upon a mountain of bare rocks raise up a signal, you men. Lift up the voice to them, wave the hand, that they may come into the entrances of the nobles."* (Isaiah 13:2) The "signal" is a rising world power that will dislodge Babylon from its place of eminence. It will be raised "upon a mountain of bare rocks"—in plain view from a great distance. Summoned to assault Babylon, that new world power will force its way through "the entrances of the nobles," the gates of that great city, and will conquer it.

3 Jehovah now says: *"I myself have issued the command to my sanctified ones. I have also called my mighty ones for expressing my anger, my eminently exultant ones. Listen! A crowd in the mountains, something like a numerous people! Listen! The uproar of kingdoms, of nations gathered together! Jehovah of armies is mustering the army of war."* (Isaiah 13:3, 4) Who are these "sanctified ones" appointed to bring down haughty Babylon? They are combined national armies, "nations gathered together." They descend against Babylon from a distant mountainous region. *"They are coming from the land far away, from the extremity of the heavens."* (Isaiah 13:5) In what sense are they sanctified? Certainly not in the sense of being holy. They are pagan armies with no interest in serving Jehovah. However, in the Hebrew Scriptures, "sanctified" means "set apart for use by God." Jehovah can sanctify the armies of the nations and use their selfish ambitions in order to express his anger. He used Assyria in this way.

---

3. (a) Who are the "sanctified ones" that Jehovah will raise up? (b) In what sense are pagan armies "sanctified"?

He will use Babylon similarly. (Isaiah 10:5; Jeremiah 25:9) And he will use other nations to punish Babylon.

4 Babylon is not yet the dominant world power. Yet, issuing a proclamation through Isaiah, Jehovah looks to the time when she will occupy that position, and he foretells her fall. He says: *"Howl, you people, for the day of Jehovah is near! As a despoiling from the Almighty it will come." (Isaiah 13:6)* Yes, Babylon's boasting will be replaced by grief-filled howling. Why? Because of "the day of Jehovah," the day when Jehovah executes judgment against her.

5 How, though, will it be possible for Babylon to be despoiled? When Jehovah's time for this comes, the city will appear to be secure. Invading armies will first have to deal with the natural defenses provided by the Euphrates River, which runs through the center of the city and is tapped to fill a protective moat and to supply the city with drinking water. Then there will be Babylon's massive double walls, which are seemingly impregnable. Moreover, the city will be well stocked with food. The book *Daily Bible Illustrations* says that Nabonidus—the last king of Babylon—"had taken immense pains to store the town with provisions, and it was reckoned to contain enough [food] to sustain the inhabitants for twenty years."

6 However, appearances can be deceptive. Isaiah says: *"That is why all hands themselves will drop down, and the whole heart itself of mortal man will melt. And people have become disturbed. Convulsions and birth pains themselves grab hold; like a woman that is giving birth they*

4, 5. (a) What does Jehovah foretell for Babylon? (b) What will those attacking Babylon have to deal with?
6. What will unexpectedly happen when the foretold assault on Babylon occurs?

have labor pains. They look at each other in amazement. Their faces are inflamed faces." **(Isaiah 13:7, 8)** When the conquering armies invade the city, the ease of its inhabitants will be replaced by pain as sudden and intense as that of a woman giving birth. Their hearts will melt with fear. Paralyzed, their hands will drop down, unable to make a defense. Their faces will be "inflamed" with fear and anguish. In amazement they will look at one another, wondering how their great city could fall.

7 Nevertheless, fall it will. Babylon is to face a day of reckoning, a "day of Jehovah," that will be painful indeed. The supreme Judge will express his anger and bring well-deserved judgment upon Babylon's sinful inhabitants. The prophecy says: *"Look! The day of Jehovah itself is coming, cruel both with fury and with burning anger, in order to make the land an object of astonishment, and that it may annihilate the land's sinners out of it."* **(Isaiah 13:9)** Babylon's prospects are gloomy. It is as though the sun, moon, and stars all cease giving light. *"For the very stars of the heavens and their constellations of Kesil will not flash forth their light; the sun will actually grow dark at its going forth, and the moon itself will not cause its light to shine."* *—Isaiah 13:10.*

8 Why such a fate for this proud city? Jehovah says: *"I shall certainly bring home its own badness upon the productive land, and their own error upon the wicked themselves. And I shall actually cause the pride of the presumptuous ones to cease, and the haughtiness of the tyrants I shall abase."* **(Isaiah 13:11)** The outpouring of Jehovah's wrath will be punishment for Babylon's cruelty to God's

---

7. What "day of Jehovah" is coming, and what will be the results for Babylon?
8. Why does Jehovah decree the fall of Babylon?

people. The whole land will suffer because of the badness of the Babylonians. No longer will these proud tyrants openly defy Jehovah!

9 Jehovah says: *"I shall make mortal man rarer than refined gold, and earthling man rarer than the gold of Ophir."* (*Isaiah 13:12*) Yes, the city will come to be depopulated, waste. Jehovah continues: *"That is why I shall cause heaven itself to become agitated, and the earth will rock out of its place at the fury of Jehovah of armies and at the day of his burning anger."* (*Isaiah 13:13*) Babylon's "heaven," her multitude of gods and goddesses, will be agitated, unable to help the city in its time of need. "The earth," the Babylonian Empire, will be rocked out of place, passing into history as just another dead empire. *"It must occur that, like a gazelle chased away and like a flock without anyone to collect them together, they will turn, each one to his own people; and they will flee, each one to his own land."* (*Isaiah 13:14*) All of Babylon's foreign supporters will forsake her and flee, hoping to set up new relationships with the conquering world power. Babylon will finally experience the agony of a conquered city, an agony that she inflicted on so many others in the days of her glory: *"Every one that is found will be pierced through, and every one that is caught in the sweep will fall by the sword; and their very children will be dashed to pieces before their eyes. Their houses will be pillaged, and their own wives will be raped."—Isaiah 13:15, 16.*

God's Instrument of Destruction

10 Which power will Jehovah use to bring about the fall of Babylon? Some 200 years ahead of time, Jehovah reveals the answer: *"Here I am arousing against them the*

---

9. What awaits Babylon on Jehovah's day of judgment?
10. Whom will Jehovah use to defeat Babylon?

Medes, who account silver itself as nothing and who, as respects gold, take no delight in it. And their bows will dash even young men to pieces. And the fruitage of the belly they will not pity; for sons their eye will not feel sorry. And Babylon, the decoration of kingdoms, the beauty of the pride of the Chaldeans, must become as when God overthrew Sodom and Gomorrah." (Isaiah 13:17-19)

Magnificent Babylon will fall, and Jehovah's instrument for bringing this about will be armies from the distant,

mountainous country of Media.* Eventually, Babylon will be as desolate as the grossly immoral cities of Sodom and Gomorrah.—Genesis 13:13; 19:13, 24.

11 In Isaiah's day, both Media and Babylon are under the Assyrian yoke. About a century later, in 632 B.C.E., Media

---

* Isaiah mentions only the Medes by name, but a number of nations will be allies against Babylon—Media, Persia, Elam, and other smaller nations. (Jeremiah 50:9; 51:24, 27, 28) Neighboring nations refer to both Medes and Persians as "the Mede." Further, in Isaiah's day, Media is the dominant power. Only under Cyrus does Persia become dominant.

11, 12. (a) How does Media become a world power? (b) What unusual trait does the prophecy mention about Media's armies?

Fallen Babylon will become the haunt of desert creatures

and Babylon join forces and overthrow Nineveh, the capital of Assyria. This opens the way for Babylon to become the predominant world power. Little does she realize that about 100 years after that, Media will destroy her! Who but Jehovah God could make such a bold prediction?

12 When identifying his chosen instrument of destruction, Jehovah says that Media's armies "account silver itself as nothing and . . . as respects gold, take no delight in it." What an unusual trait for battle-hardened soldiers! Bible scholar Albert Barnes says: "Few, indeed, have been the invading armies which were not influenced by the hope of spoil." Do the Median armies prove Jehovah true in this regard? Yes. Consider this comment found in *The Bible-Work,* prepared by J. Glentworth Butler: "Unlike most nations that have ever waged war, the Medes, and especially the Persians, thought less of gold than of conquest and glory."* In view of this, it is not surprising that when he releases the Israelites from Babylonian exile, the Persian ruler Cyrus restores to them thousands of gold and silver vessels that Nebuchadnezzar looted from Jerusalem's temple. —Ezra 1:7-11.

13 While the Median and the Persian warriors have little passion for spoil, they are nevertheless ambitious. They do not intend to remain second to any nation on the world stage. Moreover, Jehovah puts "despoiling" into their hearts. (Isaiah 13:6) Hence, with their metal bows—which can be used not only to shoot arrows but also to strike and crush enemy soldiers, the offspring of Babylonian mothers—they are determined to conquer Babylon.

---

* It appears, however, that later on the Medes and the Persians developed a great love for luxury.—Esther 1:1-7.

13, 14. (a) Although not interested in spoil, for what are the Median and the Persian warriors ambitious? (b) How does Cyrus overcome the vaunted defenses of Babylon?

14 Cyrus, leader of the Medo-Persian armies, is undeterred by Babylon's fortifications. On the night of October 5/6, 539 B.C.E., he orders the diverting of the waters of the Euphrates River. As the water level falls, the invaders stealthily make their way into the city, walking along the riverbed through thigh-deep water. Babylon's inhabitants are caught unawares, and Babylon falls. (Daniel 5:30) Jehovah God inspires Isaiah to prophesy these events, leaving no doubt that He is directing matters.

15 How complete will the destruction of Babylon be? Listen to Jehovah's pronouncement: *"She will never be inhabited, nor will she reside for generation after generation. And there the Arab will not pitch his tent, and no shepherds will let their flocks lie down there. And there the haunters of waterless regions will certainly lie down, and their houses must be filled with eagle owls. And there the ostriches must reside, and goat-shaped demons themselves will go skipping about there. And jackals must howl in her dwelling towers, and the big snake will be in the palaces of exquisite delight. And the season for her is near to come, and her days themselves will not be postponed."* (Isaiah 13:20-22) Utter desolation will be the city's fate.

16 This did not happen immediately in 539 B.C.E. Still, today it is very clear that everything Isaiah foretold regarding Babylon has come true. Babylon "is now, and has been for centuries, a scene of wide desolation, and is a heap of ruins," says one Bible commentator. Then he adds: "It is impossible to behold this scene and not be reminded how exactly the predictions of Isaiah and Jeremiah have been fulfilled." Clearly, no man in Isaiah's day could have foretold Babylon's fall and her eventual desolation. After all, Babylon's fall to the Medes and the Persians occurred some

---

15. What future awaits Babylon?
16. The present condition of Babylon gives us what confidence?

200 years after Isaiah wrote his book! And her final desolation came centuries later. Does this not strengthen our faith in the Bible as the inspired Word of God? (2 Timothy 3:16) Moreover, since Jehovah fulfilled prophecies in times past, we can have absolute confidence that Bible prophecies yet unfulfilled will be realized in God's due time.

"Rest From Your Pain"

17 Babylon's fall will be a relief for Israel. It will mean release from captivity and the opportunity to return to the Promised Land. Hence, Isaiah now says: *"Jehovah will show mercy to Jacob, and he is yet certain to choose Israel; and he will actually give them rest upon their soil, and the alien resident must be joined to them, and they must attach themselves to the house of Jacob. And peoples will actually take them and bring them to their own place, and the house of Israel must take them to themselves as a possession upon the soil of Jehovah as menservants and as maidservants; and they must become the captors of those holding them captive, and they must have in subjection those who were driving them to work."* (Isaiah 14:1, 2) "Jacob" here refers to Israel as a whole—all 12 tribes. Jehovah will show mercy to "Jacob" by allowing the nation to return home. They will be accompanied by thousands of foreigners, many of whom will serve the Israelites as temple servants. Some Israelites will even come to have authority over their former captors.*

18 Gone will be the anguish of living in exile. Instead,

---

* For example, Daniel was appointed as a high official in Babylon under the Medes and the Persians. And about 60 years later, Esther became queen of the Persian King Ahasuerus, and Mordecai became prime minister of the whole Persian Empire.

17, 18. The defeat of Babylon will mean what blessings for Israel?

Jehovah will give his people *"rest from [their] pain and from [their] agitation and from the hard slavery in which [they] were made a slave."* (*Isaiah 14:3*) Having been freed from the physical burdens of slavery, Israel will no longer suffer the pain and agitation of living among worshipers of false gods. (Ezra 3:1; Isaiah 32:18) Commenting on this, the book *Lands and Peoples of the Bible* says: "To the Babylonian his gods were altogether such as himself, in all the worst aspects of his character. They were cowards, drunkards and imbeciles." What a relief to escape such a degraded religious environment!

19 Nevertheless, Jehovah's mercy is not unconditional. His people must express remorse for their wickedness, which moved God to punish them so severely. (Jeremiah 3:25) Open, heartfelt confession will bring Jehovah's forgiveness. (See Nehemiah 9:6-37; Daniel 9:5.) This same principle holds true today. Since "there is no man that does not sin," all of us need Jehovah's mercy. (2 Chronicles 6:36) Jehovah, the merciful God, lovingly invites us to confess our sins to him, to repent, and to cease any wrong course, in order that we may get healed. (Deuteronomy 4:31; Isaiah 1:18; James 5:16) This not only helps to restore us to his favor but also brings us comfort.—Psalm 51:1; Proverbs 28:13; 2 Corinthians 2:7.

A "Proverbial Saying" Against Babylon

20 More than 100 years before Babylon's rise as the preeminent world power, Isaiah foretells the world's reaction to her fall. Prophetically, he commands Israelites who have been freed from captivity to her: *"You must raise up this proverbial saying against the king of Babylon and say:*

---

19. What is needed if Israel is to enjoy Jehovah's forgiveness, and what do we learn from this?
20, 21. How do Babylon's neighbors rejoice at her fall?

'How has the one driving others to work come to a stop, the oppression come to a stop! Jehovah has broken the rod of the wicked ones, the staff of the ruling ones, the one striking peoples in fury with a stroke incessantly, the one subduing nations in sheer anger with a persecution without restraint.'" (Isaiah 14:4-6) Babylon has built up quite a reputation as a conqueror, an oppressor who turns free people into slaves. How fitting that her fall be celebrated with a "proverbial saying" directed primarily at the Babylonian dynasty—starting with Nebuchadnezzar and ending with Nabonidus and Belshazzar—that presided over the glory days of the great city!

21 What a difference her fall will make! *"The whole earth has come to rest, has become free of disturbance. People have become cheerful with joyful cries. Even the juniper trees have also rejoiced at you, the cedars of Lebanon, saying, 'Ever since you have lain down, no woodcutter comes up against us.'"* (Isaiah 14:7, 8) The kings of the nations round about were, to Babylon's rulers, like trees to be cut down and used for their own purposes. Well, all of that is finished. The Babylonian woodcutter has cut his last tree!

22 So astonishing is the fall of Babylon that the grave itself reacts: *"Even Sheol underneath has become agitated at you in order to meet you on coming in. At you it has awakened those impotent in death, all the goatlike leaders of the earth. It has made all the kings of the nations get up from their thrones. All of them speak up and say to you, 'Have you yourself also been made weak like us? Is it to us that you have been made comparable? Down to Sheol your pride has been brought, the din of your stringed instruments. Beneath you, maggots are spread out as a couch; and worms are your covering.'"* (Isaiah 14:9-11)

---

22. In a poetic sense, how is Sheol affected by the fall of the Babylonian dynasty?

What a powerful poetic image! It is as if the common grave of mankind were to wake up all those kings who preceded the Babylonian dynasty into death so that they can greet the newcomer. They mock the Babylonian ruling power, which is now helpless, lying on a bed of maggots instead of on a costly divan, covered with worms instead of expensive linens.

"Like a Carcass Trodden Down"

23 Isaiah continues the proverbial saying: *"O how you have fallen from heaven, you shining one, son of the dawn! How you have been cut down to the earth, you who were disabling the nations!"* (Isaiah 14:12) Selfish pride prompts Babylon's kings to elevate themselves above those around them. Like a star shining brightly in the early morning sky, they arrogantly wield power and authority. A particular source of pride is Nebuchadnezzar's conquest of Jerusalem, a feat that Assyria failed to accomplish. The proverbial utterance portrays the proud dynasty of Babylon as saying: *"To the heavens I shall go up. Above the stars of God I shall lift up my throne, and I shall sit down upon the mountain of meeting, in the remotest parts of the north. I shall go up above the high places of the clouds; I shall make myself resemble the Most High."* (Isaiah 14:13, 14) Could there be anything more outrageous?

24 In the Bible the kings of the royal line of David are likened to stars. (Numbers 24:17) From David on, those "stars" ruled from Mount Zion. After Solomon built the temple in Jerusalem, the name Zion came to apply to the whole city. Under the Law covenant, all male Israelites were obliged to travel to Zion three times a year. Thus, it became "the mountain of meeting." By determining to subjugate the Judean kings and then remove them from

23, 24. What extreme arrogance is shown by Babylon's kings?

that mountain, Nebuchadnezzar is declaring his intention to put himself above those "stars." He does not give Jehovah credit for his victory over them. Rather, in effect, he arrogantly puts himself in Jehovah's place.

25 What a reversal is in store for the proud Babylonian dynasty! Babylon is far from being elevated above the stars of God. Rather, Jehovah says: *"Down to Sheol you will be brought, to the remotest parts of the pit. Those seeing you will gaze even at you; they will give close examination even to you, saying, 'Is this the man that was agitating the earth, that was making kingdoms rock, that made the productive land like the wilderness and that overthrew its very cities, that did not open the way homeward even for his prisoners?'"* (Isaiah 14:15-17) The ambitious dynasty will come down to Hades (Sheol), just like any human.

26 Where, then, will be the power that conquered kingdoms, destroyed productive land, and overthrew cities without number? Where will be the world power that took captives and never allowed them to go back home? Why, the Babylonian dynasty will not even have a decent burial! Jehovah says: *"All other kings of the nations, yes, all of them, have lain down in glory, each one in his own house. But as for you, you have been thrown away without a burial place for you, like a detested sprout, clothed with killed men stabbed with the sword that are going down to the stones of a pit, like a carcass trodden down. You will not become united with them in a grave, because you brought your own land to ruin, you killed your own people. To time indefinite the offspring of evildoers will not be named."* (Isaiah 14:18-20) In the ancient world, it was considered a disgrace for a king to be deprived of an honorable burial. So, what about Babylon's royal dynasty? It is true that individual kings are probably interred

25, 26. How does the Babylonian dynasty meet a disgraceful end?

with honor, but the imperial dynasty of kings that descended from Nebuchadnezzar is discarded "like a detested sprout." It is as if the dynasty were thrown into an unmarked grave—like a mere foot soldier slain in battle. What a humiliation!

27 The proverbial saying ends with final orders to the conquering Medes and Persians: *"Make ready, you men, a slaughtering block for his own sons because of the error of their forefathers, that they may not rise up and actually take possession of the earth and fill the face of the productive land with cities." (Isaiah 14:21)* The fall of Babylon will be permanent. The Babylonian dynasty will be rooted out. There will be no renaissance. Future generations of Babylonians will suffer because of "the error of their forefathers."

28 The judgment pronounced against the Babylonian dynasty provides a valuable lesson for us. The root of the Babylonian kings' sin was their endless ambition. (Daniel 5:23) Their hearts were filled with a desire for power. They wanted to dominate others. (Isaiah 47:5, 6) And they lusted after glory from men, which rightly belongs to God. (Revelation 4:11) This is a warning to any in authority—even in the Christian congregation. Ambition and selfish pride are characteristics that Jehovah will not tolerate, either in individuals or in nations.

29 The pride of the Babylonian rulers was a reflection of the spirit of "the god of this system of things," Satan the

---

27. In what way do future generations of Babylonians suffer for the error of their forefathers?
28. What was the root of the sin of the Babylonian kings, and what do we learn from this?
29. The pride and ambition of the Babylonian rulers was a reflection of what?

Like ancient Babylon, Babylon the Great will become a heap of ruins

Devil. (2 Corinthians 4:4) He too lusts for power and longs to place himself above Jehovah God. As was the case with the king of Babylon and the people he subjugated, Satan's unholy ambition has resulted in misery and suffering for all mankind.

30 Moreover, in the book of Revelation, we read of another Babylon—"Babylon the Great." (Revelation 18:2) This organization, the world empire of false religion, has also shown a prideful, oppressive, and cruel spirit. As a result, she too has to face a "day of Jehovah" and be destroyed in God's due time. (Isaiah 13:6) Since 1919 the message has sounded around the earth: "Babylon the Great has fallen!" (Revelation 14:8) When she was unable to hold God's people in captivity, she experienced a fall. Soon she will be completely destroyed. Of ancient Babylon, Jehovah commanded: "Pay back to her according to her activity. According to all that she has done, do to her. For it is against Jehovah that she has acted presumptuously, against the Holy One of Israel." (Jeremiah 50:29; James 2:13) Babylon the Great will receive a similar judgment.

31 Hence, Jehovah's final statement of this prophecy in the book of Isaiah applies not only to ancient Babylon but also to Babylon the Great: *"I will rise up against them . . . And I will cut off from Babylon name and remnant and progeny and posterity . . . And I will make her a possession of porcupines and reedy pools of water, and I will sweep her with the broom of annihilation." (Isaiah 14:22, 23)* The desolated ruins of ancient Babylon show what Jehovah will soon do to Babylon the Great. What a comfort for lovers of true worship! What an encouragement to strive never to allow the satanic characteristics of pride, arrogance, or cruelty to develop in us!

---

30. What other Babylon is mentioned in the Bible, and what spirit has she shown?
31. What will soon happen to Babylon the Great?

CHAPTER FIFTEEN

Jehovah's Counsel Against the Nations

Isaiah 14:24–19:25

JEHOVAH can use the nations to discipline his people for their wickedness. Even so, he does not excuse those nations for their unnecessary cruelty, their pride, and their animosity toward true worship. Thus, long in advance he inspires Isaiah to record "the pronouncement against Babylon." (Isaiah 13:1) However, Babylon is a future threat. In Isaiah's day, Assyria is oppressing God's covenant people. Assyria destroys the northern kingdom of Israel and devastates much of Judah. But Assyria's triumph is limited. Isaiah writes: *"Jehovah of armies has sworn, saying: 'Surely just as I have figured, so it must occur . . . in order to break the Assyrian in my land and that I may tread him down on my own mountains; and that his yoke may actually depart from upon them and that his very load may depart from upon their shoulder.'" (Isaiah 14:24, 25)* Not long after Isaiah utters this prophecy, the Assyrian threat is removed from Judah.

2 What, though, of other nations that are enemies of God's covenant people? They too must be judged. Isaiah declares: *"This is the counsel that is counseled against all the earth, and this is the hand that is stretched out against*

---

1. What judgment proclamation against Assyria does Isaiah record?
2, 3. (a) In ancient times, against whom does Jehovah stretch out his hand? (b) What does it mean that Jehovah stretches out his hand against "all the nations"?

all the nations. For Jehovah of armies himself has coun-
seled, and who can break it up? And his hand is the one
stretched out, and who can turn it back?" **(Isaiah 14:26,**
27) Jehovah's "counsel" is more than mere advice. It is
his firm determination, his decree. (Jeremiah 49:20, 30)
God's "hand" is his applied power. In the final verses of
Isaiah chapter 14 and in chapters 15 to 19, Jehovah's counsel is against Philistia, Moab, Damascus, Ethiopia, and
Egypt.

3 However, Isaiah says that Jehovah's hand is stretched
out against "all the nations." Hence, while these prophecies of Isaiah are first fulfilled in ancient times, they also
apply in principle during "the time of the end" when Jehovah stretches out his hand against all the kingdoms of
the earth. (Daniel 2:44; 12:9; Romans 15:4; Revelation 19:
11, 19-21) Long in advance, the almighty God, Jehovah,
confidently reveals his counsel. No one can turn back his
stretched-out hand.—Psalm 33:11; Isaiah 46:10.

"A Flying Fiery Snake" Against Philistia

4 The Philistines receive attention first. *"In the year that*
King Ahaz died this pronouncement occurred: 'Do not re-
joice, O Philistia, any one of you, just because the staff of
the one striking you has been broken. For out of the root of
the serpent there will come forth a poisonous snake, and
its fruit will be a flying fiery snake.'"—Isaiah 14:28, 29.

5 King Uzziah was strong enough to contain the threat
posed by Philistia. (2 Chronicles 26:6-8) To them, he
was like a serpent, and his staff kept striking that un-

---

4. What are some details of Jehovah's pronouncement against Philistia?

5, 6. (a) In what way was Uzziah like a serpent to the Philistines?
(b) What does Hezekiah prove to be against Philistia?

Philistine warriors charging their enemies (Egyptian carving from the 12th century B.C.E.)

friendly neighbor. After Uzziah died—'his staff was broken'—the faithful Jotham ruled, but "the people were yet acting ruinously." Next, Ahaz became king. Things changed, and the Philistines conducted successful military raids on Judah. (2 Chronicles 27:2; 28:17, 18) Now, however, things are changing again. In 746 B.C.E., King Ahaz dies and the young Hezekiah takes the throne. If the Philistines feel that things will continue in their favor, they are sadly mistaken. Hezekiah proves to be a deadly foe. A descendant of Uzziah (the "fruit" from his "root"), Hezekiah is like "a flying fiery snake"—rapidly darting to the attack, striking in a lightninglike fashion, and producing a burning effect, as if injecting his victims with venom.

6 This is an apt description of the new king. "It was [Hezekiah] that struck down the Philistines clear to Gaza and also its territories." (2 Kings 18:8) According to the annals of Assyrian King Sennacherib, the Philistines become subjects of Hezekiah. *"The lowly ones"*—the weakened kingdom of Judah—get to enjoy security and material plenty, while Philistia suffers famine.—*Read Isaiah 14:30, 31.*

7 It seems that ambassadors are present in Judah—perhaps seeking an alliance against Assyria. What should they be told? *"What will anyone say in answer to the messengers of the nation?"* Should Hezekiah seek security

---

7. What declaration of faith must Hezekiah make to the ambassadors present in Jerusalem?

Stone relief of a Moabite warrior or god (between 11th and 8th century B.C.E.)

in foreign alliances? No! He should tell the messengers: *"Jehovah himself has laid the foundation of Zion, and in her the afflicted ones of his people will take refuge." (Isaiah 14:32)* The king must have full trust in Jehovah. The foundation of Zion is firm. The city will survive as a safe haven from the Assyrian menace.—Psalm 46:1-7.

8 Like Philistia, some nations today viciously oppose God's worshipers. Christian Witnesses of Jehovah have been confined in prisons and concentration camps. They have been banned. A number have been killed. Opponents continue to "make sharp attacks on the soul of the righteous one." (Psalm 94:21) To their enemies, this Christian group may seem "lowly" and "poor." However, with Jehovah's support, they enjoy spiritual plenty, while their enemies suffer famine. (Isaiah 65:13, 14; Amos 8:11) When Jehovah stretches out his hand against the modern-day Philistines, these "lowly ones" will be secure. Where? In association with "the household of God," of which Jesus is the sure foundation cornerstone. (Ephesians 2:19, 20) And they will be under the protection of "heavenly Jerusalem," Jehovah's celestial Kingdom, which has Jesus Christ as King.—Hebrews 12:22; Revelation 14:1.

---

8. (a) How have some nations today been like Philistia? (b) As he did in ancient times, what has Jehovah done to support his people today?

Moab Is Silenced

9 East of the Dead Sea is another neighbor of Israel —Moab. Unlike the Philistines, the Moabites are related to Israel, being descendants of Abraham's nephew Lot. (Genesis 19:37) Despite that relationship, Moab has a history of enmity with Israel. For example, back in the days of Moses, the king of Moab hired the prophet Balaam, hoping that he would curse the Israelites. When that failed, Moab used immorality and Baal worship to ensnare Israel. (Numbers 22:4-6; 25:1-5) Little wonder, then, that Jehovah now inspires Isaiah to record *"the pronouncement against Moab"*!—*Isaiah 15:1a.*

10 Isaiah's prophecy is directed against numerous cities and locations in Moab, including Ar, Kir (or Kir-hareseth), and Dibon. (*Isaiah 15:1b, 2a*) Moabites will mourn for Kir-hareseth's raisin cakes, perhaps a principal product of the city. (*Isaiah 16:6, 7*) Sibmah and Jazer, famous for vine cultivation, will be smitten. (*Isaiah 16:8-10*) Eglath-shelishiyah, whose name may mean "A Heifer of Three Years Old," will be like a sturdy young cow uttering pitiful cries of anguish. (*Isaiah 15:5*) The grass of the land will dry up while the *"waters of Dimon"* become full of blood because of the slaughter of the Moabites. The *"waters of Nimrim"* will become *"sheer desolations,"* in either a figurative sense or a literal sense—likely because enemy forces dam up their streams.—*Isaiah 15:6-9.*

11 Moabites will gird themselves with sackcloth, the garment of mourning. They will shave their heads bald to symbolize shame and lamentation. Their beards will be *"clipped,"* showing extreme grief and humiliation. (*Isaiah 15:2b-4*) Isaiah himself, certain of the fulfillment of these

---

9. Against whom is the next pronouncement made, and how has this people proved to be an enemy of God's people?
10, 11. What will happen to Moab?

judgments, feels deep emotions. Like the vibrating strings of a harp, his inward parts are moved with pity because of the message of woe against Moab.—*Isaiah 16:11, 12.*

12 When will this prophecy be fulfilled? Soon. *"This is the word that Jehovah spoke concerning Moab formerly. And now Jehovah has spoken, saying: 'Within three years, according to the years of a hired laborer, the glory of Moab must also be disgraced with much commotion of every sort, and those who remain over will be a trifling few, not mighty.' "(Isaiah 16:13, 14)* In harmony with this, there is archaeological evidence that during the eighth century B.C.E., Moab suffered grievously and many of its sites were depopulated. Tiglath-pileser III mentioned Salamanu of Moab among the rulers who paid tribute to him. Sennacherib received tribute from Kammusunadbi, king of Moab. Assyrian monarchs Esar-haddon and Ashurbanipal referred to Moabite Kings Musuri and Kamashaltu as being their subjects. Centuries ago, the Moabites ceased to exist as a people. Ruins of cities thought to be Moabite have been found, but little physical evidence of this once-powerful enemy of Israel has thus far been unearthed.

Modern-Day "Moab" Perishes

13 Today there is a worldwide organization similar to ancient Moab. It is Christendom, the principal part of "Babylon the Great." (Revelation 17:5) Both Moab and Israel descended from Abraham's father, Terah. Similarly, Christendom, like the congregation of anointed Christians today, claims to have roots in the first-century Christian congregation. (Galatians 6:16) However, Christendom—like Moab—is corrupt, promoting spiritual immorality and the worship of gods other than the one true God, Jehovah.

12. How were Isaiah's words against Moab fulfilled?
13. What organization today can be compared with Moab?

(James 4:4; 1 John 5:21) As a class, Christendom's leaders oppose those who preach the good news of the Kingdom. —Matthew 24:9, 14.

14 Moab was eventually silenced. The same will happen to Christendom. Jehovah, using a modern-day equivalent of Assyria, will cause her to be desolated. (Revelation 17: 16, 17) However, there is hope for people in this modern-day "Moab." In the midst of prophesying against Moab, Isaiah says: *"In loving-kindness a throne will certainly be firmly established; and one must sit down upon it in true-ness in the tent of David, judging and seeking justice and being prompt in righteousness." (Isaiah 16:5)* In 1914, Jehovah firmly established the throne of Jesus, a Ruler in the line of King David. Jesus' kingship is an expression of Jehovah's loving-kindness and, in fulfillment of God's covenant with King David, will last forever. (Psalm 72:2; 85:10, 11; 89:3, 4; Luke 1:32) Many meek ones have left modern-day "Moab" and have submitted themselves to Jesus in order to gain life. (Revelation 18:4) How comforting for these to know that Jesus will 'make clear to the nations what justice is'!—Matthew 12:18; Jeremiah 33:15.

Damascus Becomes a Decaying Ruin

15 Next, Isaiah records *"the pronouncement against Damascus." (Read Isaiah 17:1-6.)* Damascus, to the north of Israel, is "the head of Syria." (Isaiah 7:8) During the reign of King Ahaz of Judah, Rezin of Damascus in league with Pekah of Israel invades Judah. At Ahaz' request, however, Assyrian Tiglath-pileser III wars against

---

14. Despite Jehovah's counsel against the modern-day "Moab," what hope is there for individual members of that organization?
15, 16. (a) What hostile steps do Damascus and Israel take against Judah, and with what result for Damascus? (b) Who is included in the pronouncement against Damascus? (c) What can Christians today learn from Israel's example?

Syrian warrior riding a camel (ninth century B.C.E.)

Damascus, conquering it and exiling many of its inhabitants. Thereafter, Damascus ceases to be a threat to Judah.—2 Kings 16:5-9; 2 Chronicles 28:5, 16.

16 Likely because of Israel's alliance with Damascus, Jehovah's pronouncement against Damascus also includes expressions of judgment against the unfaithful northern kingdom. (Isaiah 17:3-6) Israel will become like a field at harvesttime with very little grain or like an olive tree from which most of the olives have been shaken from the branches. (Isaiah 17:4-6) What a sobering example for those who are dedicated to Jehovah! He expects exclusive devotion and accepts only heartfelt sacred service. And he hates those who turn against their brothers.—Exodus 20:5; Isaiah 17:10, 11; Matthew 24:48-50.

Full Confidence in Jehovah

17 Isaiah now says: *"In that day earthling man will look up to his Maker, and his own eyes will gaze at the Holy One of Israel himself. And he will not look to the altars, the work of his hands; and at what his fingers have made he will not*

17, 18. (a) How do some in Israel react to Jehovah's pronouncements, but what is the general response? (b) How do events today resemble those of Hezekiah's day?

gaze, either at the sacred poles or at the incense stands." *(Isaiah 17:7, 8)* Yes, some in Israel heed Jehovah's warning pronouncement. For example, when Hezekiah sends an invitation to the inhabitants of Israel to join Judah in a celebration of the Passover, some Israelites respond and travel south to join their brothers in pure worship. (2 Chronicles 30:1-12) Still, most of Israel's inhabitants mock the messengers bearing the invitation. The country is incurably apostate. Hence, Jehovah's counsel against her is fulfilled. Assyria destroys Israel's cities, the land becomes waste, the pastures unproductive.—*Read Isaiah 17:9-11.*

18 What of today? Israel was an apostate nation. Hence, the way Hezekiah tried to help individuals in that nation to return to true worship reminds us of how true Christians today try to help individuals in the apostate organization of Christendom. Since 1919, couriers from "the Israel of God" have gone through Christendom, inviting people to share in pure worship. (Galatians 6:16) Most have refused. Many have mocked the messengers. Some, though, have responded. They now number into the millions, and they delight in 'gazing at the Holy One of Israel,' being educated by him. (Isaiah 54:13) They abandon worship at the unholy altars—devotion to and trust in man-made gods—and eagerly turn to Jehovah. (Psalm 146: 3, 4) Like Isaiah's contemporary Micah, each one of them says: "As for me, it is for Jehovah that I shall keep on the lookout. I will show a waiting attitude for the God of my salvation. My God will hear me."—Micah 7:7.

19 What a contrast to those who put their trust in mortal man! Turbulent waves of violence and upheaval buffet humanity in these last days. "The sea" of restless, rebellious humanity churns up discontent and revolution. (Isaiah 57:20; Revelation 8:8, 9; 13:1) Jehovah will *"rebuke"* this

---

19. Whom will Jehovah rebuke, and what will this mean for them?

noisy crowd. His heavenly Kingdom will destroy every trouble-making organization and individual, and these will *"flee far away . . . like a thistle whirl before a storm wind."*—*Isaiah 17:12, 13;* Revelation 16:14, 16.

20 The result? Isaiah says: *"At evening time, why, look! there is sudden terror. Before morning—it is no more. This is the share of those pillaging us, and the lot belonging to those plundering us."* (*Isaiah 17:14*) Many are plundering Jehovah's people, treating them harshly and disrespectfully. Because they are not—and do not wish to be—a part of the world's mainstream religions, true Christians

---

20. Despite being 'plundered' by the nations, what confidence do true Christians have?

"The sea" of rebellious humanity churns up discontent and revolution

are viewed as easy prey by biased critics and fanatic opponents. But God's people are confident that the "morning" when their tribulations will end is fast approaching. —2 Thessalonians 1:6-9; 1 Peter 5:6-11.

Ethiopia Brings a Gift to Jehovah

21 On at least two occasions, Ethiopia, to the south of Egypt, has been involved in military action against Judah. (2 Chronicles 12:2, 3; 14:1, 9-15; 16:8) Now Isaiah predicts judgment on that nation: *"Ha for the land of the whirring insects with wings, which is in the region of the rivers of Ethiopia!" (Read Isaiah 18:1-6.)** Jehovah decrees that Ethiopia will be 'cut off, removed, and lopped off.'

22 Secular history tells us that in the latter part of the eighth century B.C.E., Ethiopia conquered Egypt and ruled it for some 60 years. Assyrian Emperors Esar-haddon and Ashurbanipal invaded in turn. With the destruction of Thebes by Ashurbanipal, Assyria subjugated Egypt, thus ending Ethiopian dominance over the Nile Valley. (See also Isaiah 20:3-6.) What about in modern times?

23 In Daniel's prophecy of "the time of the end," the aggressive "king of the north" is described as having Ethiopia and Libya "at his steps," that is, responsive to his direction. (Daniel 11:40-43) Ethiopia is also mentioned as being in the battle forces of "Gog of the land of Magog."

------

* Some scholars suggest that the expression "land of the whirring insects with wings" refers to the locusts that occasionally swarm in Ethiopia. Others point out that the Hebrew word for "whirring," *tsela·tsal'*, resembles in sound the name given to the tsetse fly, *tsal-tsalya*, by the Galla, a Hamitic people living in modern Ethiopia.

21, 22. Which nation next receives a judgment pronouncement, and how are Isaiah's inspired words fulfilled?
23. What part does the modern-day "Ethiopia" play, and why does it meet its end?

(Ezekiel 38:2-5, 8) Gog's forces, including the king of the north, meet their end when they attack Jehovah's holy nation. Hence, Jehovah's hand will also be stretched out against the modern-day "Ethiopia" because of its opposition to Jehovah's sovereignty.—Ezekiel 38:21-23; Daniel 11:45.

24 Yet, the prophecy also says: *"In that time a gift will be brought to Jehovah of armies, from a people drawn out and scoured, even from a people fear-inspiring everywhere . . . to the place of the name of Jehovah of armies, Mount Zion." (Isaiah 18:7)* Although the nations do not recognize Jehovah's sovereignty, they have at times acted in ways that benefit Jehovah's people. In some lands the authorities have enacted legislation and rendered court decisions giving legal rights to faithful worshipers of Jehovah. (Acts 5:29; Revelation 12:15, 16) And there are other gifts. "Kings will bring gifts to you yourself. . . . Bronzeware things will come out of Egypt; Cush [Ethiopia] itself will quickly stretch out its hands with gifts to God." (Psalm 68:29-31) Today, millions of modern-day "Ethiopians" who fear Jehovah are bringing "a gift" in the form of worship. (Malachi 1:11) They are sharing in the immense task of preaching the good news of the Kingdom in all the earth. (Matthew 24:14; Revelation 14:6, 7) What a fine gift to offer to Jehovah!—Hebrews 13:15.

The Heart of Egypt Melts

25 Judah's immediate neighbor to the south is Egypt, long an enemy of God's covenant people. Isaiah chapter 19 recounts the unsettled state of affairs in Egypt during Isaiah's lifetime. There is civil war in Egypt, with "city against city, kingdom against kingdom." (Isaiah 19:2, 13,

24. In what ways has Jehovah received "gifts" from the nations?
25. In fulfillment of Isaiah 19:1-11, what happens to ancient Egypt?

14) Historians present evidence of rival dynasties ruling different parts of the country at the same time. The vaunted wisdom of Egypt, with her 'valueless gods and charmers,' does not save her from "the hand of a hard master." (Isaiah 19:3, 4) Egypt is successively conquered by Assyria, Babylon, Persia, Greece, and Rome. All these events fulfill the prophecies of Isaiah 19:1-11.

26 However, in the Bible, Egypt often symbolizes Satan's world. (Ezekiel 29:3; Joel 3:19; Revelation 11:8) Therefore, does Isaiah's *"pronouncement against Egypt"* have a larger fulfillment? Yes, indeed! The opening words of the prophecy should give everyone cause to take notice: *"Look! Jehovah is riding on a swift cloud and coming into Egypt. And the valueless gods of Egypt will certainly quiver because of him, and the very heart of Egypt will melt in the midst of it."* *(Isaiah 19:1)* Jehovah will soon move against Satan's organization. At that time, the gods of this system of things will be seen to be valueless. (Psalm 96:5; 97:7) "The very heart of Egypt will melt" in fear. Jesus foretold that time: "There will be . . . anguish of nations, not knowing the way out because of the roaring of the sea and its agitation, while men become faint out of fear and expectation of the things coming upon the inhabited earth."—Luke 21:25, 26.

27 Of the time leading up to his execution of judgment, Jehovah says prophetically: *"I will goad Egyptians against Egyptians, and they will certainly war each one against his brother, and each one against his companion, city against city, kingdom against kingdom."* *(Isaiah 19:2)* Since the establishment of God's Kingdom in 1914, "the sign of [Jesus'] presence" has been marked by nation rising against nation and kingdom against kingdom.

---

26. In the larger fulfillment, how will inhabitants of modern-day "Egypt" react to Jehovah's acts of judgment?
27. What internal divisions were foretold for "Egypt," and how is this being fulfilled today?

Tribal massacres, bloody genocides, and so-called ethnic cleansings have claimed millions of lives during these last days. Such "pangs of distress" will only get worse as the end draws nearer.—Matthew 24:3, 7, 8.

28 *"The spirit of Egypt must become bewildered in the midst of it, and I shall confuse its own counsel. And they will be certain to resort to the valueless gods and to the charmers and to the spirit mediums and to the professional foretellers of events." (Isaiah 19:3)* When Moses appeared before Pharaoh, the priests of Egypt were put to shame, unable to match Jehovah in power. (Exodus 8:18, 19; Acts 13:8; 2 Timothy 3:8) Similarly, in the day of judgment, false religion will be unable to save this corrupt system. (Compare Isaiah 47:1, 11-13.) Eventually, Egypt came under *"a hard master,"* Assyria. *(Isaiah 19:4)* This foreshadows the bleak future facing this system of things.

29 What, though, of the political leaders? Can they help? *"The princes of Zoan are indeed foolish. As regards the wise ones of Pharaoh's counselors, their counsel is something unreasonable." (Read Isaiah 19:5-11.)* How unreasonable to hope that human counselors will be of any use in the day of judgment! Even with all the world's knowledge at their disposal, they lack godly wisdom. (1 Corinthians 3:19) They have rejected Jehovah and have turned to science so-called, philosophy, money, pleasure, and other substitute gods. As a result, they have no knowledge of God's purposes. They are deceived and disconcerted. Their works are in vain. *(Read Isaiah 19:12-15.)* "The wise ones have become ashamed. They have become terrified and will be caught. Look! They have rejected the very word of Jehovah, and what wisdom do they have?"—Jeremiah 8:9.

---

28. In the day of judgment, what will false religion be able to do to save this system of things?
29. When Jehovah's day comes, of what use will politicians be?

A Sign and a Witness to Jehovah

30 However, while "Egypt's" leaders are weak, *"like wom-en,"* there are still some individuals who look for godly wisdom. Jehovah's anointed ones and their companions 'declare abroad God's excellencies.' (*Isaiah 19:16;* 1 Peter 2:9) They are doing what they can to warn people of the coming demise of Satan's organization. Looking ahead to this situation, Isaiah says: *"The ground of Judah must be-come to Egypt a cause for reeling. Everybody to whom one mentions it is in dread because of the counsel of Jehovah of*

---

30. In what way will 'the ground of Judah become to Egypt a cause for reeling'?

The priests of Egypt were unable to match Jehovah in power

armies that he is counseling against him." (Isaiah 19:17)
The faithful messengers of Jehovah go forth telling people
the truth—including the announcement of the plagues
foretold by Jehovah. (Revelation 8:7-12; 16:2-12) This is
disturbing to the religious leaders of the world.

31 What is the surprising result of this proclamation
work? *"In that day there will prove to be five cities in
the land of Egypt speaking the language of Canaan and
swearing to Jehovah of armies. The City of Tearing Down
will one city be called." (Isaiah 19:18)* In ancient times this
prophecy was apparently fulfilled when the Hebrew language was spoken in Egyptian cities by Jews who had fled
there. (Jeremiah 24:1, 8-10; 41:1-3; 42:9–43:7; 44:1) Today,
there are people in the territory of modern-day "Egypt"
who have learned to speak the "pure language" of Bible
truth. (Zephaniah 3:9) One of the five figurative cities is
called "The City of Tearing Down," signifying that part
of the "pure language" is related to exposing and "tearing
down" Satan's organization.

32 Thanks to the proclamation work of Jehovah's people,
his great name will certainly become known in this system of things. *"In that day there will prove to be an altar to Jehovah in the midst of the land of Egypt, and a pillar to Jehovah beside its boundary." (Isaiah 19:19)* These
words point to the position of anointed Christians, who
are in a covenant relationship with God. (Psalm 50:5) As
"an altar" they are offering their sacrifices; as "a pillar and
support of the truth," they are bearing witness to Jehovah.
(1 Timothy 3:15; Romans 12:1; Hebrews 13:15, 16) They
are "in the midst of the land," being found—along with

---

31. How does it come to pass that "the language of Canaan" is spoken in cities of Egypt (a) in ancient times? (b) in modern times?
32. (a) What "altar" is in the midst of the land of Egypt? (b) How
are the anointed like "a pillar" beside Egypt's boundary?

their "other sheep" companions—in more than 230 countries and islands of the sea. But they are "no part of the world." (John 10:16; 17:15, 16) They are, as it were, standing on the boundary between this world and the Kingdom of God, prepared to cross that boundary and receive their heavenly reward.

33 Isaiah continues: *"It must prove to be for a sign and for a witness to Jehovah of armies in the land of Egypt; for they will cry out to Jehovah because of the oppressors, and he will send them a savior, even a grand one, who will actually deliver them." (Isaiah 19:20)* As "a sign" and "a witness," the anointed take the lead in the preaching work and exalt Jehovah's name in this system of things. (Isaiah 8:18; Hebrews 2:13) Throughout the world the cries of oppressed people can be heard, but by and large, human governments are unable to help them. However, Jehovah will send a Grand Savior, the King Jesus Christ, to liberate all the meek ones. When these last days reach their climax at the war of Armageddon, he will bring relief and everlasting blessings to God-fearing humans.—Psalm 72:2, 4, 7, 12-14.

34 In the meantime, it is God's will that all sorts of people gain accurate knowledge and be saved. (1 Timothy 2:4) Hence, Isaiah writes: *"Jehovah will certainly become known to the Egyptians; and the Egyptians must know Jehovah in that day, and they must render sacrifice and gift and must make a vow to Jehovah and pay it. And Jehovah will certainly deal Egypt a blow. There will be a dealing of a blow and a healing; and they must return to Jehovah,*

---

33. In what ways are the anointed "a sign" and "a witness" in "Egypt"?

34. (a) How will Jehovah come to be known to "the Egyptians," and what sacrifice and gift will they give to him? (b) When will Jehovah deal a blow to "Egypt," and what healing will follow?

and he must let himself be entreated by them and must heal them." (Isaiah 19:21, 22) People from all nations of Satan's world, individual "Egyptians," come to know Jehovah and render him sacrifice, "the fruit of lips which make public declaration to his name." (Hebrews 13:15) They make a vow to Jehovah by dedicating themselves to him, and they pay their vow by living a life of loyal service. Following the "blow" that Jehovah will deal this system of things at Armageddon, he will use his Kingdom to heal humankind. During Jesus' Millennial Reign, mankind will be elevated to spiritual, mental, moral, and physical perfection—healing indeed!—Revelation 22:1, 2.

"Blessed Be My People"

35 The prophet then foresees a remarkable development: *"In that day there will come to be a highway out of Egypt to Assyria, and Assyria will actually come into Egypt, and Egypt into Assyria; and they will certainly render service, Egypt with Assyria. In that day Israel will come to be the third with Egypt and with Assyria, namely, a blessing in the midst of the earth, because Jehovah of armies will have blessed it, saying: 'Blessed be my people, Egypt, and the work of my hands, Assyria, and my inheritance, Israel.'" (Isaiah 19:23-25)* Yes, one day friendly relations will exist between Egypt and Assyria. How?

36 When Jehovah rescued his people from the nations in times past, he made for them highways to freedom, so to speak. (Isaiah 11:16; 35:8-10; 49:11-13; Jeremiah 31:21) A limited fulfillment of this prophecy took place after the defeat of Babylon when exiles from Assyria and Egypt, as well as from Babylon, were brought back to the Promised Land. (Isaiah 11:11) But what of modern times?

35, 36. In fulfillment of Isaiah 19:23-25, what connections came to exist in ancient times between Egypt, Assyria, and Israel?

37 Today, the remnant of anointed spiritual Israelites is "a blessing in the midst of the earth." They promote true worship and are declaring the Kingdom message to people in all the nations. Some of these nations are like Assyria, heavily militaristic. Other nations are more liberal, perhaps like Egypt—at one time "the king of the south" in Daniel's prophecy. (Daniel 11:5, 8) Millions of individuals from the militaristic nations and the more liberal nations have taken up the way of true worship. Thus, people from all nations are united in 'rendering service.' There are no nationalistic divisions among these ones. They love one another, and it can truly be said that 'Assyria comes into Egypt and Egypt into Assyria.' It is as if there were a highway from one to the other.—1 Peter 2:17.

38 How, though, does Israel "come to be the third with Egypt and with Assyria"? Early in "the time of the end," most of those serving Jehovah on earth were members of "the Israel of God." (Daniel 12:9; Galatians 6:16) Since the 1930's, a great crowd of "other sheep," with an earthly hope, have appeared. (John 10:16a; Revelation 7:9) Coming out of the nations—foreshadowed by Egypt and Assyria—they stream to Jehovah's house of worship and invite others to join them. (Isaiah 2:2-4) They perform the same preaching work as their anointed brothers, endure similar tests, manifest the same faithfulness and integrity, and feed at the same spiritual table. Truly, the anointed and the "other sheep" are "one flock, one shepherd." (John 10:16b) Can anyone doubt that Jehovah, viewing their zeal and endurance, is pleased with their activity? Little wonder that he pronounces a benediction on them, saying: "Blessed be my people"!

---

37. How do millions today live as though there were a highway between "Assyria" and "Egypt"?
38. (a) How will Israel "come to be the third with Egypt and with Assyria"? (b) Why does Jehovah say "Blessed be my people"?

CHAPTER SIXTEEN

Trust in Jehovah for Guidance and Protection

Isaiah 20:1-6

AS SEEN in earlier chapters of this book, God's people face a frightening threat in the eighth century B.C.E. The blood-thirsty Assyrians are ravaging one land after another, and it is only a matter of time before they attack the southern kingdom of Judah. To whom will the land's inhabitants turn for protection? They are in a covenant relationship with Jehovah and should rely on him for help. (Exodus 19:5, 6) That is what King David did. He acknowledged: "Jehovah is my crag and my stronghold and the Provider of escape for me." (2 Samuel 22:2) Evidently, though, many in the eighth century B.C.E. do not put trust in Jehovah as their stronghold. They are more inclined to look to Egypt and Ethiopia, hoping that these two nations will provide a bulwark against the threatened Assyrian invasion. They are wrong.

2 Through his prophet Isaiah, Jehovah warns that seeking refuge in Egypt or in Ethiopia will be disastrous. The prophet's inspired words provide a salutary lesson for his contemporaries and contain a valuable lesson for us about the importance of trusting in Jehovah.

A Land of Bloodshed

3 The Assyrians were known for their military might. The

1, 2. What danger do God's people face in the eighth century B.C.E., and to whom are many of them inclined to turn for protection?
3. Describe the emphasis that Assyria put on military power.

The Assyrians used to blind some of their captives

book *Ancient Cities* notes: "They worshiped strength, and would say their prayers only to colossal idols of stone, lions and bulls whose ponderous limbs, eagle wings, and human heads were symbols of strength, courage, and victory. Fighting was the business of the nation, and the priests were incessant fomenters of war." It is with good reason that the Bible prophet Nahum described Nineveh, Assyria's capital, as "the city of bloodshed."—Nahum 3:1.

4 The war tactics of the Assyrians were unusually cruel. Carved reliefs from those days show Assyrian warriors leading off captives by means of hooks stuck through the noses or the lips. With spears they blinded some captives. One inscription tells of a conquest in which the Assyrian army dismembered its captives and made two mounds outside the city—one of heads and the other of limbs. The children of the conquered were burned in fire. The fear

---

4. How did the Assyrians strike terror in the hearts of other nations?

inspired by such cruelty must have served the Assyrians well in a military sense, discouraging resistance by those who stood in the way of their armies.

The War Against Ashdod

5 In Isaiah's day the Assyrian Empire reached an unprecedented level of power under King Sargon.* For many years, critics doubted the existence of this ruler, as they knew of no mention of him in secular sources. In time, however, archaeologists uncovered the ruins of Sargon's palace, and the Bible's account was vindicated.

6 Isaiah briefly describes one of Sargon's military campaigns: *"Tartan came to Ashdod, when Sargon the king of Assyria sent him, and he proceeded to war against Ashdod and to capture it." (Isaiah 20:1)*# Why does Sargon order an attack on the Philistine city of Ashdod? For one thing, Philistia is an ally of Egypt, and Ashdod, home to a temple of Dagon, is located on the road that runs along the coast from Egypt through Palestine. The city is thus in a strategic location. Its capture can be viewed as a preliminary step to the conquest of Egypt. In addition, Assyrian records report that Azuri, Ashdod's king, was conspiring against Assyria. Hence, Sargon has the rebellious king removed and puts the king's younger brother, Ahimiti, on the throne. Still, that does not settle matters. Another revolt breaks out, and

---

* Historians refer to this king as Sargon II. An earlier king, not of Assyria, but of Babylon, is designated as "Sargon I."

"Tartan" is not a name but a title designating the commander in chief of the Assyrian army, likely the second most powerful person in the empire.

---

5. Who was a powerful Assyrian ruler in Isaiah's day, and how was the Bible's account of him vindicated?

6, 7. (a) Likely, for what reasons does Sargon order an attack on Ashdod? (b) How does the fall of Ashdod affect Philistia's neighbors?

this time Sargon takes more forceful action. He orders an attack on Ashdod, which is besieged and conquered. Likely, Isaiah 20:1 is alluding to this event.

7 The fall of Ashdod casts a grim shadow over her neighbors, especially Judah. Jehovah knows that his people are inclined to look to "an arm of flesh," such as Egypt or Ethiopia to the south. Therefore, he commissions Isaiah to act out a dire warning.—2 Chronicles 32:7, 8.

"Naked and Barefoot"

8 Jehovah tells Isaiah: *"Go, and you must loosen the sackcloth from off your hips; and your sandals you should draw from off your feet."* Isaiah complies with Jehovah's command. *"He proceeded to do so, walking about naked and barefoot."* (*Isaiah 20:2*) Sackcloth is a coarse garment often worn by the prophets, sometimes in conjunction with a warning message. It is also worn in times of crisis or upon hearing calamitous news. (2 Kings 19:2; Psalm 35:13; Daniel 9:3) Does Isaiah really walk around naked in the sense of being without any protective covering at all? Not necessarily. The Hebrew word translated "naked" can also refer to one's being partially or scantily clothed. (1 Samuel 19:24, footnote) So Isaiah may have merely taken off his outer garment, while retaining the short tunic that was commonly worn close to the body. Male captives are often represented in this manner in Assyrian sculptures.

9 The meaning of Isaiah's unusual action is not left in doubt: *"Jehovah went on to say: 'Just as my servant Isaiah has walked about naked and barefoot three years as a sign and a portent against Egypt and against Ethiopia, so the king of Assyria will lead the body of captives of*

8. What inspired prophetic act does Isaiah carry out?
9. What is the prophetic meaning of Isaiah's action?

Egypt and the exiles of Ethiopia, boys and old men, naked and barefoot, and with buttocks stripped, the nakedness of Egypt.'" (Isaiah 20:3, 4) Yes, the Egyptians and Ethiopians will soon be carried off captive. No one will be spared. Even "boys and old men"—the children and the elderly—will be stripped of all their possessions and taken into exile. By means of this bleak imagery, Jehovah warns the inhabitants of Judah that it will be futile for them to put their trust in Egypt and Ethiopia. The downfall of these nations will lead to their "nakedness"—their ultimate humiliation!

Hope Crumbles, Beauty Fades

10 Next, Jehovah prophetically describes the response of his people as they realize that Egypt and Ethiopia, their hoped-for refuge, has proved powerless before the Assyrians. *"They will certainly be terrified and be ashamed of Ethiopia their looked-for hope and of Egypt their beauty. And the inhabitant of this coastland will be certain to say in that day, 'There is how our looked-for hope is, to which we fled for assistance, in order to be delivered because of the king of Assyria! And how shall we ourselves escape?'"—Isaiah 20:5, 6.*

11 Judah seems like a mere strip of coastland when compared with the powers of Egypt and Ethiopia. Perhaps some of the inhabitants of "this coastland" are enamored with Egypt's beauty—its impressive pyramids, its towering temples, and its spacious villas with their surrounding gardens, orchards, and ponds. The magnificent architecture of Egypt seems to be evidence of stability and permanence. Surely this land cannot be devastated! Likely, the Jews are

---

10, 11. (a) What will the response of Judah be when she realizes that Egypt and Ethiopia are powerless before Assyria? (b) Why may the inhabitants of Judah be inclined to trust in Egypt and Ethiopia?

*Some may be impressed by man's achievements,
but it is better to trust in Jehovah*

also impressed by the archers, chariots, and horsemen of Ethiopia.

12 In view of the acted-out warning of Isaiah and the prophetic words of Jehovah, any of God's professed people who are inclined to trust in Egypt and Ethiopia have some serious thinking to do. How much better to put their trust in Jehovah rather than in earthling man! (Psalm 25:2; 40:4) As things work out, Judah suffers terribly at the hand of the king of Assyria, and later, she sees her temple and capital city destroyed by Babylon. Yet, "a tenth," "a holy seed," is left, like the stump of a massive tree. (Isaiah 6:13) When the time comes, Isaiah's message will greatly

12. In whom should Judah put her trust?

strengthen the faith of that small group who continue to trust in Jehovah!

Put Your Trust in Jehovah

13 The warning in Isaiah concerning the futility of trusting in Egypt and Ethiopia is not just dead history. It has practical value for our day. We are living in "critical times hard to deal with." (2 Timothy 3:1) Financial disasters, widespread poverty, political uncertainty, civil unrest, and small- or large-scale wars have devastating effects—not only on those who spurn God's rulership but also on those who worship Jehovah. The question facing each one is, 'To whom will I turn for help?'

14 Some might be impressed by today's financial wizards, politicians, and scientists, who talk of solving man's problems using man's ingenuity and technology. However, the Bible plainly states: "It is better to take refuge in Jehovah than to trust in nobles." (Psalm 118:9) All man's schemes for peace and security will come to naught for the reason aptly stated by the prophet Jeremiah: "I well know, O Jehovah, that to earthling man his way does not belong. It does not belong to man who is walking even to direct his step." —Jeremiah 10:23.

15 It is imperative, therefore, that servants of God not be unduly impressed by any seeming strength or wisdom of this world. (Psalm 33:10; 1 Corinthians 3:19, 20) The only hope for distressed humankind rests with the Creator, Jehovah. Those who put their trust in him will be saved. As the inspired apostle John wrote, "the world is passing away and so is its desire, but he that does the will of God remains forever."—1 John 2:17.

13. What pressures affect all—both believers and unbelievers—today?
14. Why should we put trust only in Jehovah?
15. Where lies the only hope for distressed mankind?

CHAPTER SEVENTEEN

"Babylon Has Fallen!"

THE Bible may be likened to a great piece of music with a dominant theme and with minor themes introduced to add to the distinctiveness of the whole. In a similar way, the Bible has a major theme—the vindication of Jehovah's sovereignty by means of the Messianic Kingdom government. It also has other important, recurring themes. One of these is the fall of Babylon.

2 That theme is introduced in Isaiah chapters 13 and 14. It recurs in chapter 21 and again in chapters 44 and 45. A century later, Jeremiah enlarges on the same theme, and the book of Revelation brings it to a thundering conclusion. (Jeremiah 51:60-64; Revelation 18:1–19:4) Every serious student of the Bible needs to be concerned about this important subsidiary theme of God's Word. Isaiah chapter 21 helps in this regard, for it supplies fascinating details about the prophesied fall of that great world power. Later, we will see that Isaiah chapter 21 stresses another important Bible theme—one that helps us assess our vigilance as Christians today.

"A Hard Vision"

3 Isaiah chapter 21 opens on an ominous note: *"The*

1, 2. (a) What is the overall theme of the Bible, but what important subsidiary theme appears in Isaiah? (b) How does the Bible develop the theme of the fall of Babylon?
3. Why is Babylon termed "the wilderness of the sea," and what does that title portend regarding her future?

*pronouncement against the wilderness of the sea: Like
storm winds in the south in moving onward, from the wilderness it is coming, from a fear-inspiring land." (Isaiah
21:1)* Straddling the Euphrates River is Babylon, with its
eastern half in the region between the two great rivers Euphrates and Tigris. It is some distance from the actual sea.
Why, then, is it called "the wilderness of the sea"? Because the region of Babylon used to flood annually, creating a vast, marshy "sea." However, the Babylonians have
controlled this watery wilderness by creating a complex
system of dikes, sluices, and canals. They ingeniously use
these waters as part of the city's defense system. Still,
no human works will save Babylon from divine judgment. A wilderness she had been—a wilderness she will
again become. Calamity is heading her way, brewing like
one of the fierce storms that sometimes blow in upon Israel from the fearsome wilderness to the south.—Compare
Zechariah 9:14.

4 As we learned in Chapter 14 of this book, ancient Babylon has a modern counterpart—"Babylon the Great," the
world empire of false religion. In Revelation, Babylon the
Great is likewise portrayed in connection with "a wilderness" and "waters." The apostle John is carried away to
a wilderness to be shown Babylon the Great. He is told
that she "sits on many waters" representing "peoples and
crowds and nations and tongues." (Revelation 17:1-3, 5,
15) Popular support has always been a key to the survival of false religion, but such "waters" will not protect her
in the end. Like her ancient counterpart, she will end up
empty, neglected, and desolate.

---

4. How does the Revelation vision of "Babylon the Great" include
the elements of "waters" and "a wilderness," and what do the "waters" mean?

5 In Isaiah's day Babylon is not yet the dominant world power, but Jehovah already foresees that when her time comes, she will abuse her power. Isaiah proceeds: *"There is a hard vision that has been told to me: The treacherous dealer is dealing treacherously, and the despoiler is despoiling." (Isaiah 21:2a)* Babylon will indeed despoil and deal treacherously with the nations she conquers, including Judah. The Babylonians will sack Jerusalem, pillage its temple, and take its people captive to Babylon. There, these helpless captives will be treated treacherously, ridiculed for their faith, and offered no hope of return to their homeland.—2 Chronicles 36:17-21; Psalm 137:1-4.

6 Yes, Babylon richly deserves this "hard vision," which will mean hard times for her. Isaiah continues: *"Go up, O Elam! Lay siege, O Media! All sighing due to her I have caused to cease." (Isaiah 21:2b)* Those oppressed by this treacherous empire will have relief. At last, an end to their sighing! (Psalm 79:11, 12) By what means will this relief come? Isaiah names two nations that will attack Babylon: Elam and Media. Two centuries later, in 539 B.C.E., Cyrus the Persian will lead a combined force of Persians and Medes against Babylon. As for Elam, Persian monarchs will possess at least part of that land prior to 539 B.C.E.* The Persian forces will thus include Elamites.

7 Note how Isaiah describes the effect of this vision

---

* The Persian King Cyrus was at times designated "King of Anshan" —Anshan being a region or city in Elam. The Israelites of Isaiah's day —the eighth century B.C.E.—may have been unfamiliar with Persia, whereas they would have known of Elam. This may explain why Isaiah here names Elam instead of Persia.

---

5. How does Babylon come to earn a reputation as being "treacherous" and a "despoiler"?
6. (a) What sighing will Jehovah cause to cease? (b) What nations are foretold to attack Babylon, and how is this fulfilled?
7. How does Isaiah's vision affect him, signifying what?

upon him: *"That is why my hips have become full of severe pains. Convulsions themselves have grabbed hold of
me, like the convulsions of a woman that is giving birth.
I have become disconcerted so that I do not hear; I have
become disturbed so that I do not see. My heart has wandered about; a shuddering itself has terrified me. The twilight for which I had an attachment has been made for me
a trembling."* (Isaiah 21:3, 4) The prophet, it seems, enjoys the twilight hours, a lovely time for quiet contempla-
tion. But nightfall has now lost its charm, bringing instead
only fear, pain, and trembling. He suffers convulsions like
those of a woman in labor, and his heart "has wandered
about." One scholar renders this phrase "my heart beats
wildly," noting that the expression refers to "a feverish
and irregular beating of the pulse." Why such distress? Evidently, Isaiah's feelings are prophetic. On the night of October 5/6, 539 B.C.E., the Babylonians will experience similar terror.

8 As darkness falls on that fateful night, terror is the last
thing on the Babylonians' minds. Some two centuries in
advance, Isaiah foretells: *"Let there be a setting of the table
in order, an arranging of the location of seats, an eating, a
drinking!"* (Isaiah 21:5a) Yes, the arrogant King Belshazzar is hosting a feast. Seats are arranged for a thousand of
his grandees, as well as many wives and concubines. (Daniel 5:1, 2) The revelers know that there is an army outside
the walls, but they believe that their city is impregnable.
Her massive walls and deep moat appear to make her capture impossible; her many gods make it unthinkable. So
let there be "an eating, a drinking!" Belshazzar gets drunk,
and he probably is not alone. The besotted state of the

----

8. As prophesied, how do the Babylonians act, even though their enemies are outside the walls?

high officials is suggested by the need to rouse them, as Isaiah's next words prophetically show.

9 ***"Get up, you princes, anoint the shield."*** **(Isaiah 21:5b)** Suddenly, the party is over. The princes have to rouse themselves! The aged prophet Daniel has been called to the scene, and he sees how Jehovah throws Babylonian King Belshazzar into a state of terror similar to that described by Isaiah. The king's grandees are plunged into confusion as the combined forces of Medes, Persians, and Elamites breach the city's defenses. Babylon falls quickly! What, though, does it mean to "anoint the shield"?

9. Why does it become necessary to "anoint the shield"?

"Let there be . . . an eating, a drinking!"

The Bible sometimes refers to a nation's king as its shield because he is the defender and protector of the land.* (Psalm 89:18) So this verse in Isaiah is likely foretelling the need for a new king. Why? Because Belshazzar is killed that "very night." Thus, there is a need to "anoint the shield," or appoint a new king.—Daniel 5:1-9, 30.

10 All lovers of true worship draw comfort from this account. Modern-day Babylon, Babylon the Great, is as much a treacherous dealer and despoiler as was her ancient counterpart. To this day religious leaders conspire to have Jehovah's Witnesses banned, persecuted, or punitively taxed. But as this prophecy reminds us, Jehovah sees all such treacherous dealing, and he will not let it go unpunished. He will bring an end to all religions that misrepresent him and mistreat his people. (Revelation 18:8) Is such a thing possible? To build our faith, we have only to see how his warnings regarding the fall of both ancient Babylon and her modern-day counterpart have already been fulfilled.

"She Has Fallen!"

11 Jehovah now speaks to the prophet. Isaiah reports:

---

* Many Bible commentators think that the words "anoint the shield" refer to the ancient military practice of oiling leather shields before battle so that most blows will glance off. While this is a possible interpretation, it should be noted that on the night the city fell, the Babylonians barely had time to put up a fight, let alone prepare for battle by greasing their shields!

10. What comfort can worshipers of Jehovah draw from the fulfillment of Isaiah's prophecy regarding the treacherous dealer?
11. (a) What is the responsibility of a watchman, and who has been active as a watchman today? (b) What is represented by the war chariot of asses and that of camels?

The watchman "proceeded to call out like a lion"

"This is what Jehovah has said to me: 'Go, post a lookout that he may tell just what he sees.'" **(Isaiah 21:6)** These words introduce another important theme of this chapter—that of the lookout, or watchman. This is of interest to all true Christians today, for Jesus urged his followers to "keep on the watch." "The faithful and discreet slave" has never stopped telling what it sees regarding the nearness of God's day of judgment and the dangers of this corrupt world. (Matthew 24:42, 45-47) What does Isaiah's visionary watchman see? *"He saw a war chariot with a span of steeds, a war chariot of asses, a war chariot of camels. And he paid strict attention, with much attentiveness."* **(Isaiah 21:7)** These single war chariots likely represent columns of

"I am standing constantly by day, and . . . all the nights"

chariots advancing in battle formation with the speed of trained steeds. The war chariot of asses and that of camels fittingly represent the two powers, Media and Persia, that will unite to launch this attack. Furthermore, history confirms that the Persian army used both asses and camels in warfare.

12 The watchman, then, is compelled to make a report. *"He proceeded to call out like a lion: 'Upon the watchtower, O Jehovah, I am standing constantly by day, and at my guardpost I am stationed all the nights. And here, now, there is coming a war chariot of men, with a span of steeds!'"* (Isaiah 21:8, 9a) The visionary watchman calls out courageously, "like a lion." It takes courage to call out a judgment message against so formidable a nation as Babylon. Something else is required as well—endurance. The watchman remains at his post day and night, never letting his vigilance flag. Similarly, the watchman class in these last days has needed courage and endurance. (Revelation 14:12) All true Christians need these qualities.

13 Isaiah's visionary watchman sees a war chariot advancing. What is the news? *"He began to speak up and say: 'She has fallen! Babylon has fallen, and all the graven images of her gods he has broken to the earth!'"* (Isaiah 21: 9b) What a thrilling report! At last, this treacherous despoiler of God's people has fallen!* In what sense, though,

---

* Isaiah's prophecy regarding Babylon's fall is so accurate that some Bible critics have theorized that it must have been written after the event. But as Hebrew scholar F. Delitzsch notes, such speculation is unnecessary if we accept that a prophet might be inspired to foretell events hundreds of years in advance.

---

12. Isaiah's visionary watchman displays what qualities, and who need these qualities today?
13, 14. (a) How does ancient Babylon fare, and in what sense are her idols broken? (b) How and when did Babylon the Great suffer a similar fall?

are Babylon's graven images and idols broken? Will the Medo-Persian invaders march into Babylon's temples and smash the innumerable idols? No, nothing of the sort is needed. Babylon's idol gods will be broken in that they are exposed as powerless to protect the city. And Babylon will experience a fall when she becomes unable to continue oppressing God's people.

14 What of Babylon the Great? By engineering the oppression of God's people during World War I, she effectively held them in exile for a time. Their preaching work was virtually brought to a halt. The president and other prominent officers of the Watch Tower Society were imprisoned on false charges. But 1919 saw an astounding reversal. The officers were released from prison, the headquarters office was reopened, and the preaching work was recommenced. Thus, Babylon the Great fell in that her hold over God's people was broken.* In Revelation, this fall is twice heralded by an angel using the words of the announcement at Isaiah 21:9.—Revelation 14:8; 18:2.

15 Isaiah concludes this prophetic message on a note of compassion toward his own people. He says: *"O my threshed ones and the son of my threshing floor, what I have heard from Jehovah of armies, the God of Israel, I have reported to you people." (Isaiah 21:10)* In the Bible, threshing often symbolizes the disciplining and refining of God's people. God's covenant people will become 'sons of the threshing floor,' where wheat is forcibly separated from the chaff, leaving only the refined, desirable grains. Isaiah is not gloating over this discipline. Rather, he has compassion for these future 'sons of the threshing floor,'

---

* See *Revelation—Its Grand Climax At Hand!,* pages 164-9.

15, 16. In what sense are Isaiah's people "threshed ones," and what can we learn from Isaiah's attitude toward them?

some of whom will spend their entire lives as captives in a foreign land.

16 This may serve as a useful reminder to all of us. In the Christian congregation today, some may be inclined to lose their compassion for wrongdoers. And those who receive discipline may often be prone to resent it. However, if we keep in mind that Jehovah disciplines his people in order to refine them, we will neither belittle the discipline and those who humbly undergo it nor resist it when it comes our way. Let us accept godly discipline as an expression of God's love.—Hebrews 12:6.

Inquiring of the Watchman

17 The second prophetic message of Isaiah chapter 21 brings the figure of the watchman to the fore. It begins: *"The pronouncement against Dumah: To me there is one calling out from Seir: 'Watchman, what about the night? Watchman, what about the night?'"* (Isaiah 21:11) Where is this Dumah? There were evidently several towns with that name in Bible times, but none of them are intended here. Dumah is not found in Seir, which is another name for Edom. However, "Dumah" means "Silence." So it seems that, as was the case in the previous pronouncement, the region is given a name suggestive of its future. Edom, long a vindictive enemy of God's people, will end up in silence—the silence of death. Before that happens, though, some will anxiously inquire about the future.

18 At the time of the writing of Isaiah, Edom lies in the path of the powerful Assyrian army. Some in Edom yearn to know when the night of oppression will end for them. The answer? *"The watchman said: 'The morning has*

_____

17. Why is Edom appropriately termed "Dumah"?
18. How is the pronouncement, "The morning has to come, and also the night," fulfilled upon ancient Edom?

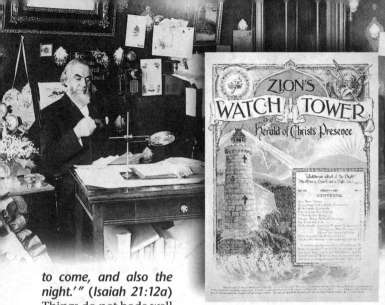

to come, and also the night.'" (Isaiah 21:12a)
Things do not bode well
for Edom. A glimmer of morning will show on the horizon, but it will be brief, illusory. Night—another dark time of oppression—will follow quickly on the heels of morning. What an apt picture of Edom's future! The Assyrian oppression will end, but Babylon will succeed Assyria as a world power and will decimate Edom. (Jeremiah 25:17, 21; 27:2-8) This cycle will be repeated. Babylonian oppression will be followed by Persian and then Greek oppression. There will then be a brief "morning" during Roman times, when the Herods—Edomite in origin—gain power in Jerusalem. But that "morning" will not last. Finally, Edom will descend permanently into silence, vanishing from history. The name Dumah will fittingly describe her at last.

¹⁹ The watchman concludes his brief message with the

19. When the watchman says, "If you people would inquire, inquire. Come again!" what may he mean?

words: *"If you people would inquire, inquire. Come again!"* *(Isaiah 21:12b)* The expression "Come again!" may refer to the endless succession of 'nights' ahead of Edom. Or because the expression may also be translated "return," the prophet may be suggesting that any Edomites who want to escape the nation's doom should repent and "return" to Jehovah. In either case, the watchman invites further inquiries.

20 This short pronouncement has meant a great deal to Jehovah's people in modern times.* We understand that mankind is deep into the dark night of spiritual blindness and alienation from God that will lead to the destruction of this system of things. (Romans 13:12; 2 Corinthians 4:4) During this nighttime, any glimmerings of hope that mankind can somehow bring about peace and security are like those illusory gleamings of dawn that are followed only by still darker times. A genuine dawn is approaching —the dawn of Christ's Millennial Reign over this earth. But as long as the night lasts, we must follow the lead of the watchman class by staying spiritually alert and courageously announcing the nearness of the end of this corrupt system of things.—1 Thessalonians 5:6.

Night Falls on the Desert Plain

21 The final pronouncement of Isaiah chapter 21 is directed against "the desert plain." It begins: *"The pronouncement against the desert plain: In the forest in the*

---

* During the first 59 years of its publication, the *Watchtower* magazine featured Isaiah 21:11 on its cover. The same scripture provided the theme of the last written sermon of Charles T. Russell, the Watch Tower Society's first president. (See illustration on preceding page.)

---

20. Why is the pronouncement recorded at Isaiah 21:11, 12 significant to Jehovah's people today?
21. (a) What play on words may be intended in the phrase "the pronouncement against the desert plain"? (b) What are the caravans of men of Dedan?

desert plain you will spend the night, O caravans of men of Dedan." (Isaiah 21:13) The desert plain referred to is evidently Arabia, for the pronouncement is directed at a number of Arab tribes. The word for "desert plain" is sometimes rendered "evening," a very similar word in Hebrew. Some suggest that this is a play on words, as if a dark evening—a time of trouble—is about to fall upon this region. The pronouncement opens with a nocturnal scene featuring caravans of men of Dedan, a prominent Arab tribe. Such caravans follow trade routes from one desert oasis to the next, bearing spices, pearls, and other treasures. But here we see them forced to leave their well-traveled tracks to spend the nights in hiding. Why?

22 Isaiah explains: *"To meet the thirsty one bring water. O you inhabitants of the land of Tema, confront the one fleeing away with bread for him. For because of the swords they have fled away, because of the drawn sword, and because of the bent bow and because of the heaviness of the war." (Isaiah 21:14, 15)* Yes, the crushing burden of war will fall upon these Arab tribes. Tema, located on one of the most well-watered oases in the region, is forced to bring water and bread to the hapless refugees of war. When will this trouble come?

23 Isaiah continues: *"This is what Jehovah has said to me: 'Within yet a year, according to the years of a hired laborer, all the glory of Kedar must even come to its end. And the ones remaining over of the number of bowmen, the mighty men of the sons of Kedar, will become few, for Jehovah himself, the God of Israel, has spoken it.'" (Isaiah 21: 16, 17)* Kedar is so prominent a tribe that it is sometimes used to represent all of Arabia. Jehovah has determined that the bowmen and mighty men of this tribe will dwin-

---

22, 23. (a) What crushing burden is about to befall the Arab tribes, and with what effect upon them? (b) How soon will this disaster come, and at whose hands?

dle in number to a mere remnant. When? "Within yet a year," no more, just as a hired laborer works no more than the amount of time for which he is paid. Precisely how all of this was fulfilled is uncertain. Two Assyrian rulers —Sargon II and Sennacherib—claimed credit for subjugating Arabia. Either may well have decimated these proud Arab tribes, as foretold.

24 We can be sure, however, that this prophecy was fulfilled to the letter. Nothing can make that point more forcefully than the closing words of the pronouncement: "Jehovah himself, the God of Israel, has spoken it." To people in Isaiah's day, it may seem unlikely that Babylon will ascend above Assyria and then be toppled from power during the debauched merrymaking of a single evening. It may seem equally unlikely that powerful Edom will end up in deathly silence or that a night of hardship and privation will fall on the wealthy Arab tribes. But Jehovah says it will, and so it happens. Today, Jehovah tells us that the world empire of false religion will come to nothing. This is not just a possibility; it is a certainty. Jehovah himself has spoken it!

25 Let us, then, be like the watchman. Let us remain vigilant, as if posted on a lofty watchtower, scanning the horizon for any sign of impending danger. Let us ally ourselves closely with the faithful watchman class, the remaining anointed Christians on earth today. Let us join them in courageously calling out just what we see—the overwhelming evidence that Christ is ruling in heaven; that he will soon bring an end to mankind's long, dark night of alienation from God; and that thereafter he will usher in the true dawn, the Millennial Reign over a paradise earth!

---

24. How can we be sure that Isaiah's prophecy against Arabia was fulfilled?
25. How may we imitate the example of the watchman?

CHAPTER EIGHTEEN

Lessons About Unfaithfulness

Isaiah 22:1-25

IMAGINE what it was like to be in an ancient city under siege. Outside the walls is the enemy—strong and ruthless. You know that other cities have already fallen to him. Now he is determined to conquer and plunder your city and rape and kill its inhabitants. The enemy armies are far too powerful to confront directly in combat; you can only hope that the walls of the city will keep them out. As you look out over the walls, you can see siege towers brought by the enemy. They also have siege engines capable of hurling boulders to smash your defenses. You see their battering rams and scaling ladders, their archers and chariots, their hordes of soldiers. What a terrifying sight!

2 In Isaiah chapter 22, we read about such a siege—a siege against Jerusalem. When does it happen? It is difficult to pinpoint any one siege in which all the features described are fulfilled. Evidently, the prophecy is best understood as a generic description of the various sieges that will befall Jerusalem, a general warning of what lies ahead.

3 In the face of the siege that Isaiah describes, what are the inhabitants of Jerusalem doing? As God's covenant people, are they crying out to Jehovah to save them? No, they are showing a very unwise attitude, one like that

1. What might it have been like to be inside an ancient city under siege?
2. When does the siege described in Isaiah chapter 22 happen?
3. How are Jerusalem's inhabitants reacting to the siege that Isaiah describes?

When Zedekiah flees, he is captured and blinded

found today among many who claim to worship God.

A City Under Siege

4 In chapter 21 of Isaiah, each of the three judgment messages was introduced with the expression "The pronouncement." (Isaiah 21:1, 11, 13) Chapter 22 opens the same way: *"The pronouncement of the valley of the vision: What is the matter with you, then, that you have gone up in your entirety to the roofs?" (Isaiah 22:1)* "The valley of the vision" refers to Jerusalem. The city is called the valley because even though elevated, it is surrounded by higher mountains. It is associated with "the vision" because many divine visions and revelations are given there. For this reason, the city's inhabitants should pay heed to Jehovah's words. Instead, they have ignored him and have strayed into false worship. The enemy besieging the city is an instrument of God's judgment against his wayward people.—Deuteronomy 28:45, 49, 50, 52.

---

4. (a) What is "the valley of the vision," and why does it have this name? (b) What is the spiritual condition of the inhabitants of Jerusalem?

5 Notice that the inhabitants of Jerusalem have 'gone up in their entirety to the roofs' of their houses. In ancient times, the roofs of Israelite homes were flat and families often congregated there. Isaiah does not tell why they do so on this occasion, but his words indicate disapproval. Likely, then, they have gone to the roofs to appeal to their false gods. This is their custom in the years leading up to the destruction of Jerusalem in 607 B.C.E.—Jeremiah 19: 13; Zephaniah 1:5.

6 Isaiah continues: *"With turmoil you were full, a boisterous city, an exultant town. Your slain ones are not those slain with the sword, nor those dead in battle."* (Isaiah 22:2)

---

5. Likely, why do the people go up to their roofs?
6. (a) What conditions prevail inside Jerusalem? (b) Why do some exult, but what lies ahead?

Prospects are grim for Jews trapped in Jerusalem

Multitudes have flocked to the city, and it is in turmoil. People in the streets are noisy and fearful. Some, though, are exulting, perhaps because they feel secure or they believe that the danger is passing.* To exult at this time, however, is foolish. Many in the city are going to die a death far more cruel than by the edge of the sword. A city under siege is cut off from outside sources of food. Stockpiles within the city dwindle. Starving people and crowded conditions lead to epidemics. Many in Jerusalem will thus die by famine and pestilence. This happens both in 607 B.C.E. and in 70 C.E. —2 Kings 25:3; Lamentations 4:9, 10.#

---

* In 66 C.E., many Jews exulted when the Roman armies besieging Jerusalem withdrew.

According to first-century historian Josephus, in 70 C.E., famine in Jerusalem was so severe that people ate leather, grass, and hay. In one reported instance, a mother roasted and ate her own son.

7 In this crisis, what lead do Jerusalem's rulers give? Isaiah answers: ***"All your dictators themselves have fled at one time. Without need of a bow they have been taken prisoner. All those of you who have been found have been taken prisoner together. Far off they had run away."*** **(Isaiah 22:3)** The rulers and the mighty men run away and are then caught! Without even a bow bending against them, they are captured and led off as prisoners. This happens in 607 B.C.E. After Jerusalem's wall is breached, King Zedekiah flees by night with his mighty men. The enemy learns of this, pursues them, and catches up with them on the plains of Jericho. The mighty men scatter. Zedekiah is seized, blinded, bound in copper fetters, and dragged off to Babylon. (2 Kings 25:2-7) What a tragic consequence of his unfaithfulness!

Dismay at the Calamity

8 This prophecy moves Isaiah deeply. He says: ***"Turn your gaze away from me. I will show bitterness in weeping. Do not you people insist on comforting me over the despoiling of the daughter of my people."*** **(Isaiah 22:4)** Isaiah grieved over the prophesied fate of Moab and Babylon. (Isaiah 16:11; 21:3) Now his dismay and lamentation are even more intense as he contemplates the disaster coming upon his own people. He is inconsolable. Why? ***"For it is the day of confusion and of downtreading and of confounding that the Sovereign Lord, Jehovah of armies, has in the valley of the vision. There is the demolisher of the wall, and the cry to the mountain."*** **(Isaiah 22:5)** Jerusalem will be filled with wild confusion. People will wander about panic-stricken, without purpose. As the enemy begins to

---

7. What do Jerusalem's rulers do during the siege, and what happens to them?
8. (a) How does Isaiah react to the prophecy foretelling calamity upon Jerusalem? (b) What will be the scene in Jerusalem?

break through the city walls, there will be a "cry to the mountain." Does this mean that the city's inhabitants will cry out to God in his holy temple on Mount Moriah? Perhaps. In view of their unfaithfulness, however, it probably means no more than that their cries of terror will echo in the surrounding mountains.

9 What sort of enemy is threatening Jerusalem? Isaiah tells us: *"Elam itself has taken up the quiver, in the war chariot of earthling man, with steeds; and Kir itself has uncovered the shield."* (Isaiah 22:6) The foes are fully armed. They have archers whose quivers are filled with arrows. Warriors are readying their shields for battle. There are chariots and battle-trained horses. The army includes soldiers from Elam, located north of what is now the Persian Gulf, and from Kir, probably located close to Elam. Mention of those lands indicates the great distance from which the invaders come. It also indicates that Elamite archers may have been in the army threatening Jerusalem in Hezekiah's day.

Attempts at Defense

10 Isaiah describes the developing situation: *"It will occur that the choicest of your low plains must become full of war chariots, and the very steeds must without fail set themselves in position at the gate, and one will remove the screen of Judah."* (Isaiah 22:7, 8a) Chariots and horses crowd the plains outside the city of Jerusalem and position themselves to attack the gates of the city. What is "the screen of Judah" that is removed? Likely, it is a gate of the city, the capture of which bodes ill for the defenders.*

---

* Alternatively, "the screen of Judah" might refer to something else that protects the city, such as fortresses where arms are stored and soldiers quartered.

9. Describe the army threatening Jerusalem.
10. What development bodes ill for the city?

When this defensive screen is removed, the city is open to its attackers.

11 Isaiah now focuses on the attempts by the people to defend themselves. Their first thought—weapons! *"You will look in that day toward the armory of the house of the forest, and you people will certainly see the very breaches of the City of David, for they will actually be many. And you will collect the waters of the lower pool." (Isaiah 22:8b, 9)* Weapons are stored in the armory of the house of the forest. This armory was built by Solomon. Since it was constructed of cedars from Lebanon, it became known as "the House of the Forest of Lebanon." (1 Kings 7:2-5) Breaches in the wall are examined. Water is collected—an important measure of defense. The people need water to live. Without it, a city cannot stand. Notice, though, that nothing is said of their looking to Jehovah for deliverance. Rather, they rely on their own resources. May we never make that mistake!—Psalm 127:1.

12 What can be done about those breaches in the city wall? *"The houses of Jerusalem you will actually count. You will also pull down the houses to make the wall unattainable." (Isaiah 22:10)* Houses are evaluated to see to which ones might be demolished to provide materials for repairing the breaches. This is an effort to prevent the enemy from gaining complete control of the wall.

A Faithless People

13 *"There will be a collecting basin that you must make between the two walls for the waters of the old pool. And you will certainly not look at the grand maker of it,*

11, 12. What defensive measures do the inhabitants of Jerusalem take?

13. How do the people try to ensure a supply of water, but whom do they forget?

and the one forming it long ago you will certainly not see." *(Isaiah 22:11)* The efforts to collect water, described both here and in verse 9, remind us of the action King Hezekiah took to protect the city against the invading Assyrians. (2 Chronicles 32:2-5) However, the people of the city in this prophecy of Isaiah are absolutely faithless. As they work on the defense of the city, they give no thought to the Creator, unlike Hezekiah.

14 Isaiah continues: *"The Sovereign Lord, Jehovah of armies, will call in that day for weeping and for mourning and for baldness and for girding on sackcloth. But, look! exultation and rejoicing, the killing of cattle and the slaughtering of sheep, the eating of flesh and the drinking of wine, 'Let there be eating and drinking, for tomorrow we shall die.' "* *(Isaiah 22:12, 13)* The inhabitants of Jerusalem show no remorse for their rebellion against Jehovah. They do not weep, cut their hair, or wear sackcloth as a sign of repentance. If they were doing so, likely Jehovah would spare them the coming horrors. Instead, they abandon themselves to sensual enjoyment. The same attitude exists today among many who do not put faith in God. Because they have no hope—either of a resurrection from the dead or of life in the future Paradise earth—they pursue lives of self-indulgence, saying: "Let us eat and drink, for tomorrow we are to die." (1 Corinthians 15:32) How shortsighted! If only they would put their trust in Jehovah, they would have a lasting hope!—Psalm 4:6-8; Proverbs 1:33.

15 The besieged inhabitants of Jerusalem will not know

---

14. Despite Jehovah's warning message, what unwise attitude do the people have?
15. (a) What is Jehovah's judgment message against Jerusalem, and who carries out his judgment? (b) Why will Christendom suffer a fate similar to that of Jerusalem?

security. Isaiah says: *"In my ears Jehovah of armies has revealed himself: ' "This error will not be atoned for in your behalf until you people die," the Sovereign Lord, Jehovah of armies, has said.'"* (Isaiah 22:14) Because of the hardheartedness of the people, there will be no pardon. Without fail, death will come. This is a certainty. The Sovereign Lord, Jehovah of armies, has said it. In fulfillment of Isaiah's prophetic words, calamity comes twice upon unfaithful Jerusalem. It is destroyed by the armies of Babylon and later by those of Rome. So, too, calamity will come upon unfaithful Christendom, whose members claim to worship God but actually disown him by their works. (Titus 1:16) The sins of Christendom, along with those of the world's other religions that flout God's righteous ways, have "massed together clear up to heaven." Like the error of apostate Jerusalem, their error is too great to be atoned for.—Revelation 18:5, 8, 21.

A Selfish Steward

16 The prophet now turns his attention from an unfaithful people to an unfaithful individual. Isaiah writes: *"This is what the Sovereign Lord, Jehovah of armies, has said: 'Go, enter in to this steward, to Shebna, who is over the house, "What is there of interest to you here, and who is there of interest to you here, that you have hewed out for yourself here a burial place?" On a height he is hewing out his burial place; in a crag he is cutting out a residence for himself.'"* —Isaiah 22:15, 16.

17 Shebna is 'steward over the house,' probably the house of King Hezekiah. As such, he has an influential position, second only to the king. Much is expected of him. (1 Co-

---

16, 17. (a) Who now receives a warning message from Jehovah, and why? (b) Because of his lofty aspirations, what will happen to Shebna?

rinthians 4:2) Yet, when he should be giving first attention to the affairs of the nation, Shebna is pursuing glory for himself. He is having a luxurious tomb—comparable to that of a king—carved for himself high on a crag. Jehovah, observing this, inspires Isaiah to warn the unfaithful steward: *"Look! Jehovah is hurling you down with violent hurling, O able-bodied man, and grasping you forcibly. Without fail he will wrap you up tightly, like a ball for a wide land. There you will*

Eliakim is made "a peg in a lasting place" by Hezekiah

die, and there the chariots of your glory will be the dishonor of the house of your master. And I will push you away from your position; and from your official standing one will tear you down." (Isaiah 22:17-19) Because of his self-centeredness, Shebna will not have even an ordinary tomb in Jerusalem. Instead, he will be hurled like a ball, to die in a distant land. In this there is a warning to all of those entrusted with authority among God's people. Abuse of power will lead to the loss of that authority and possibly to banishment.

18 How, though, will Shebna be removed from his

---

18. Who will replace Shebna, and what does it mean that this one will receive Shebna's official garments and the key of the house of David?

position? Through Isaiah, Jehovah explains: *"It must occur in that day that I will call my servant, namely, Eliakim the son of Hilkiah. And I will clothe him with your robe, and your sash I shall firmly bind about him, and your dominion I shall give into his hand; and he must become a father to the inhabitant of Jerusalem and to the house of Judah. And I will put the key of the house of David upon his shoulder, and he must open without anyone's shutting, and he must shut without anyone's opening."* (Isaiah 22:20-22) Replacing Shebna, Eliakim will be given the steward's official garments along with the key of the house of David. The Bible uses the term "key" to symbolize authority, government, or power. (Compare Matthew 16:19.) In ancient times, a king's adviser, entrusted with the keys, might have general supervision of the royal chambers, even deciding on candidates for the king's service. (Compare Revelation 3:7, 8.) Thus, the office of steward is important, and much is expected of whoever serves in it. (Luke 12:48) Shebna may be capable, but because he is unfaithful, Jehovah will replace him.

Two Symbolic Pegs

19 Finally, Jehovah uses symbolic language to describe the transfer of power from Shebna to Eliakim. He states: *"'I will drive him [Eliakim] in as a peg in a lasting place, and he must become as a throne of glory to the house of his father. And they must hang upon him all the glory of the house of his father, the descendants and the offshoots, all the vessels of the small sort, the vessels of the bowl sort as well as all the vessels of the large jars. In that day,' is the utterance of Jehovah of armies, 'the peg [Sheb-*

19, 20. (a) How will Eliakim prove to be a blessing to his people? (b) What will happen to those who continue to look to Shebna?

na] that is driven in a lasting place will be removed, and it must be hewn down and fall, and the load that is upon it must be cut off, for Jehovah himself has spoken it.'"—Isaiah 22:23-25.

20 In these verses the first peg is Eliakim. He will become "a throne of glory" to the house of his father, Hilkiah. Unlike Shebna, he will not disgrace his father's house or reputation. Eliakim will be a lasting support to household vessels, that is, to others in the king's service. (2 Timothy 2:20, 21) In contrast, the second peg refers to Shebna. Though he may seem secure, he will be removed. Any who continue to look to him will fall.

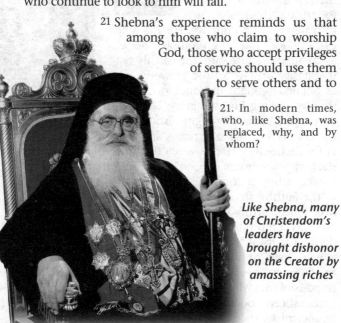

21 Shebna's experience reminds us that among those who claim to worship God, those who accept privileges of service should use them to serve others and to

21. In modern times, who, like Shebna, was replaced, why, and by whom?

Like Shebna, many of Christendom's leaders have brought dishonor on the Creator by amassing riches

In modern times a faithful steward class has been appointed over Jesus' household

bring praise to Jehovah. They should not abuse their position in order to enrich themselves or gain personal prominence. For example, Christendom has long promoted herself as an appointed steward, the earthly representative of Jesus Christ. However, just as Shebna brought dishonor on his father by seeking his own glory, Christendom's leaders have brought dishonor on the Creator by amassing riches and power for themselves. Hence, when the time of judgment "to start with the house of God" came in 1918, Jehovah removed Christendom. Another steward was identified —"the faithful steward, the discreet one"—and appointed over Jesus' earthly household. (1 Peter 4:17; Luke 12:42-44) This composite class has shown itself worthy of shouldering the royal "key" of the house of David. Like a trustworthy "peg," it has proved to be a reliable support for all the different "vessels," anointed Christians with different responsibilities who look to it for spiritual sustenance. The "other sheep" too, like 'the alien resident within the gates' of ancient Jerusalem, depend on this "peg," the modern-day Eliakim.—John 10:16; Deuteronomy 5:14.

22 Eliakim replaced Shebna when Sennacherib and his hordes were threatening Jerusalem. Similarly, "the faithful steward, the discreet one," has been appointed to serve during the time of the end, which will come to a conclusion when Satan and his forces move for a final attack on "the Israel of God" and their other sheep companions. (Galatians 6:16) As in Hezekiah's day, that attack will end in destruction for the enemies of righteousness. Those who support themselves on the "peg in a lasting place," the faithful steward, will survive, just as faithful inhabitants of Jerusalem survived the Assyrian invasion of Judah. How wise, then, not to cling to the discredited "peg" of Christendom!

23 What happens to Shebna? We have no record of how the prophecy about him, recorded at Isaiah 22:18, was fulfilled. When he exalts himself and is then disgraced, he resembles Christendom, but he may have learned from the discipline. In this, he is very different from Christendom. When the Assyrian Rabshakeh demands Jerusalem's surrender, Hezekiah's new steward, Eliakim, leads the delegation that goes out to meet him. However, Shebna is at his side as secretary to the king. Evidently, Shebna is still in the king's service. (Isaiah 36:2, 22) What a fine lesson for those who lose positions of service in God's organization! Rather than being bitter and resentful, they are wise to continue serving Jehovah in whatever capacity he allows. (Hebrews 12:6) By so doing, they will avoid the disaster that will befall Christendom. They will enjoy God's favor and blessing throughout eternity.

---

22. (a) Why was the replacing of Shebna as steward timely? (b) In modern times, why was the appointing of "the faithful steward, the discreet one," timely?
23. What eventually happens to Shebna, and what can we learn from this?

CHAPTER NINETEEN

Jehovah Profanes the Pride of Tyre

Isaiah 23:1-18

SHE was "perfect in beauty" and abundant in "wealth of every kind." (Ezekiel 27:4, 12, *An American Translation*) Her large fleet of ships sailed across the sea to faraway places. She became "very glorious in the heart of the open sea," and with her "valuable things," she "made earth's kings rich." (Ezekiel 27:25, 33) In the seventh century B.C.E., such was the stature of Tyre—a Phoenician city on the eastern end of the Mediterranean.

2 Yet, destruction was in the offing for Tyre. Some 100 years before Ezekiel described her, the prophet Isaiah foretold the downfall of this Phoenician stronghold and the grief of those depending upon her. Isaiah also prophesied that after some time God would turn his attention to the city, granting her renewed prosperity. How were the prophet's words fulfilled? And what can we learn from all that happened to Tyre? Having a clear understanding of what befell her and why such things happened will strengthen our faith in Jehovah and his promises.

"Howl, You Ships of Tarshish!"

3 Under the title, *"The pronouncement of Tyre,"* Isaiah

1, 2. (a) What kind of city was ancient Tyre? (b) What did Isaiah prophesy for Tyre?

3, 4. (a) Where was Tarshish, and what was the relationship between Tyre and Tarshish? (b) Why will the sailors trading with Tarshish have reason to "howl"?

declares: *"Howl, you ships of Tarshish! for it has been de-spoiled from being a port, from being a place to en-ter in." (Isaiah 23:1a)* Tarshish is believed to have been a part of Spain, far from Tyre in the eastern Mediterranean.* Still, the Phoenicians were expert seamen, and their ships were large and seaworthy. Some historians believe that the Phoenicians were the first to notice the link between the moon and the tides and to use astronomy as a navigation-al aid. So the long distance from Tyre to Tarshish was no obstacle for them.

4 In Isaiah's day, distant Tarshish is a market for Tyre, per-haps the main source of her wealth during part of her his-tory. Spain has mines rich with deposits of silver, iron, tin, and other metals. (Compare Jeremiah 10:9; Ezekiel 27:12.) "Ships of Tarshish," likely ships from Tyre trading with Tarshish, will have good reason to "howl," lamenting the destruction of their home port.

5 How will mariners at sea learn of the downfall of Tyre? Isaiah answers: *"From the land of Kittim it has been re-vealed to them." (Isaiah 23:1b)* "The land of Kittim" like-ly refers to the island of Cyprus, about 60 miles west of the Phoenician coast. This is the last stop for the eastbound ships from Tarshish before they arrive at Tyre. Hence, the sailors will receive news of the overthrow of their be-loved home port when they make a stopover in Cyprus. What a shock for them! Grief-stricken, they will "howl" in dismay.

6 Dismay will also be felt by the people of the Phoenician

---

* Some scholars have identified Tarshish with Sardinia, an island in the western Mediterranean. Sardinia too was far from Tyre.

---

5. Where will mariners coming from Tarshish learn of the fall of Tyre?
6. Describe the relationship between Tyre and Sidon.

seacoast. The prophet says: *"Be silent, you inhabitants of the coastland. The merchants from Sidon, the ones crossing over the sea—they have filled you. And on many waters has been the seed of Shihor, the harvest of the Nile, her revenue; and it came to be the profit of the nations."* (*Isaiah 23:2, 3*) The "inhabitants of the coastland"—Tyre's neighbors—will be silent in utter amazement at the calamitous fall of Tyre. Who are "the merchants from Sidon" who "have filled" these inhabitants, making them rich? Tyre was originally a colony of the seaport city of Sidon, just 22 miles to the north. On her coins, Sidon describes herself as the mother of Tyre. Although Tyre has eclipsed Sidon in wealth, she is still a "daughter of Sidon," and her inhabitants still call themselves Sidonians. (Isaiah 23:12) Hence, the expression "the merchants from Sidon" probably refers to the commercial inhabitants of Tyre.

7 Engaging in commercial enterprise, the wealthy Sidonian merchants traverse the Mediterranean Sea. They carry to many places the seed, or grain, of Shihor, the easternmost branch of the Nile River in the delta region of Egypt. (Compare Jeremiah 2:18.) "The harvest of the Nile" also includes other produce from Egypt. Trading and bartering in such goods is highly profitable for these seafaring merchants as well as for the nations with which they do business. The Sidonian traders fill Tyre with revenue. Indeed, they will grieve at her desolation!

8 Isaiah next addresses Sidon with the words: *"Be ashamed, O Sidon; because the sea, O you stronghold of the sea, has said: 'I have not had birth pains, and I have not given birth, nor have I brought up young men, raised up virgins.'"* (*Isaiah 23:4*) After the destruction of Tyre,

_____

7. How have Sidonian merchants spread wealth?
8. What effect will Tyre's destruction have on Sidon?

the coastline where the city formerly stood will look barren and desolate. The sea will appear to cry out in anguish, like a mother who has lost her children and is so distraught that she now disclaims ever having had them. Sidon will be ashamed at what happens to her daughter.

9 Yes, the news of the destruction of Tyre will cause widespread grief. Isaiah says: *"Just as at the report pertaining to Egypt, people will likewise be in severe pains at the report on Tyre."* (Isaiah 23:5) The pain of the mourning ones will be comparable to that resulting from the report about Egypt. Which report does the prophet mean? Possibly the fulfillment of his earlier "pronouncement against Egypt."* (Isaiah 19:1-25) Or perhaps the prophet means the report of the destruction of Pharaoh's army in Moses' day, which caused widespread consternation. (Exodus 15:4, 5, 14-16; Joshua 2:9-11) In any case, those hearing the report of Tyre's destruction will be in severe pains. They are invited to flee to distant Tarshish for refuge and are commanded to make a noisy expression of their grief: *"Cross over to Tarshish; howl, you inhabitants of the coastland."* —Isaiah 23:6.

Exultant "From Her Early Times"

10 Tyre is an ancient city, as Isaiah reminds us when he asks: *"Is this your city that was exultant from days of long ago, from her early times?"* (Isaiah 23:7a) Tyre's prosperous history extends at least as far back as Joshua's time. (Joshua 19:29) Over the years, Tyre has become famous as a manufacturer of metal objects, glassware, and purple

---

* See Chapter 15, pages 200-207, of this book.

---

9. The grief of the people following the fall of Tyre will be comparable to the consternation following what other events?
10-12. Describe the wealth, antiquity, and influence of Tyre.

dye. Robes of Tyrian purple command the highest prices, and Tyre's costly fabrics are sought after by the nobility. (Compare Ezekiel 27:7, 24.) Tyre is also a trading center for overland caravans as well as a great import-export depot.

11 Moreover, the city is militarily strong. L. Sprague de Camp writes: "Although not especially warlike—they were businessmen, not soldiers—the Phoenicians defended their cities with fanatical courage and stubbornness. These qualities, as well as their naval might, enabled the Tyrians to hold out against the Assyrian army, the strongest of its time."

12 Indeed, Tyre makes her mark on the Mediterranean world. *"Her feet used to bring her far away to reside as an alien." (Isaiah 23:7b)* Phoenicians travel to distant places, setting up trading posts and ports of call, which in some instances grow into colonies. For example, Carthage, on the north coast of Africa, is a colony of Tyre. In time, it will surpass Tyre and rival Rome for influence in the Mediterranean world.

Her Pride Will Be Profaned

13 In view of Tyre's antiquity and wealth, the next question is fitting: *"Who is it that has given this counsel against Tyre, the bestower of crowns, whose merchants were princes, whose tradesmen were the honorable ones of the earth?" (Isaiah 23:8)* Who dares to speak against the city that has appointed powerful individuals to positions of high authority in her colonies and elsewhere —thus becoming "the bestower of crowns"? Who dares to speak against the metropolis whose merchants are princes and whose tradesmen are honorable ones? Said Maurice

---

13. Why is the question raised as to who dares to pronounce judgment against Tyre?

Chehab, former director of antiquities at the National Museum of Beirut, Lebanon: "From the ninth to the sixth century B.C., Tyre retained the position of importance known to London at the beginning of the twentieth century." So who dares to speak against this city?

14 The inspired reply will cause consternation in Tyre. Isaiah says: *"Jehovah of armies himself has given this counsel, to profane the pride of all beauty, to treat with contempt all the honorable ones of the earth." (Isaiah 23:9)* Why does Jehovah pronounce judgment against this wealthy, ancient city? Is it because its inhabitants are worshipers of the false god Baal? Is it because of Tyre's relationship with Jezebel—the daughter of King Ethbaal of Sidon, including Tyre—who married King Ahab of Israel and massacred the prophets of Jehovah? (1 Kings 16:29, 31; 18:4, 13, 19) The answer to both questions is no. Tyre is condemned because of her arrogant pride—she has grown fat at the expense of other peoples, including the Israelites. In the ninth century B.C.E., through the prophet Joel, Jehovah said to Tyre and other cities: "The sons of Judah and the sons of Jerusalem you have sold to the sons of the Greeks, for the purpose of removing them far from their own territory." (Joel 3:6) Can God overlook Tyre's treating his covenant people as mere trading commodities?

15 The passing of a hundred years will not change Tyre. When the army of King Nebuchadnezzar of Babylon destroys Jerusalem in 607 B.C.E., Tyre will exult: "Aha! She [Jerusalem] has been broken, the doors of the peoples! The trend will certainly be to me. I shall be filled—she has been devastated." (Ezekiel 26:2) Tyre will rejoice, expecting to benefit from the destruction of Jerusalem. With

---

14. Who pronounces judgment against Tyre, and why?
15. How will Tyre react when Jerusalem falls to Nebuchadnezzar?

the Judean capital no longer a competitor, she will expect more trade for herself. Jehovah will treat with contempt self-proclaimed "honorable ones," who pridefully stand with the enemies of his people.

16 Isaiah continues Jehovah's condemnation of Tyre: ***"Cross over your land like the Nile River, O daughter of Tarshish. There is no shipyard any longer. His hand he has stretched out over the sea; he has caused kingdoms to be agitated. Jehovah himself has given a command against Phoenicia, to annihilate her strongholds. And he says: 'You must never again exult, O oppressed one, the virgin daughter of Sidon. Get up, cross over to Kittim itself. Even there it will not be restful for you.'"—Isaiah 23:10-12.***

17 Why is Tyre called the "daughter of Tarshish"? Perhaps because after the defeat of Tyre, Tarshish will be the more powerful of the two.* The inhabitants of ruined Tyre will be scattered like a river in flood, its banks broken down and its waters overflowing into all the neighboring plains. Isaiah's message to the "daughter of Tarshish" underscores the severity of what will happen to Tyre. Jehovah himself stretches out his hand and gives the command. No one can alter the outcome.

18 Isaiah also speaks of Tyre as "the virgin daughter of

---

* Alternatively, the "daughter of Tarshish" may refer to the inhabitants of Tarshish. One reference work says: "The natives of Tarshish are now free to travel and trade as freely as the Nile when it flows in all directions." Still, the emphasis is on the drastic repercussions of the fall of Tyre.

16, 17. What will happen to the inhabitants of Tyre when the city falls? (See footnote.)
18. Why is Tyre called "the virgin daughter of Sidon," and how will her state change?

Tyre would submit to Babylon, not Assyria

Sidon," indicating that she has not previously been seized and ravished by foreign conquerors and still enjoys an unsubdued state. (Compare 2 Kings 19:21; Isaiah 47:1; Jeremiah 46:11.) Now, though, she is to be annihilated, and like refugees, some of her residents will cross over to the Phoenician colony of Kittim. Nevertheless, having lost their economic power, they will find no rest there.

The Chaldeans Will Despoil Her

19 Which political power will execute Jehovah's judgment upon Tyre? Isaiah proclaims: *"Look! The land of the Chaldeans. This is the people—Assyria did not prove to be the one—they founded her for the desert haunters. They have erected their siege towers; they have stripped bare her dwelling towers; one has set her as a crumbling ruin. Howl, you ships of Tarshish, for your stronghold has been despoiled." (Isaiah 23:13, 14)* The Chaldeans—not the Assyrians—will conquer Tyre. They will erect their siege towers, level the dwelling places of Tyre, and make that stronghold of the ships of Tarshish a crumbling heap of ruins.

20 True to the prophecy, not long after the fall of Jerusalem, Tyre rebels against Babylon, and Nebuchadnezzar lays siege to the city. Believing herself impregnable, Tyre resists. In the course of the siege, the heads of Babylon's soldiers are "made bald" from the chafing of their helmets and their shoulders are "rubbed bare" from carrying materials used in the construction of siegeworks. (Ezekiel 29: 18) The siege is costly to Nebuchadnezzar. The mainland city of Tyre is destroyed, yet its spoil eludes him. The bulk of the treasures of Tyre have been transferred to a small is-

___

19, 20. Who is prophesied to be the conqueror of Tyre, and how is that prophecy fulfilled?

land about half a mile from the shore. Lacking a fleet of ships, the Chaldean king is unable to take the island. After 13 years, Tyre capitulates, but she will survive and see the fulfillment of further prophecies.

"She Must Return to Her Hire"

21 Isaiah goes on to prophesy: *"It must occur in that day that Tyre must be forgotten seventy years, the same as the days of one king." (Isaiah 23:15a)* Following the destruction of the mainland city by the Babylonians, the island-city of Tyre will "be forgotten." True to the prophecy, for the duration of "one king"—the Babylonian Empire—the island-city of Tyre will not be an important financial power. Jehovah, through Jeremiah, includes Tyre among the nations that will be singled out to drink the wine of His rage. He says: "These nations will have to serve the king of Babylon seventy years." (Jeremiah 25:8-17, 22, 27) True, the island-city of Tyre is not subject to Babylon for a full 70 years, since the Babylonian Empire falls in 539 B.C.E. Evidently, the 70 years represents the period of Babylonia's greatest domination—when the Babylonian royal dynasty boasts of having lifted its throne even above "the stars of God." (Isaiah 14:13) Different nations come under that domination at different times. But at the end of 70 years, that domination will crumble. What will then happen to Tyre?

22 Isaiah continues: *"At the end of seventy years it will happen to Tyre as in the song of a prostitute: 'Take a harp, go around the city, O forgotten prostitute. Do your best at playing on the strings; make your songs many, in order that you may be remembered.' And it must occur at the*

---

21. In what way is Tyre "forgotten," and for how long?
22, 23. What will happen to Tyre when she comes out from under Babylonian domination?

end of seventy years that Jehovah will turn his attention to Tyre, and she must return to her hire and commit prostitution with all the kingdoms of the earth upon the surface of the ground."—Isaiah 23:15b-17.

23 Following the fall of Babylon in 539 B.C.E., Phoenicia becomes a satrapy of the Medo-Persian Empire. The Persian monarch, Cyrus the Great, is a tolerant ruler. Under this new rulership, Tyre will resume her former activity and try hard to regain recognition as a world commercial center—just as a prostitute who has been forgotten and has lost her clientele seeks to attract new clients by going around the city, playing her harp and singing her songs. Will Tyre succeed? Yes, Jehovah will grant her success. In time, the island-city will become so prosperous that toward the end of the sixth century B.C.E., the prophet Zechariah will say: "Tyre proceeded to build a rampart for herself, and to pile up silver like dust and gold like the mire of the streets."—Zechariah 9:3.

'Her Profit Must Become Something Holy'

24 How remarkable are the following prophetic words! *"Her profit and her hire must become something holy to Jehovah. It will not be stored up, nor be laid up, because her hire will come to be for those dwelling before Jehovah, for eating to satisfaction and for elegant covering." (Isaiah 23:18)* How does Tyre's material profit become something holy? Jehovah maneuvers matters so that it is used according to his will—for the eating to satisfaction of his people and for their covering. This comes about following the Israelites' return from Babylonian exile. The people of Tyre assist them by supplying cedar timbers for rebuilding the

---

24, 25. (a) How does Tyre's profit become something holy to Jehovah? (b) Despite Tyre's helping God's people, what prophecy does Jehovah inspire regarding her?

temple. They also resume trade with the city of Jerusalem.
—Ezra 3:7; Nehemiah 13:16.

25 Despite this, Jehovah inspires a further pronouncement against Tyre. Zechariah prophesies concerning the
now wealthy island-city: "Look! Jehovah himself will dis-
possess her, and into the sea he will certainly strike down
her military force; and in the fire she herself will be devoured." (Zechariah 9:4) This is fulfilled in July 332 B.C.E.
when Alexander the Great demolishes that proud mistress
of the sea.

Avoid Materialism and Pride

26 Jehovah condemned Tyre for her pride, a characteristic that he despises. "Lofty eyes" are listed first among the
seven things that Jehovah hates. (Proverbs 6:16-19) Paul
associated pride with Satan the Devil, and Ezekiel's description of proud Tyre has elements that describe Satan himself. (Ezekiel 28:13-15; 1 Timothy 3:6) Why was
Tyre proud? Ezekiel, addressing Tyre, says: "Your heart began to be haughty because of your wealth." (Ezekiel 28:5)
The city was dedicated to trade and the amassing of money. Tyre's success in this made her unbearably haughty.
Through Ezekiel, Jehovah said to "the leader of Tyre":
"Your heart has become haughty, and you keep saying, 'I
am a god. In the seat of god I have seated myself.'"
—Ezekiel 28:2.

27 Nations can succumb to pride and a wrong view of
wealth—and so can individuals. Jesus gave a parable that
showed how subtle this snare can be. He spoke of a rich
man whose fields produced very well. Delighted, the man

---

26. Why did God condemn Tyre?
27, 28. What trap can humans fall into, and how did Jesus illustrate
this?

planned to build larger storehouses for his produce and happily looked forward to a long life of comfort. But this did not happen. God said to him: "Unreasonable one, this night they are demanding your soul from you. Who, then, is to have the things you stored up?" Yes, the man died, and his wealth availed him nothing.—Luke 12:16-20.

28 Jesus concluded the parable, saying: "So it goes with the man that lays up treasure for himself but is not rich toward God." (Luke 12:21) Being wealthy was not wrong in itself, and having a good harvest was no sin. The man's error lay in his making these the main things in his life. His whole confidence was in his riches. When looking to the future, he did not take Jehovah God into account.

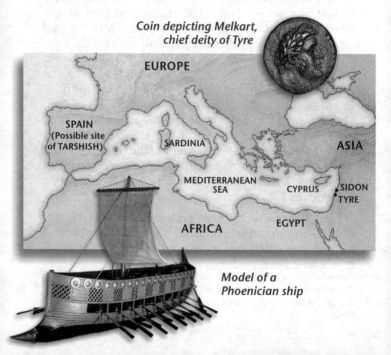

Coin depicting Melkart, chief deity of Tyre

Model of a Phoenician ship

29 James very strongly made the same point. He said: "Come, now, you who say: 'Today or tomorrow we will journey to this city and will spend a year there, and we will engage in business and make profits,' whereas you do not know what your life will be tomorrow. For you are a mist appearing for a little while and then disappearing. Instead, you ought to say: 'If Jehovah wills, we shall live and also do this or that.'" (James 4:13-15) Then, James showed the relationship between wealth and pride when he continued, saying: "You take pride in your self-assuming brags. All such taking of pride is wicked."—James 4:16.

30 Again, doing business is not a sin. The sin is the pride, the arrogance, the confidence in self that gaining wealth can engender. Wisely, the ancient proverb said: "Give me neither poverty nor riches." Poverty can make life very bitter. But riches can lead a person to "deny [God] and say: 'Who is Jehovah?'"—Proverbs 30:8, 9.

31 We live in a world where many have fallen victim to greed and selfishness. Because of the prevailing commercial climate, much emphasis is placed on wealth. Hence, a Christian does well to examine himself to be sure that he is not falling into the same trap that ensnared the commercial city of Tyre. Does he spend so much of his time and energy in material pursuits that he is, in fact, a slave of riches? (Matthew 6:24) Is he envious of some who may have more or better possessions than he has? (Galatians 5: 26) If he happens to be wealthy, does he proudly feel that he deserves more attention or privileges than others do? (Compare James 2:1-9.) If he is not rich, is he "determined to *be* rich," whatever the cost? (1 Timothy 6:9) Is he so occupied with business matters that he leaves only a very

---

29, 30. How did James warn against reliance on self?
31. What questions does a Christian do well to ask himself?

small corner in his life for serving God? (2 Timothy 2:4) Does he become so consumed with the pursuit of wealth that he ignores Christian principles in his business practices?—1 Timothy 6:10.

32 Whatever our economic situation, the Kingdom should always have first place in our lives. It is vital that we never lose sight of the words of the apostle John: "Do not be loving either the world or the things in the world. If anyone loves the world, the love of the Father is not in him." (1 John 2:15) True, we have to use the world's economic arrangements in order to survive. (2 Thessalonians 3:10) Hence, we 'use the world'—but we do not use it "to the full." (1 Corinthians 7:31) If we have an excessive love of material things—the things in the world—we no longer love Jehovah. Chasing after "the desire of the flesh and the desire of the eyes and the showy display of one's means of life" is incompatible with doing the will of God.* And it is doing the will of God that leads to eternal life.—1 John 2:16, 17.

33 The trap of putting the pursuit of material things ahead of all else ensnared Tyre. She was successful in a material sense, became very proud, and was punished for her pride. Her example stands as a warning to nations and individuals today. How much better to follow the admonition of the apostle Paul! He urges Christians "not to be high-minded, and to rest their hope, not on uncertain riches, but on God, who furnishes us all things richly for our enjoyment."—1 Timothy 6:17.

---

* "Showy display" is a translation of the Greek word *a·la·zo·ni'a*, which is described as "an impious and empty presumption which trusts in the stability of earthly things."—*The New Thayer's Greek-English Lexicon.*

---

32. What warning did John give, and how can we apply it?
33. How can Christians avoid the trap that ensnared Tyre?

CHAPTER TWENTY

Jehovah Is King

Isaiah 24:1-23

BABYLON, Philistia, Moab, Syria, Ethiopia, Egypt, Edom, Tyre, Assyria—all will experience Jehovah's wrath. Isaiah has foretold the calamities that will befall these hostile nations and cities. What, though, of Judah? Will the inhabitants of Judah be exempt from punishment for their sinful ways? The historical record answers with a resounding no!

2 Consider what happened to Samaria, the capital of the ten-tribe kingdom of Israel. That nation did not keep its covenant with God. It did not keep separate from the lewd practices of the nations round about. Instead, the inhabitants of Samaria "kept doing bad things to offend Jehovah . . . Therefore Jehovah got very incensed against Israel, so that he removed them from his sight." Forcibly removed from its land, "Israel went off its own soil into exile in Assyria." (2 Kings 17:9-12, 16-18, 23; Hosea 4:12-14) What happened to Israel bodes ill for her sister kingdom, Judah.

Isaiah Foretells the Desolation of Judah

3 Some kings of Judah were faithful, but most were not. Even under a faithful king, such as Jotham, the people did not turn completely away from false worship. (2 Kings 15:32-35) A climax in the wickedness of Judah is reached during the reign of bloodthirsty King Manasseh, who according to Jewish tradition, murders the faithful prophet

---

1, 2. (a) Who will experience Jehovah's wrath? (b) Will Judah be exempt from punishment, and how do we know?
3. (a) Why does Jehovah forsake the two-tribe kingdom of Judah? (b) What is Jehovah determined to do?

Isaiah by commanding that he be sawed apart. (Compare Hebrews 11:37.) This wicked king "kept seducing Judah and the inhabitants of Jerusalem to do worse than the nations that Jehovah had annihilated from before the sons of Israel." (2 Chronicles 33:9) Under Manasseh's rule the land becomes even more polluted than when the Canaanites controlled it. Hence, Jehovah declares: "Here I am bringing a calamity upon Jerusalem and Judah, of which if anyone hears both his ears will tingle. . . . I shall simply wipe Jerusalem clean just as one wipes the handleless bowl clean, wiping it clean and turning it upside down. And I shall indeed forsake the remnant of my inheritance and give them into the hand of their enemies, and they will simply become plunder and pillage to all their enemies, for the reason that they did what was bad in my eyes and were continually offending me."—2 Kings 21:11-15.

4 Like a bowl that is turned upside down, allowing all its contents to spill out, the land will be emptied of its human inhabitants. This coming desolation of Judah and Jerusalem is again the subject of prophecy by Isaiah. He begins: ***"Look! Jehovah is emptying the land and laying it waste, and he has twisted the face of it and scattered its inhabitants." (Isaiah 24:1)*** This prophecy is fulfilled when Jerusalem and its temple are destroyed by the invading Babylonian armies under King Nebuchadnezzar and when the inhabitants of Judah are decimated by sword, famine, and pestilence. Most of the Jewish survivors are taken captive to Babylon, and the few left behind flee to Egypt. Thus the land of Judah is wrecked and completely depopulated. Not even domestic animals remain. The deserted land becomes a wilderness with dreary ruins inhabited only by wild beasts and birds.

5 Will anyone in Judah receive preferential treatment

---

4. What will Jehovah do to Judah, and how is this prophecy fulfilled?
5. Will anyone be exempt from Jehovah's judgment? Explain.

during the coming judgment? Isaiah answers: *"It must come to be the same for the people as for the priest; the same for the servant as for his master; the same for the maidservant as for her mistress; the same for the buyer as for the seller; the same for the lender as for the borrower; the same for the interest taker as for the one paying the interest. Without fail the land will be emptied, and without fail it will be plundered, for Jehovah himself has spoken this word."* **(Isaiah 24:2, 3)** Wealth and privileges of temple service will make no difference. No exceptions will be made. The land is so corrupted that everyone surviving —priests, servants and masters, buyers and sellers—must go into exile.

6 In order that there be no misunderstanding, Isaiah describes the completeness of this coming disaster and explains the reason for it: *"The land has gone to mourning, has faded away. The productive land has withered, has faded away. The high ones of the people of the land have withered. And the very land has been polluted under its inhabitants, for they have bypassed the laws, changed the regulation, broken the indefinitely lasting covenant. That is why the curse itself has eaten up the land, and those inhabiting it are held guilty. That is why the inhabitants of the land have decreased in number, and very few mortal men have remained over."* **(Isaiah 24:4-6)** When the Israelites were given the land of Canaan, they found it to be "a land flowing with milk and honey." (Deuteronomy 27:3) Still, they continued to be dependent on Jehovah's blessing. If they faithfully kept his statutes and commandments, the land would "give its yield," but if they bypassed his laws and commandments, their efforts to cultivate the land would be "expended for nothing" and the earth would "not give its yield." (Leviticus 26:3-5, 14, 15, 20) Jehovah's curse would 'eat up the land.' (Deuteronomy 28:15-20,

---

6. Why does Jehovah withdraw his blessing from the land?

Music and rejoicing will no longer be heard in the land

38-42, 62, 63) Judah must now expect to experience that curse.

7 Some 800 years before Isaiah's day, the Israelites willingly entered into a covenant relationship with Jehovah and agreed to abide by it. (Exodus 24:3-8) The terms of that Law covenant stipulated that if they obeyed Jehovah's commandments, they would experience his rich blessing but if they violated the covenant, they would lose his blessing and be taken captive by their enemies. (Exodus 19:5, 6; Deuteronomy 28:1-68) This Law covenant, given through Moses, was to remain in force for an indefinite, unspecified time. It would safeguard the Israelites until the appearance of the Messiah.—Galatians 3:19, 24.

8 But the people have "broken the indefinitely lasting covenant." They have bypassed the divinely given laws, ignoring them. They have "changed the regulation," following legal practices different from those that Jehovah gave. (Exodus 22:25; Ezekiel 22:12) Hence, the people will be re-

---

7. How would the Law covenant be a blessing for the Israelites?
8. (a) How have the people "bypassed the laws" and "changed the regulation"? (b) In what ways are "the high ones" the first to 'wither'?

moved from the land. No mercy will be shown in the coming judgment. Among the first to 'wither' because of Jehovah's withdrawing his protection and favor will be "the high ones," the nobility. In fulfillment of this, as the destruction of Jerusalem approaches, first the Egyptians and then the Babylonians make Judean kings their vassals. Subsequently, King Jehoiachin and other members of the royal family are among the first ones taken into Babylonian captivity.—2 Chronicles 36:4, 9, 10.

Rejoicing Leaves the Land

9 The nation of Israel is an agricultural society. From the time that the Israelites entered the Promised Land, they have settled down to a life of cultivating crops and herding livestock. Thus, agriculture occupies an important place in the legislation given to Israel. A compulsory sabbath rest is commanded for the land every seventh year to allow fertility to be restored to the soil. (Exodus 23:10, 11; Leviticus 25:3-7) The three annual festivals that the nation is commanded to celebrate are timed to coincide with agricultural seasons.—Exodus 23:14-16.

10 Vineyards are common throughout the land. The Scriptures list wine, a product of the vine, as a gift from God that "makes the heart of mortal man rejoice." (Psalm 104:15) Each one 'sitting under his own vine and fig tree,' denotes prosperity, peace, and security under God's righteous rule. (1 Kings 4:25; Micah 4:4) A successful vintage season is considered a blessing and is a cause for singing and rejoicing. (Judges 9:27; Jeremiah 25:30) The opposite is also true. When the vines wither or produce no grapes and the vineyards become desolate wastes of thorns, it is evidence that Jehovah has withdrawn his blessing—a time of great sorrow.

9, 10. (a) What role does agriculture play in Israel? (b) What is the significance of each one 'sitting under his own vine and fig tree'?

11 Appropriately, then, Isaiah uses vineyards and their products to illustrate the conditions resulting from Jehovah's withdrawing his blessing from the land: *"The new wine has gone to mourning, the vine has withered, all those glad at heart have gone to sighing. The exultation of the tambourines has ceased, the noise of the highly elated ones has discontinued, the exultation of the harp has ceased. It is with no song that they drink wine; the intoxicating liquor becomes bitter to those drinking it. The deserted town has been broken down; every house has been shut up from entering. There is an outcry in the streets for want of wine. All rejoicing has passed away; the exultation of the land has departed. In the city an astonishing condition has been left behind; the gate has been crushed to a mere rubble heap."—Isaiah 24:7-12.*

12 The tambourine and the harp are pleasant instruments used to praise Jehovah and express joy. (2 Chronicles 29: 25; Psalm 81:2) Their music will not be heard at this time of divine punishment. There will be no joyful grape harvests. There will be no happy sounds in the desolated ruins of Jerusalem, with its gate "crushed to a mere rubble heap" and its houses "shut up," so that no one can enter. What grim prospects for inhabitants of a land that by nature has been so fertile!

A Remnant "Cry Out Joyfully"

13 In order to harvest olives, the Israelites beat the trees with rods so that the fruit will fall. According to God's Law,

---

11, 12. (a) How does Isaiah illustrate the conditions that will result from Jehovah's judgment? (b) What grim prospects does Isaiah describe?
13, 14. (a) What are Jehovah's laws on harvesting? (b) How does Isaiah use the laws on harvesting to illustrate that some will survive Jehovah's judgment? (c) Although there are dark seasons of trial coming, of what can faithful Judeans be certain?

Some will survive Jehovah's judgment, just as fruit remains on a tree after the harvest

they are forbidden to go over the boughs of the trees to collect the remaining olives. Nor should they gather the leftover grapes after harvesting their vineyards. The remnants of the harvest are to be left for the poor—"for the alien resident, for the fatherless boy and for the widow"—to glean. (Deuteronomy 24:19-21) Drawing on these well-known laws, Isaiah illustrates the comforting fact that there will be survivors of Jehovah's coming judgment: *"Thus it will become in the midst of the land, in among the peoples, like the beating off of the olive tree, like the gleaning when the grape gathering has come to an end. They themselves will raise their voice, they will cry out joyfully. In the superiority of Jehovah they will certainly cry out shrilly from the sea. That is why in the region of light they must glorify Jehovah, in the islands of the sea the name of Jehovah, the God of Israel. From the extremity of the land there are melodies that we have heard: 'Decoration to the Righteous One!' "*—Isaiah 24:13-16a.

14 Just as some fruit remains on the tree or vine after harvesting, so there will be some who are left over after Jehovah's execution of judgment—"the gleaning when the grape gathering has come to an end." As recorded in verse 6, the prophet has already spoken of these, saying

that "very few mortal men have remained over." Still, few as they are, there are to be survivors of the destruction of Jerusalem and Judah, and later a remnant will return from captivity to repopulate the land. (Isaiah 4:2, 3; 14:1-5) Though righthearted ones will experience dark seasons of trial, they can be sure that there will be deliverance and joy ahead. The survivors will see Jehovah's prophetic word unfold and will realize that Isaiah has been a true prophet of God. They will be filled with joy as they witness the fulfillment of the restoration prophecies. From wherever they have been scattered—be it the islands of the Mediterranean in the West, Babylon in "the region of light" (the sunrise, or the East), or any other distant place—they will praise God because they have been preserved, and they will sing: "Decoration to the Righteous One!"

No Escape From Jehovah's Judgment

15 For now, though, rejoicing is premature. Isaiah brings his contemporaries back to the present, stating: *"But I say: 'For me there is leanness, for me there is leanness! Woe to me! The treacherous dealers have dealt treacherously. Even with treachery the treacherous dealers have dealt treacherously.' Dread and the hollow and the trap are upon you, you inhabitant of the land. And it must occur that anyone fleeing from the sound of the dreaded thing will fall into the hollow, and anyone coming up from inside the hollow will be caught in the trap. For the very floodgates on high will actually be opened, and the foundations of the land will rock. The land has absolutely burst apart, the land has absolutely been shaken up, the land has absolutely been sent staggering. The land absolutely moves unsteadily like a drunken man, and it has swayed to and fro like a lookout hut. And its transgression has become heavy upon it,*

15, 16. (a) How does Isaiah feel about what will happen to his people? (b) What will befall the unfaithful inhabitants of the land?

and it must fall, so that it will not rise up again."—Isaiah 24:16b-20.

16 Isaiah is filled with grief over what will befall his people. The state of affairs around him causes feelings of sickness and woe. Treacherous ones abound and cause dread to the inhabitants of the land. When Jehovah withdraws his protection, unfaithful inhabitants of Judah will experience terror both day and night. They will be uncertain of their lives. There will be no escaping the disaster that will befall them for forsaking Jehovah's commandments and ignoring godly wisdom. (Proverbs 1:24-27) Calamity will come even though treacherous ones in the land, trying to convince the people that everything

Isaiah is filled with grief over what will befall his people

will be all right, use falsehood and deceit to lead them on a course to destruction. (Jeremiah 27:9-15) Enemies from outside will come in and plunder them and carry them away captive. All of this is very distressing to Isaiah.

17 Yet, the prophet is bound to declare that there will be

---

17. (a) Why will no escape be possible? (b) When Jehovah's judgment power is released from the heavens, what will happen to the land?

no escape. Wherever people try to flee, they will be caught. Some may escape one calamity, but they will be caught in another—there will be no security. It will be just as with a hunted animal that escapes falling into a pit only to be caught in a snare. (Compare Amos 5:18, 19.) Jehovah's judgment power will be released from the heavens and will shake the very foundations of the land. Like a drunken man, the land reels and falls, heavy with guilt and unable to rise again. (Amos 5:2) Jehovah's judgment is final. Utter destruction and ruin will befall the land.

Jehovah Will Reign in Glory

18 Isaiah's prophecy now takes on a greater scope, pointing to the final outworking of Jehovah's purpose: *"It must occur in that day that Jehovah will turn his attention upon the army of the height in the height, and upon the kings of the ground upon the ground. And they will certainly be gathered with a gathering as of prisoners into the pit, and be shut up in the dungeon; and after an abundance of days they will be given attention. And the full moon has become abashed, and the glowing sun has become ashamed, for Jehovah of armies has become king in Mount Zion and in Jerusalem and in front of his elderly men with glory."—Isaiah 24:21-23.*

19 "The army of the height" may refer to the demonic "world rulers of this darkness, . . . the wicked spirit forces in the heavenly places." (Ephesians 6:12) These have had a powerful influence on the world powers. (Daniel 10:13, 20; 1 John 5:19) Their goal is to turn people away from Jehovah and his pure worship. How well they succeed in seducing Israel to follow the corrupt practices of the nations that

_____
18, 19. (a) To what may "the army of the height" refer, and how are these gathered "in the dungeon"? (b) Likely, how will "the army of the height" be given attention "after an abundance of days"? (c) How does Jehovah give attention to "the kings of the ground"?

Neither the sun nor the moon will match Jehovah in glory

surround them and thus merit God's divine judgment! But Satan and his demons must answer to God when he finally turns his attention to them and to the rulers on earth, "the kings of the ground upon the ground," whom they have influenced to turn against God and to transgress his laws. (Revelation 16:13, 14) Speaking symbolically, Isaiah says that they will be gathered and "shut up in the dungeon." "After an abundance of days," perhaps when

Satan and his demons (but not "the kings of the ground upon the ground") are temporarily released at the end of the Thousand Year Reign of Jesus Christ, God will bring upon them the final punishment they deserve.—Revelation 20:3, 7-10.

20 This part of Isaiah's prophecy thus left the Jews with a wonderful assurance. In Jehovah's due time, he would bring about the fall of ancient Babylon and restore the Jews to their homeland. In 537 B.C.E., when he demonstrates his power and sovereignty in this way in behalf of his people, it could truly be said to them: "Your God has become king!" (Isaiah 52:7) In modern times, Jehovah 'became king' in 1914 when he installed Jesus Christ as King in His heavenly Kingdom. (Psalm 96:10) He also 'became king' in 1919 when he demonstrated the power of his kingship by liberating spiritual Israel from bondage to Babylon the Great.

21 Jehovah will again "become king" when he brings an end to Babylon the Great and the rest of this wicked system of things. (Zechariah 14:9; Revelation 19:1, 2, 19-21) Afterward, Jehovah's Kingdom rule will be so magnificent that neither the gleaming full moon at night nor the glowing sun at high noon will match it in glory. (Compare Revelation 22:5.) They will be ashamed, so to speak, to compare themselves to the glorious Jehovah of armies. Jehovah will reign supreme. His almighty power and glory will be manifest to all. (Revelation 4:8-11; 5:13, 14) What a marvelous prospect! At that time, the call of Psalm 97:1 will resound throughout the earth in its grandest fulfillment: "Jehovah himself has become king! Let the earth be joyful. Let the many islands rejoice."

---

20. In both ancient and modern times, how and when does Jehovah "become king"?
21. (a) How will 'the full moon become abashed and the glowing sun become ashamed'? (b) What resounding call will have its grandest fulfillment?

CHAPTER TWENTY-ONE

Jehovah's Hand Becomes High

Isaiah 25:1–27:13

ISAIAH has deep love for Jehovah and delights in praising him. He cries out: *"O Jehovah, you are my God. I exalt you, I laud your name."* What helps the prophet to have such fine appreciation for his Creator? A major factor is his knowledge of Jehovah and of his activities. Isaiah's next words reveal this knowledge: *"For you have done wonderful things, counsels from early times, in faithfulness, in trustworthiness." (Isaiah 25:1)* Like Joshua before him, Isaiah knows that Jehovah is faithful and trustworthy and that all his "counsels"—the things he purposes—come true.—Joshua 23:14.

2 The counsels of Jehovah include his judgment declarations against Israel's enemies. Isaiah now pronounces one of these: *"You have made a city a pile of stones, a fortified town a crumbling ruin, a dwelling tower of strangers to be no city, which will not be rebuilt even to time indefinite." (Isaiah 25:2)* What is this unnamed city? Isaiah may be referring to Ar of Moab—Moab has long been at enmity with God's people.* Or he may be referring to another, stronger city—Babylon.—Isaiah 15:1; Zephaniah 2:8, 9

3 How will Jehovah's enemies react when his counsel

---

* The name Ar probably means "City."

---

1. Why does Isaiah have appreciation for Jehovah?
2. What counsel of Jehovah does Isaiah now pronounce, and what may be the object of this counsel?
3. In what way do Jehovah's enemies glorify him?

against their strong city comes true? *"Those who are a strong people will glorify you; the town of the tyrannical nations, they will fear you."* (*Isaiah 25:3*) It is understandable that the enemies of the almighty God will fear him. How, though, do they glorify him? Will they abandon their false gods and adopt pure worship? Hardly! Rather, like Pharaoh and Nebuchadnezzar, they glorify Jehovah when they are compelled to recognize his overwhelming superiority.—Exodus 10:16, 17; 12:30-33; Daniel 4:37.

4 Today "the town of the tyrannical nations" is "the great city that has a kingdom over the kings of the earth," namely, "Babylon the Great," the world empire of false religion. (Revelation 17:5, 18) The principal part of this empire is Christendom. How do the religious leaders of Christendom glorify Jehovah? By bitterly conceding the wonderful things he has accomplished in behalf of his Witnesses. Particularly in 1919 when Jehovah restored his servants to dynamic activity after their release from spiritual captivity to Babylon the Great, these leaders "became frightened and gave glory to the God of heaven."—Revelation 11:13.*

5 Although fearsome when viewed by his enemies, Jehovah is a refuge to the meek and humble who want to serve him. Religious and political tyrants may try everything to break the faith of true worshipers, but they fail because these have absolute confidence in Jehovah. Eventually, he easily silences his opposers, doing so as if he were covering the burning desert sun with a cloud or blocking the force of a rainstorm with a wall.—*Read Isaiah 25:4, 5.*

---

* See *Revelation—Its Grand Climax At Hand!,* page 170.

---

4. What "town of the tyrannical nations" exists today, and how does even she have to glorify Jehovah?
5. How does Jehovah protect those who have absolute confidence in him?

'A Banquet for All the Peoples'

6 Like a loving father, Jehovah not only protects but also feeds his children, especially in a spiritual way. After liberating his people in 1919, he set before them a victory banquet, an abundant supply of spiritual food: *"Jehovah of armies will certainly make for all the peoples, in this mountain, a banquet of well-oiled dishes, a banquet of wine kept on the dregs, of well-oiled dishes filled with marrow, of wine kept on the dregs, filtered."—Isaiah 25:6.*

7 The banquet is spread in Jehovah's "mountain." What is this mountain? It is "the mountain of the house of Jehovah" to which all nations stream "in the final part of the days." It is Jehovah's "holy mountain," where his faithful worshipers do no harm and cause no ruin. (Isaiah 2:2; 11:9) In this elevated place of worship, Jehovah spreads his lush banquet for faithful ones. And the spiritual good things now supplied so generously foreshadow the physical good things that will be provided when God's Kingdom becomes the sole government of mankind. Then hunger will be no more. "There will come to be plenty of grain on the earth; on the top of the mountains there will be an overflow."—Psalm 72:8, 16.

8 Those who now partake of the divinely provided spiritual feast have glorious prospects. Listen to Isaiah's next words. Comparing sin and death to a suffocating "woven work," or "envelopment," he says: *"In this mountain [Jehovah] will certainly swallow up the face of the envelopment that is enveloping over all the peoples, and the woven work that is interwoven upon all the nations. He will actually swallow up death forever, and the Sovereign Lord*

6, 7. (a) What kind of feast does Jehovah spread, and for whom? (b) What does the banquet prophesied by Isaiah foreshadow?
8, 9. (a) What two great enemies of mankind will be removed? Explain. (b) What will God do to remove the reproach of his people?

Jehovah will certainly wipe the tears from all faces."—Isaiah 25:7, 8a.

9 Yes, no more sin and death! (Revelation 21:3, 4) Moreover, the lying reproach that Jehovah's servants have endured for thousands of years will also be done away with. *"The reproach of his people he will take away from all the earth, for Jehovah himself has spoken it." (Isaiah 25:8b)* How will this happen? Jehovah will remove the source of that reproach, Satan and his seed. (Revelation 20:1-3) Little wonder that God's people will be moved to exclaim: *"Look! This is our God. We have hoped in him, and he will save us. This is Jehovah. We have hoped in him. Let us be joyful and rejoice in the salvation by him."—Isaiah 25:9.*

The Haughty Are Abased

10 Jehovah saves those of his people who manifest humility. However, Israel's neighbor Moab is proud, and Jehovah detests pride. (Proverbs 16:18) Moab, therefore, is slated for humiliation. *"The hand of Jehovah will settle down on this mountain, and Moab must be trodden down in its place as when a straw heap is trodden down in a manure place. And he must slap out his hands in the midst of it as when a swimmer slaps them out to swim, and he must abase its haughtiness with the tricky movements of his hands. And the fortified city, with your high walls of security, he must lay low; he must abase it, bring it into contact with the earth, to the dust."—Isaiah 25:10-12.*

11 Jehovah's hand will "settle down" on the mountain of Moab. The result? Haughty Moab is to be slapped and trodden down as "in a manure place." In Isaiah's time, straw is trampled into piles of dung to make fertilizer; so

----

10, 11. What harsh treatment does Jehovah reserve for Moab?

"A banquet of well-oiled dishes"

Isaiah foretells humiliation for Moab, despite her high, seemingly secure walls.

12 Why does Jehovah single out Moab for such harsh counsel? The Moabites are descendants of Lot, the nephew of Abraham and a worshiper of Jehovah. Thus, they are not only neighbors of God's covenant nation but also relatives. Despite this, they have adopted false gods and manifested hard-set enmity toward Israel. They deserve their fate. In this, Moab is like the enemies of Jehovah's servants today. She is especially like Christendom, which claims to have roots in the first-century Christian congregation but which, as seen earlier, is the principal part of Babylon the Great.

A Song of Salvation

13 What of God's people? Thrilled to have Jehovah's favor and protection, they raise their voices in song. *"In that day this song will be sung in the land of Judah: 'We have a strong city. He sets salvation itself for walls and rampart. Open the gates, you men, that the righteous nation that is keeping faithful conduct may enter.'"* (Isaiah 26: 1, 2) While these words no doubt had a fulfillment in ancient times, they also have a clear fulfillment today. Jehovah's "righteous nation," spiritual Israel, is endowed with a strong, citylike organization. What a cause for rejoicing, for song!

14 What kind of people come into this "city"? The song gives the answer: *"The inclination that is well supported you [God] will safeguard in continuous peace, because it is in you that one is made to trust. Trust in Jehovah, you people, for all times, for in Jah Jehovah is the Rock of times in-*

---

12. Why is Moab singled out for Jehovah's judgment declaration?
13, 14. What "strong city" does God's people have today, and who are allowed to enter it?

definite." (Isaiah 26:3, 4) "The inclination" Jehovah supports is the desire to obey his righteous principles and to trust in him, not in the floundering commercial, political, and religious systems of the world. "Jah Jehovah" is the only reliable Rock of security. Those having full confidence in Jehovah receive his protection and enjoy "continuous peace."—Proverbs 3:5, 6; Philippians 4:6, 7.

15 What a contrast to what happens to the enemies of God's people! *"He has laid low those inhabiting the height, the elevated town. He abases it, he abases it to the earth; he brings it in touch with the dust. The foot will trample it down, the feet of the afflicted one, the steps of the lowly ones." (Isaiah 26:5, 6)* Again, Isaiah may be here referring to an "elevated town" in Moab, or he may mean some other city, such as Babylon, which is certainly elevated in haughtiness. Whatever the case, Jehovah has turned the tables on "the elevated town," and his 'lowly and afflicted ones' trample it. Today this prophecy aptly fits Babylon the Great, particularly Christendom. In 1919 this "elevated town" was forced to release Jehovah's people—a humiliating fall—and they, in turn, have taken to trampling upon their old captor. (Revelation 14:8) How? By publicly announcing

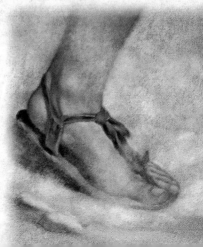

---

15. How has "the elevated town" been abased today, and in what way do "the feet of the afflicted one" trample it?

Babylon is trampled under the feet of those who were prisoners

Jehovah's coming vengeance upon her.—Revelation 8:7-12; 9:14-19.

Desiring Righteousness and Jehovah's "Memorial"

16 After this triumphant song, Isaiah reveals the depth of his own devotion and the rewards of serving the God of righteousness. (*Read Isaiah 26:7-9.*) The prophet provides a fine example of 'hoping in Jehovah' and of having a deep desire for Jehovah's *"name"* and *"memorial."* What is Jehovah's memorial? Exodus 3:15 says: "Jehovah . . . is my name to time indefinite, and this is the memorial of me to generation after generation." Isaiah cherishes Jehovah's name and all that it stands for, including His righteous standards and ways. Those who cultivate a similar love for Jehovah are assured of his blessing.—Psalm 5:8; 25:4, 5; 135:13; Hosea 12:5.

17 Not all, however, love Jehovah and his lofty standards. (*Read Isaiah 26:10.*) The wicked, even when invited, stubbornly refuse to learn righteousness in order to enter *"the land of straightforwardness,"* the land occupied by Jehovah's morally and spiritually straightforward servants. Consequently, the wicked *"will not see the eminence of Jehovah."* They will not live to enjoy the blessings that will flow to mankind after Jehovah's name has been sanctified. Even in the new world, when the whole earth will be a "land of straightforwardness," some may fail to respond to Jehovah's loving-kindness. The names of such ones will not be written in the book of life.—Isaiah 65:20; Revelation 20:12, 15.

---

16. What fine example of devotion does Isaiah set?
17. What privileges will be withheld from the wicked?

"Enter into your interior rooms"

18 *"O Jehovah, your hand has become high, but they do not behold it. They will behold and be ashamed at the zeal for your people. Yes, the very fire for your own adversaries will eat them up." (Isaiah 26:11)* In Isaiah's day, the hand of Jehovah has shown itself to be exalted when Jehovah protects his people by acting against their enemies. But most have not recognized this. Such ones, spiritually blind by choice, will eventually be forced to "behold," or acknowledge, Jehovah when they are eaten up by the fire of his zeal. (Zephaniah 1:18) God later says to Ezekiel: "They will have to know that I am Jehovah."—Ezekiel 38:23.

"Whom Jehovah Loves He Disciplines"

19 Isaiah knows that any peace and prosperity that his fellow countrymen enjoy is due to Jehovah's blessing. *"O Jehovah, you will adjudge peace to us, because even all our works you have performed for us." (Isaiah 26:12)* In spite of this and in spite of Jehovah's having set before his people the opportunity to become "a kingdom of priests and a holy nation," Judah has had a checkered history. (Exodus 19:6) Repeatedly, her people have turned to the worship of false gods. As a result, time after time they have been disciplined. Such discipline, however, is evidence of Jehovah's love because "whom Jehovah loves he disciplines." —Hebrews 12:6.

20 Often, Jehovah disciplines his people by allowing other nations, *"other masters,"* to dominate them. *(Read Isaiah 26:13.)* In 607 B.C.E., he allows the Babylonians to take them into exile. Does this benefit them? Suffering in itself does not benefit a person. However, if the sufferer learns from what happens, repents, and gives Jehovah

---

18. In what way are some in Isaiah's day blind by choice, and when will they be forced to "behold" Jehovah?
19, 20. Why and how has Jehovah disciplined his people, and who have benefited from such discipline?

exclusive devotion, *then* he benefits. (Deuteronomy 4:25-31) Do any Jews show godly repentance? Yes! Isaiah says prophetically: *"By you only shall we make mention of your name."* After their return from exile in 537 B.C.E., the Jews often need discipline for other sins, but they never again fall prey to worshiping gods of stone.

21 What of Judah's captors? *"Impotent in death, they will not rise up. Therefore you have turned your attention that you might annihilate them and destroy all mention of them." (Isaiah 26:14)* Babylon will suffer for the cruelties visited upon Jehovah's chosen nation. By means of the Medes and the Persians, Jehovah will overturn proud Babylon and free his exiled people. That great city, Babylon, will be rendered impotent, as good as dead. Eventually, she will cease to exist.

22 In the modern fulfillment, a remnant of chastened spiritual Israel was set free from Babylon the Great and restored to Jehovah's service in 1919. Revitalized, anointed Christians threw themselves into their preaching work. (Matthew 24:14) In turn, Jehovah has blessed them with increase, even bringing in a great crowd of "other sheep" to serve with them. (John 10:16) *"You have added to the nation; O Jehovah, you have added to the nation; you have glorified yourself. You have extended afar all the borders of the land. O Jehovah, during distress they have turned their attention to you; they have poured out a whisper of prayer when they had your disciplining."—Isaiah 26:15, 16.*

"They Will Rise Up"

23 Isaiah returns to the situation facing Judah while she

---

21. What will happen to those who have oppressed God's people?
22. In modern times, how have God's people been blessed?
23. (a) What outstanding demonstration of Jehovah's power occurs in 537 B.C.E.? (b) What similar demonstration occurred in 1919 C.E.?

is still captive to Babylon. He compares the nation to a woman who is in labor but who without help is unable to give birth. *(Read Isaiah 26:17, 18.)* That help comes in 537 B.C.E., and Jehovah's people return to their homeland, eager to rebuild the temple and restore true worship. In effect, the nation is raised from the dead. *"Your dead ones will live. A corpse of mine—they will rise up. Awake and cry out joyfully, you residents in the dust! For your dew is as the dew of mallows, and the earth itself will let even those impotent in death drop in birth." (Isaiah 26:19)* What a demonstration of Jehovah's power! Further, what a great demonstration there was when these words were fulfilled in a spiritual sense in 1919! (Revelation 11:7-11) And how we look forward to the time when these words are fulfilled in a literal way in the new world and those impotent in death 'hear Jesus' voice and come out' from the memorial tombs!—John 5:28, 29.

24 However, if faithful ones are to enjoy the spiritual blessings promised through Isaiah, they must obey Jehovah's commands: *"Go, my people, enter into your interior rooms, and shut your doors behind you. Hide yourself for but a moment until the denunciation passes over. For, look! Jehovah is coming forth from his place to call to account the error of the inhabitant of the land against him, and the land will certainly expose her bloodshed and will no longer cover over her killed ones." (Isaiah 26:20, 21;* compare Zephaniah 1:14.) This passage may have an initial fulfillment when the Medes and the Persians, led by King Cyrus, conquer Babylon in 539 B.C.E. According to the Greek historian Xenophon, when Cyrus enters Bab-

---

24, 25. (a) How may the Jews in 539 B.C.E. have obeyed Jehovah's command to hide themselves? (b) What may the "interior rooms" point to in modern times, and what attitude must we cultivate toward these?

ylon, he commands everyone to stay in their homes because his cavalry has "orders to cut down all whom they found out of doors." Today, the "interior rooms" of this prophecy could be closely linked with the tens of thousands of congregations of Jehovah's people around the world. Such congregations will continue to play a key role in our lives, even through "the great tribulation." (Revelation 7:14) How vital that we maintain a wholesome attitude toward the congregation and regularly associate with it!—Hebrews 10:24, 25.

25 Soon the end will come for Satan's world. How Jehovah will protect his people during that fear-inspiring time, we do not yet know. (Zephaniah 2:3) However, we do know that our survival will depend on our faith in Jehovah and our loyalty and obedience to him.

26 Looking toward that time, Isaiah prophesies: *"In that day Jehovah, with his hard and great and strong sword, will turn his attention to Leviathan, the gliding serpent, even to Leviathan, the crooked serpent, and he will certainly kill the sea monster that is in the sea." (Isaiah 27:1)* In the initial fulfillment, "Leviathan" refers to the countries to which Israel has been scattered, such as Babylon, Egypt, and Assyria. These countries will be unable to prevent the return of Jehovah's people to their homeland at the proper time. Who, though, is the modern-day Leviathan? It appears to be Satan—"the original serpent"—and his wicked system of things here on earth, his tool for warring against spiritual Israel. (Revelation 12:9, 10; 13:14, 16, 17; 18:24) "Leviathan" lost his hold on God's people in 1919, and soon he will disappear altogether when Jehovah will "certainly kill the sea monster." Meantime, nothing

---

26. What is "Leviathan" in Isaiah's day and in our day, and what happens to this "sea monster"?

"Leviathan" may try to do against Jehovah's people will have real success.—Isaiah 54:17.

"A Vineyard of Foaming Wine"

27 With another song, Isaiah now beautifully illustrates the fruitfulness of Jehovah's freed people: *"In that day*

27, 28. (a) With what has Jehovah's vineyard filled the whole earth? (b) How does Jehovah protect his vineyard?

"A Great Horn" Heralds Liberty

In 607 B.C.E., Judah's pains increase when Jehovah disciplines his wayward nation with the stroke of exile. (*Read Isaiah 27:7-11.*) The nation's error is too great to be atoned for by animal sacrifices. So, as one might scatter sheep or goats with *"a scare cry"* or might *"blast"* leaves away with a strong wind, Jehovah expels Israel from their homeland. Thereafter, even weak peoples, symbolized by the feminine sex, are able to exploit what remains in the land.

However, the time comes for Jehovah to deliver his people from captivity. He frees them as a farmer might free olives held prisoner, so to speak, on trees. *"It must occur in that day that Jehovah will beat off the fruit, from the flowing stream of the River [Euphrates] to the torrent valley of Egypt, and so you yourselves will be picked up one after the other, O sons of Israel. And it must occur in that day that there will be a blowing on a great horn, and those who are perishing in the land of Assyria and those who are dispersed in the land of Egypt will certainly come and bow down to Jehovah in the holy mountain in Jerusalem."* (*Isaiah 27:12, 13*) Following his victory in 539 B.C.E., Cyrus issues a decree freeing all the Jews in his empire, which includes those in Assyria and Egypt. (*Ezra 1:1-4*) It is as if "a great horn" sounded, echoing the anthem of freedom for God's people.

sing to her, you people: 'A vineyard of foaming wine! I, Jehovah, am safeguarding her. Every moment I shall water her. In order that no one may turn his attention against her, I shall safeguard her even night and day.'" (*Isaiah 27:2, 3*) The remnant of spiritual Israel and their hardworking associates have indeed filled the entire earth with spiritual produce. What a cause for celebration—for song! All credit goes to Jehovah, the one lovingly attending to his vineyard.—Compare John 15:1-8.

28 Truly, Jehovah's earlier anger has been replaced by joy! *"There is no rage that I have. Who will give me thornbushes and weeds in the battle? I will step on such. I will set such on fire at the same time. Otherwise let him take hold of my stronghold, let him make peace with me; peace let him make with me."* (Isaiah 27:4, 5) To ensure that his vines continue to produce an abundance of "foaming wine," Jehovah crushes and consumes as with fire any weedlike influence that could corrupt his vineyard. Hence, let no one endanger the welfare of the Christian congregation! Rather, let all 'take hold of Jehovah's stronghold,' seeking his favor and protection. In so doing, they make peace with God—something so important that Isaiah mentions it twice. The result? *"In the coming days Jacob will take root, Israel will put forth blossoms and actually sprout; and they will simply fill the surface of the productive land with produce."* (Isaiah 27:6)* What wonderful evidence of Jehovah's power the fulfillment of this verse is! Since 1919, anointed Christians have filled the earth with "produce," nourishing spiritual food. As a result, they have come to be joined by millions of loyal other sheep, who together with them "are rendering [God] sacred service day and night." (Revelation 7:15) In the midst of a corrupt world, these joyfully maintain his elevated standards. And Jehovah continues to bless them with increase. May we never lose sight of the grand privilege of partaking of "produce" and sharing it with others through our own shout of praise!

---

* Isaiah 27:7-13 is discussed in the box on page 285.

CHAPTER TWENTY-TWO

Isaiah Foretells Jehovah's 'Strange Deed'

Isaiah 28:1–29:24

FOR a brief moment, Israel and Judah feel secure. Their leaders have forged political alliances with larger, more powerful nations, in an effort to find safety in a dangerous world. Samaria, the capital of Israel, has turned to neighboring Syria, while Jerusalem, the capital of Judah, has rested her hope on ruthless Assyria.

2 In addition to putting their trust in new political allies, some in the northern kingdom may expect Jehovah to protect them—despite their continuing to use golden calves in worship. Judah is likewise convinced that she can count on Jehovah's protection. After all, is not Jehovah's temple located in Jerusalem, their capital city? But there are unexpected events ahead for both nations. Jehovah inspires Isaiah to foretell developments that will seem truly strange to his wayward people. And his words contain vital lessons for everyone today.

"The Drunkards of Ephraim"

3 Isaiah begins his prophecy with startling words: *"Woe to the eminent crown of the drunkards of Ephraim, and the fading blossom of its decoration of beauty that is upon the head of the fertile valley of those overpowered by wine! Look! Jehovah has someone strong and vigorous. Like a thunderous storm of hail, . . . he will certainly do*

1, 2. Why do Israel and Judah feel secure?
3, 4. Of what is the northern kingdom of Israel proud?

a casting down to the earth with force. With the feet the eminent crowns of the drunkards of Ephraim will be trampled down."—Isaiah 28:1-3.

4 Ephraim, the most prominent of the ten northern tribes, has come to stand for the entire kingdom of Israel. Its capital, Samaria, enjoys a beautiful and commanding location at "the head of the fertile valley." Ephraim's leaders are proud of their "eminent crown" of independence from the Davidic kingship in Jerusalem. But they are "drunkards," spiritually inebriated because of their alliance with Syria against Judah. Everything they cherish is about to be trampled under the feet of invaders.—Compare Isaiah 29:9.

5 Ephraim does not realize its precarious position. Isaiah continues: *"The fading flower of its decoration of beauty that is upon the head of the fertile valley must become like the early fig before summer, that, when the seer sees it, while it is yet in his palm, he swallows it down." (Isaiah 28:4)* Ephraim will fall into the hand of Assyria, a sweet morsel to be consumed in a single bite. Is there no hope, then? Well, as is so often the case, Isaiah's judgment prophecies are tempered with hope. Even though the nation falls, faithful individuals will survive, with Jehovah's help. *"Jehovah of armies will become as a crown of decoration and as a garland of beauty to the ones remaining over of his people, and as a spirit of justice to the one sitting in the judgment, and as mightiness to those turning away the battle from the gate."—Isaiah 28:5, 6.*

"They Have Gone Astray"

6 The day of reckoning for Samaria comes in 740 B.C.E.

5. What is Israel's precarious position, but what hope does Isaiah hold out?
6. When does Israel meet her demise, but why should Judah not gloat?

Christendom has relied on alliances with human rulers rather than on God

when the Assyrians devastate the land and the northern kingdom ceases to exist as an independent nation. What about Judah? Her land will be invaded by Assyria, and later Babylon will destroy her capital city. But during Isaiah's lifetime, Judah's temple and priesthood will remain in operation and her prophets will continue to prophesy. Should Judah gloat over the coming demise of her northern neighbor? Certainly not! Jehovah will also settle accounts with Judah and her leaders for their disobedience and lack of faith.

7 Directing his message to Judah, Isaiah continues: **"And**

7. In what way are Judah's leaders drunk, and with what results?

these also—because of wine they have gone astray and because of intoxicating liquor they have wandered about. Priest and prophet—they have gone astray because of intoxicating liquor, they have become confused as a result of the wine, they have wandered about as a result of the intoxicating liquor; they have gone astray in their seeing, they have reeled as to decision. For the tables themselves have all become full of filthy vomit—there is no place without it." (Isaiah 28:7, 8) How disgusting! Literal drunkenness in God's house would be bad enough. But these priests and prophets are spiritually intoxicated—their minds beclouded by overconfidence in human alliances. They have deceived themselves into thinking that their course is the only practical one, perhaps believing that they now have a backup plan in case Jehovah's protection proves inadequate. In their spiritually inebriated state, these religious leaders spew out revolting, unclean expressions that betray their grievous lack of genuine faith in God's promises.

8 How do Judah's leaders react to Jehovah's warning? They mock Isaiah, accusing him of speaking to them as if they were infants: *"Whom will one instruct in knowledge, and whom will one make understand what has been heard? Those who have been weaned from the milk, those moved away from the breasts? For it is 'command upon command, command upon command, measuring line upon measuring line, measuring line upon measuring line, here a little, there a little.'" (Isaiah 28:9, 10)* How repetitious and strange Isaiah sounds to them! He keeps repeating himself, saying: 'This is what Jehovah has commanded! This is what Jehovah has commanded! This

---

8. What is the response to Isaiah's message?

Jehovah carries out his 'strange deed' when he allows Babylon to destroy Jerusalem

is Jehovah's standard! This is Jehovah's standard!'* But Jehovah will soon *"speak"* to the inhabitants of Judah by means of action. He will send against them the armies of Babylon—foreigners who really do speak a different language. Those armies will certainly carry out Jehovah's "command upon command," and Judah will fall.—*Read Isaiah 28:11-13.*

Spiritual Drunkards Today

9 Were Isaiah's prophecies fulfilled only on ancient Israel and Judah? By no means! Both Jesus and Paul quoted his words and applied them to the nation of their day. (Isaiah 29:10, 13; Matthew 15:8, 9; Romans 11:8) Today, too, a situation has arisen like that of Isaiah's day.

10 This time, it is the religious leaders of Christendom who put their faith in politics. They stagger about unsteadily, like the drunkards of Israel and Judah, interfering in political matters, rejoicing at being consulted by the so-called great ones of this world. Instead of speaking pure Bible truth, they speak uncleanness. Their spiritual vision is blurred, and they are not safe guides for mankind.—Matthew 15:14.

11 How do the leaders of Christendom react when Jehovah's Witnesses draw their attention to the only true hope, God's Kingdom? They do not understand. To them, the Witnesses seem to be babbling repetitiously, like babes. The religious leaders look down on these messengers and

---

* In the original Hebrew, Isaiah 28:10 is a repetitious rhyme, rather like a child's nursery rhyme. Thus, Isaiah's message sounded repetitious and childish to the religious leaders.

9, 10. When and how have Isaiah's words had meaning for later generations?
11. How do the leaders of Christendom react to the good news of God's Kingdom?

mock them. Like the Jews of Jesus' day, they do not want God's Kingdom nor do they want their flocks to hear about it. (Matthew 23:13) Hence, they are put on notice that Jehovah will not always speak by means of his harmless messengers. The time will come when those who do not subject themselves to God's Kingdom will be "broken and ensnared and caught," yes, utterly destroyed.

"A Covenant With Death"

12 Isaiah continues his pronouncement: *"You men have said: 'We have concluded a covenant with Death; and with Sheol we have effected a vision; the overflowing flash flood, in case it should pass through, will not come to us, for we have made a lie our refuge and in falsehood we have concealed ourselves.'"* (Isaiah 28:14, 15) Judah's leaders brag that their political alliances insulate them from defeat. They feel that they have made "a covenant with Death" to leave them alone. But their hollow refuge will not shield them. Their alliances are a lie, a falsehood. Similarly today, Christendom's close relationship with the leaders of the world will not protect her when Jehovah's time for her accounting comes. Indeed, it will prove to be her undoing. —Revelation 17:16, 17.

13 Where, then, should these religious leaders be looking? Isaiah now records Jehovah's promise: *"Here I am laying as a foundation in Zion a stone, a tried stone, the precious corner of a sure foundation. No one exercising faith will get panicky. And I will make justice the measuring line and righteousness the leveling instrument; and the hail must sweep away the refuge of a lie, and the waters themselves will flood out the very place of concealment."* (Isaiah 28:16, 17) Not long after Isaiah speaks these

---

12. What is Judah's supposed "covenant with Death"?
13. Who is the "tried stone," and how has Christendom rejected him?

words, faithful King Hezekiah is enthroned in Zion, and his kingdom is saved, not by neighboring allies, but by Jehovah's intervention. However, these inspired words are not fulfilled in Hezekiah. The apostle Peter, quoting Isaiah's words, showed that Jesus Christ, a distant descendant of Hezekiah, is the "tried stone" and that no one exercising faith in Him need have any fear. (1 Peter 2:6) How sad that the leaders of Christendom, while calling themselves Christian, have done what Jesus refused to do! They have sought prominence and power in this world rather than wait on Jehovah to bring about his Kingdom under Jesus Christ the King.—Matthew 4:8-10.

14 When "the overflowing flash flood" of Babylon's armies passes through the land, Jehovah will expose Judah's political refuge as the lie that it is. *"Your covenant with Death will certainly be dissolved,"* says Jehovah. *"The overflowing flash flood, when it passes through—you must also become for it a trampling place. As often as it passes through, . . . it must become nothing but a reason for quaking to make others understand what has been heard." (Isaiah 28:18, 19)* Yes, there is a powerful lesson to be learned from what happens to those who claim to serve Jehovah but who instead put their confidence in alliances with the nations.

15 Consider the position in which these leaders of Judah now find themselves. *"The couch has proved too short for stretching oneself on, and the woven sheet itself is too narrow when wrapping oneself up." (Isaiah 28:20)* It is as if they were to lie down to take their ease, but in vain. Either their feet stick out in the cold or they pull up their legs and the cover is too narrow to wrap up in to keep warm. This was the uncomfortable situation in Isaiah's day. And it is

---

14. When will Judah's "covenant with Death" be dissolved?
15. How does Isaiah illustrate the inadequacy of Judah's protection?

the situation today for any who put their trust in Christendom's refuge of a lie. How disgusting that as a result of involving themselves in politics, some of Christendom's religious leaders have found themselves implicated in such terrible atrocities as ethnic cleansing and genocide!

Jehovah's 'Strange Deed'

16 The final outcome of affairs will be completely contrary to what Judah's religious leaders are hoping for. Jehovah will do something strange to the spiritual drunkards of Judah. *"Jehovah will rise up just as at Mount Perazim, he will be agitated just as in the low plain near Gibeon, that he may do his deed—his deed is strange—and that he may work his work—his work is unusual." (Isaiah 28:21)* In the days of King David, Jehovah gave his people notable victories over the Philistines at Mount Perazim and on the low plain of Gibeon. (1 Chronicles 14:10-16) In the days of Joshua, he even caused the sun to stand still over Gibeon so that the victory of Israel over the Amorites could be complete. (Joshua 10:8-14) That was most unusual! Now Jehovah will fight again but this time against those who profess to be his people. Could anything be more strange or unusual? Not in view of the fact that Jerusalem is the center of Jehovah's worship and the city of Jehovah's anointed king. Up to now, the royal house of David in Jerusalem has never been overthrown. Nevertheless, Jehovah will surely carry out his 'strange deed.'—Compare Habakkuk 1:5-7.

17 Therefore, Isaiah cautions: *"Do not show yourselves scoffers, in order that your bands may not grow strong, for there is an extermination, even something decided upon, that I have heard of from the Sovereign Lord, Jehovah of armies, for all the land." (Isaiah 28:22)* Although the

---

16. What is Jehovah's 'strange deed,' and why is this work unusual?
17. What effect will scoffing have on the fulfillment of Isaiah's prophecy?

leaders scoff, Isaiah's message is true. He has heard it from
Jehovah, with whom those leaders are in a covenant relationship. Similarly today, the religious leaders of Christendom scoff when they hear of Jehovah's 'strange deed.' They
even rant and rave. But the message Jehovah's Witnesses
proclaim is true. It is found in the Bible, a book that those
leaders claim to represent.

18 As for sincere individuals who do not follow those leaders, Jehovah will readjust them and restore them to his favor. **(Read Isaiah 28:23-29.)** Just as a farmer uses gentler
methods to thresh a more delicate grain, such as cumin,
so Jehovah adjusts his discipline according to the individual and the circumstances. He is never arbitrary or heavy-
handed but acts with a view to the potential rehabilitation
of erring ones. Yes, if individuals respond to Jehovah's appeal, there is hope. Similarly today, while the fate of Christendom as a whole is sealed, any individual who subjects
himself to Jehovah's Kingdom can avoid the coming ad-
verse judgment.

Woe to Jerusalem!

19 What, though, is Jehovah now speaking about? *"Woe
to Ariel, to Ariel, the town where David encamped! Add
year upon year, you people; let the festivals run the round.
And I have to make things tight for Ariel, and there must
come to be mourning and lamentation, and she must become to me as the altar hearth of God."* (Isaiah 29:1, 2)
"Ariel" possibly means "The Altar Hearth of God," and
here it evidently refers to Jerusalem. That is where the temple with its altar of sacrifice is located. The Jews follow the
routine of holding festivals and offering sacrifices there,

---

18. How does Isaiah illustrate Jehovah's balance when administering discipline?
19. In what way is Jerusalem to become an "altar hearth," and when
and how does this take place?

but Jehovah takes no pleasure in their worship. (Hosea 6:6) Rather, he decrees that the city itself is to become an "altar hearth" in a different sense. Like an altar, it will run with blood and be subjected to fire. Jehovah even describes how this will happen: *"I must encamp on all sides against you, and I must lay siege to you with a palisade and raise up against you siegeworks. And you must become low so that you will speak from the very earth, and as from the dust your saying will sound low." (Isaiah 29:3, 4)* This is fulfilled for Judah and Jerusalem in 607 B.C.E. when the Babylonian army besieges and destroys the city and burns the temple. Jerusalem is brought down as low as the ground on which she was built.

20 Before that fateful time, Judah does from time to time have a king who obeys Jehovah's Law. What then? Jehovah fights for his people. Even though the enemy may cover the land, they become like *"fine powder"* and *"chaff."* In his own due time, Jehovah disperses them *"with thunder and with quaking and with a great sound, storm wind and tempest, and the flame of a devouring fire."—Isaiah 29:5, 6.*

21 Hostile armies may eagerly anticipate sacking Jerusalem and gorging themselves on the spoils of war. But they are in for a rude awakening! Like a starving man who dreams that he is feasting and then wakes up as hungry as ever, the enemies of Judah will not enjoy the feast that they so eagerly anticipate. *(Read Isaiah 29:7, 8.)* Consider what happens to the Assyrian army under Sennacherib when it threatens Jerusalem in faithful King Hezekiah's day. (Isaiah, chapters 36 and 37) In one night, without a human hand being raised, the fear-inspiring Assyrian war machine is turned back—185,000 of its valiant warriors

20. What will be the ultimate fate of God's enemies?
21. Explain the illustration at Isaiah 29:7, 8.

dead! Dreams of conquest will again be frustrated when the war machine of Gog of Magog gears up against Jehovah's people in the near future.—Ezekiel 38:10-12; 39:6, 7.

22 At the time that Isaiah utters this portion of his prophecy, the leaders of Judah do not have faith like that of Hezekiah. They have drunk themselves into a spiritual stupor by means of their alliances with ungodly nations. *"Linger, you men, and be amazed; blind yourselves, and be blinded. They have become intoxicated, but not with wine; they have moved unsteadily, but not because of intoxicating liquor." (Isaiah 29:9)* Spiritually drunk, these leaders are unable to discern the import of the vision given to Jehovah's true prophet. Isaiah states: *"Upon you men Jehovah has poured a spirit of deep sleep; and he closes your eyes, the prophets, and he has covered even your heads, the visionaries. And for you men the vision of everything becomes*

---

22. How does Judah's spiritual drunkenness affect her?

*Those who used to be
spiritually deaf can "hear" the Word of God*

like the words of the book that has been sealed up, which they give to someone knowing the writing, saying: 'Read this out loud, please,' and he has to say: 'I am unable, for it is sealed up'; and the book must be given to someone that does not know writing, somebody saying: 'Read this out loud, please,' and he has to say: 'I do not know writing at all.'"—Isaiah 29:10-12.

23 Judah's religious leaders profess to be spiritually discreet, but they have left Jehovah. They teach instead their own twisted ideas of right and wrong, justifying their faithless and immoral activities and their leading the people into God's disfavor. By means of "something wonderful"—his 'strange deed'—Jehovah will call them to account for their hypocrisy. He says: *"For the reason that this people have come near with their mouth, and they have glorified me merely with their lips, and they have removed their heart itself far away from me, and their fear toward me becomes men's commandment that is being taught, therefore here I am, the One that will act wonderfully again with this people, in a wonderful manner and with something wonderful; and the wisdom of their wise men must perish, and the very understanding of their discreet men will conceal itself."* (Isaiah 29:13, 14) Judah's self-styled wisdom and understanding will perish when Jehovah maneuvers things for her entire apostate religious system to be wiped out by the Babylonian World Power. The same thing happened in the first century after the self-styled wise leaders of the Jews led the nation astray. Something similar will happen in our own day to Christendom.—Matthew 15:8, 9; Romans 11:8.

24 For now, however, the bragging leaders of Judah believe that they are clever enough to get away with their perversion of true worship. Are they? Isaiah tears off their

---

23. Why will Jehovah call Judah to account, and how will he do so?
24. How do the Judeans betray their lack of godly fear?

mask, exposing them as having no genuine fear of God and thus no true wisdom: *"Woe to those who are going very deep in concealing counsel from Jehovah himself, and whose deeds have occurred in a dark place, while they say: 'Who is seeing us, and who is knowing of us?' The perversity of you men! Should the potter himself be accounted just like the clay? For should the thing made say respecting its maker: 'He did not make me'? And does the very thing formed actually say respecting its former: 'He showed no understanding'?"* (*Isaiah 29:15, 16;* compare Psalm 111: 10.) No matter how well concealed they think they are, they stand "naked and openly exposed" to the eyes of God. —Hebrews 4:13.

"Deaf Ones Will Certainly Hear"

25 However, there is salvation for individuals who exercise faith. (*Read Isaiah 29:17-24;* compare Luke 7:22.) *"Deaf ones"* will *"hear the words of the book,"* the message from God's Word. Yes, this is not a healing of physical deafness. It is a spiritual healing. Isaiah once again points forward to the establishment of the Messianic Kingdom and the restoration of true worship on earth by the Messiah's rule. This has taken place in our time, and millions of sincere ones are allowing themselves to be corrected by Jehovah and are learning to praise him. What a thrilling fulfillment! Ultimately, the day will come when everyone, every breathing thing, will praise Jehovah and sanctify his holy name.—Psalm 150:6.

26 What do such "deaf ones" who hear God's Word today learn? That all Christians, especially those to whom the congregation looks as examples, must scrupulously avoid 'going astray because of intoxicating liquor.' (Isaiah 28:7) Further, we must never tire of hearing God's reminders,

---

25. In what sense will "deaf ones" hear?
26. What spiritual reminders do "deaf ones" hear today?

which help us to have a spiritual viewpoint of all things. While Christians are properly subject to governmental authorities and look to them to provide certain services, salvation comes, not from the secular world, but from Jehovah God. Also, we must never forget that like the judgment on apostate Jerusalem, God's judgment on this generation is inescapable. With Jehovah's help we can continue to proclaim his warning despite opposition, as did Isaiah. —Isaiah 28:14, 22; Matthew 24:34; Romans 13:1-4.

27 Elders and parents can learn from the way Jehovah administers discipline, always seeking to restore wrongdoers to God's favor, not merely to punish them. (Isaiah 28:26-29; compare Jeremiah 30:11.) And all of us, including young people, are reminded of how vital it is to be serving Jehovah from the heart, not just going through the motions of being a Christian in order to please men. (Isaiah 29:13) We must show that unlike the faithless inhabitants of Judah, we have a wholesome fear of Jehovah and a profound respect for him. (Isaiah 29:16) Moreover, we need to show that we are willing to be corrected by and to learn from Jehovah.—Isaiah 29:24.

28 How important it is to have faith and confidence in Jehovah and in his way of doing things! (Compare Psalm 146:3.) To most, the warning message we preach will sound childish. The prospective destruction of an organization, Christendom, that claims to serve God is a strange, an unusual, concept. But Jehovah will accomplish his 'strange deed.' Of that, there can be no doubt. Hence, through the last days of this system of things, God's servants put full trust in his Kingdom and in his appointed King, Jesus Christ. They know that Jehovah's saving acts—performed along with his 'unusual work'—will bring eternal blessings to all obedient mankind.

---

27. What lessons can Christians learn from Isaiah's prophecy?
28. How do Jehovah's servants view his saving acts?

CHAPTER TWENTY-THREE

Keep in Expectation of Jehovah

Isaiah 30:1-33

IN ISAIAH chapter 30, we read further divine pronouncements against the wicked. Nevertheless, this part of Isaiah's prophecy highlights some of Jehovah's heartwarming qualities. In fact, Jehovah's characteristics are described in such vivid terms that we can, as it were, see his comforting presence, hear his guiding voice, and feel his healing touch.—Isaiah 30:20, 21, 26.

2 Even so, Isaiah's countrymen, the apostate inhabitants of Judah, refuse to return to Jehovah. Instead, they put their trust in man. How does Jehovah feel about this? And how does this part of Isaiah's prophecy help Christians today to keep in expectation of Jehovah? (Isaiah 30:18) Let us find out.

Folly and Fatality

3 For some time the leaders of Judah have been scheming in secret to find a way to avoid coming under the yoke of Assyria. However, Jehovah has been watching. Now he exposes their scheme: " 'Woe to the stubborn sons,' is the utterance of Jehovah, 'those disposed to carry out counsel, but not that from me; and to pour out a libation, but not

---

1, 2. (a) What does Isaiah chapter 30 contain? (b) What questions will we now consider?
3. What scheme is exposed by Jehovah?

with my spirit, in order to add sin to sin; those who are setting out to go down to Egypt.' "—Isaiah 30:1, 2a.

4 What a shock for those scheming leaders to hear their plan revealed! Traveling to Egypt in order to make an alliance with her is more than hostile action against Assyria; it is rebellion against Jehovah God. In the time of King David, the nation looked to Jehovah as a stronghold and took refuge 'in the shadow of his wings.' (Psalm 27:1; 36:7) Now they *"take shelter in the stronghold of Pharaoh"* and *"take refuge in the shadow of Egypt."* (Isaiah 30:2b) They have put Egypt in the place of God! What treason!—*Read Isaiah 30:3-5.*

5 As if to answer any suggestion that the mission to Egypt is merely a casual visit, Isaiah gives more details. *"The pronouncement against the beasts of the south: Through the land of distress and hard conditions, of the lion and the leopard growling, of the viper and the flying fiery snake, on the shoulders of full-grown asses they carry their resources, and on the humps of camels their supplies."* (Isaiah 30:6a) Clearly, the journey is well planned. Envoys organize a caravan of camels and asses, which they load with costly goods and lead down to Egypt through a barren wilderness infested with growling lions and venomous snakes. Finally, the envoys reach their destination and hand their treasures to the Egyptians. They have bought protection—or so they think. However, Jehovah says: *"In behalf of the people they will prove of no benefit. And the Egyptians are mere vanity, and they will help simply for nothing. Therefore I have called this one: 'Rahab—they are for sitting still.' "* (Isaiah 30:6b, 7) "Rahab," a "sea

---

4. How have God's rebellious people put Egypt in the place of God?
5, 6. (a) Why is the alliance with Egypt a fatal mistake? (b) What earlier journey made by God's people highlights the foolishness of this trip to Egypt?

monster," came to symbolize Egypt. (Isaiah 51:9, 10) She promises everything but does nothing. Judah's alliance with her is a fatal mistake.

6 As Isaiah describes the journey of the envoys, his listeners may remember a similar journey made in the days of Moses. Their forefathers walked through that very same "fear-inspiring wilderness." (Deuteronomy 8:14-16) In Moses' day, however, the Israelites were traveling away from Egypt and out of bondage. This time the envoys travel to Egypt and, effectively, into subjection. What folly! May we never make such a bad decision and exchange our spiritual freedom for slavery!—Compare Galatians 5:1.

Opposition to the Prophet's Message

7 Jehovah tells Isaiah to write down the message that he has just delivered so that *"it may serve for a future day, for a witness to time indefinite." (Isaiah 30:8)* Jehovah's disapproval of putting alliances with man above reliance on Him must be recorded for the benefit of future generations—including our generation today. (2 Peter 3:1-4) But there is a more immediate need for a written record. *"It is a rebellious people, untruthful sons, sons who have been unwilling to hear the law of Jehovah." (Isaiah 30:9)* The people have rejected God's counsel. Hence, it must be written down so that later they cannot deny that they received a proper warning.—Proverbs 28:9; Isaiah 8:1, 2.

8 Isaiah now offers an example of the people's rebellious attitude. They *"have said to the ones seeing, 'You must not*

7. Why does Jehovah have Isaiah write down His warning to Judah?
8, 9. (a) In what way do the leaders of Judah try to corrupt Jehovah's prophets? (b) How does Isaiah demonstrate that he will not be intimidated?

In Moses' day, the Israelites escaped from Egypt.
In Isaiah's day, Judah goes to Egypt for help

see,' and to the ones having visions, 'You must not envision for us any straightforward things. Speak to us smooth things; envision deceptive things.'" (Isaiah 30:10) By ordering faithful prophets to stop speaking what is "straightforward," or true, and to speak instead what is "smooth" and "deceptive," or false, the leaders of Judah show that they want to have their ears tickled. They want to be praised, not condemned. In their opinion, any prophet not willing to prophesy according to their taste should *"turn aside from the way; deviate from the path."* (Isaiah 30:11a) He should either speak ear-pleasing things or stop preaching altogether!

9 Isaiah's opponents insist: *"Cause the Holy One of Israel to cease just on account of us."* (Isaiah 30:11b) Let Isaiah stop speaking in the name of Jehovah, "the Holy One of Israel"! This very title irritates them because Jehovah's exalted standards show up their contemptible condition. How does Isaiah react? He declares: *"This is what the Holy One of Israel has said."* (Isaiah 30:12a) Without hesitation, Isaiah speaks the very words his opposers hate to hear. He will not be intimidated. What a fine example for us! When it comes to proclaiming God's message, Christians must never compromise. (Acts 5:27-29) Like Isaiah, they keep on proclaiming: 'This is what Jehovah has said'!

The Consequences of Rebellion

10 Judah has rejected God's word, trusted in a lie, and relied upon *"what is devious."* (Isaiah 30:12b) What will be the consequences? Jehovah, instead of leaving the scene as the nation wishes, will cause the nation to cease to exist! This will happen suddenly and completely, as Isaiah stresses with an illustration. The rebelliousness of the nation is like *"a broken section about to fall down, a swelling*

10, 11. What will be the consequences of Judah's revolt?

out in a highly raised wall, the breakdown of which may come suddenly, in an instant." (Isaiah 30:13) Just as a growing bulge in a high wall will eventually cause the wall to collapse, so the increasing rebelliousness of Isaiah's contemporaries will cause the collapse of the nation.

11 With another illustration Isaiah shows the completeness of the coming destruction: *"One will certainly break it as in the breaking of a large jar of the potters, crushed to pieces without one's sparing it, so that there cannot be found among its crushed pieces a fragment of earthenware with which to rake the fire from the fireplace or to skim water from a marshy place." (Isaiah 30:14)* Judah's destruction will be so complete that nothing of value will remain—not even a potsherd big enough to scoop hot ashes from a fireplace or to skim water from a marsh. What a shameful end! The coming destruction of those who rebel against true worship today will be equally sudden and complete.—Hebrews 6:4-8; 2 Peter 2:1.

Jehovah's Offer Rejected

12 For Isaiah's listeners, though, destruction is not inevitable. There is a way out. The prophet explains: *"This is what the Sovereign Lord Jehovah, the Holy One of Israel, has said: 'By coming back and resting you people will be saved. Your mightiness will prove to be simply in keeping undisturbed and in trustfulness.' " (Isaiah 30:15a)* Jehovah is ready to save his people—if they show faith by "resting," or refraining from trying to secure salvation through human alliances, and by "keeping undisturbed," or demonstrating trust in God's protective power by not giving way to fear. *"But,"* Isaiah tells the people, *"you were not willing."—Isaiah 30:15b.*

---

12. How can the people of Judah avoid destruction?

13 Isaiah then elaborates: *"And you proceeded to say: 'No, but on horses we shall flee!' That is why you will flee. 'And on swift horses we shall ride!' That is why those pursuing you will show themselves swift."* (*Isaiah 30:16*) The Judeans think that swift horses, rather than Jehovah, will mean their salvation. (Deuteronomy 17:16; Proverbs 21: 31) However, counters the prophet, their trust will be an illusion because their enemies will overtake them. Even large numbers will not help them. *"A thousand will tremble on account of the rebuke of one; on account of the rebuke of five you will flee."* (*Isaiah 30:17a*) The armies of Judah will panic and flee at the shout of just a handful of the enemy.* In the end, only a remnant will remain, left alone, *"like a mast on the top of a mountain and like a signal on a hill."* (*Isaiah 30:17b*) True to the prophecy, when Jerusalem is destroyed in 607 B.C.E., only a remnant survive.—Jeremiah 25:8-11.

Comfort Amid Condemnation

14 While these sobering words are still echoing in the ears of Isaiah's listeners, the tone of his message changes. Threat of disaster gives way to a promise of blessings. *"Therefore Jehovah will keep in expectation of showing you favor, and therefore he will rise up to show you mercy. For Jehovah is a God of judgment. Happy are all those keeping in expectation of him."* (*Isaiah 30:18*) What heartening words! Jehovah is a compassionate Father who yearns to

---

* Note that if Judah had been faithful, the very opposite could have happened.—Leviticus 26:7, 8.

---

13. In what do the leaders of Judah put their confidence, and is such confidence justified?
14, 15. What comfort do the words of Isaiah 30:18 offer to the inhabitants of Judah in ancient times and to true Christians today?

help his children. He delights in showing mercy.—Psalm 103:13; Isaiah 55:7.

15 These reassuring words apply to the Jewish remnant who are mercifully allowed to survive the destruction of Jerusalem in 607 B.C.E. and to the few who return to the Promised Land in 537 B.C.E. However, the prophet's words also comfort Christians today. We are reminded that Jehovah will "rise up" in our behalf, bringing an end to this wicked world. Faithful worshipers can be confident that Jehovah—"a God of judgment"—will not allow Satan's world to exist for one day longer than justice requires. Therefore, "those keeping in expectation of him" have much reason to be happy.

Jehovah Comforts His People by Answering Prayers

16 Some, though, may feel discouraged because deliverance has not come as soon as they had hoped. (Proverbs 13:12; 2 Peter 3:9) May they draw comfort from Isaiah's next words, which highlight a special aspect of Jehovah's personality. *"When the very people in Zion will dwell in Jerusalem, you will by no means weep. He will without fail show you favor at the sound of your outcry; as soon as he hears it he will actually answer you." (Isaiah 30:19)* Isaiah conveys tenderness in these words by switching from the plural "you" in verse 18 to the singular "you" in verse 19. When Jehovah comforts distressed ones, he treats each person individually. As a Father, he does not ask a discouraged son, 'Why can't you be strong like your brother?' (Galatians 6:4) Instead, he listens attentively to each one. In fact, "as soon as he hears it he will actually answer." What reassuring words! Discouraged ones can be greatly strengthened if they pray to Jehovah.—Psalm 65:2.

---

16. How does Jehovah comfort discouraged ones?

Hear God's Guiding Voice by Reading His Word

17 As Isaiah continues his address, he reminds his listeners that distress will come. The people will receive *"bread in the form of distress and water in the form of oppression."* *(Isaiah 30:20a)* The distress and oppression that they will experience when under siege will become as familiar as bread and water. Even so, Jehovah is ready to come to the rescue of righthearted ones. *"Your Grand Instructor will no longer hide himself, and your eyes must become eyes seeing your Grand Instructor. And your own ears will hear a word behind you saying: 'This is the way. Walk in it, you people,' in case you people should go to the right or in case you should go to the left."—Isaiah 30:20b, 21.**

18 Jehovah is the "Grand Instructor." He has no equal as a teacher. How, though, can people 'see' and "hear" him? Jehovah reveals himself through his prophets, whose words are recorded in the Bible. (Amos 3:6, 7) Today, when faithful worshipers read the Bible, it is as if God's fatherly voice is telling them the way to go and urging them to readjust their course of conduct so as to walk in it. Each Christian should listen carefully as Jehovah speaks through the pages of the Bible and through Bible-based publications provided by "the faithful and discreet slave." (Matthew 24:45-47) Let each one apply himself to Bible reading, for 'it means his life.'—Deuteronomy 32:46, 47; Isaiah 48:17.

Contemplate Future Blessings

19 Those responding to the voice of the Grand In-

---

* This is the only place in the Bible where Jehovah is called "Grand Instructor."

17, 18. Even in difficult times, how does Jehovah provide guidance?
19, 20. What blessings are in store for those who respond to the voice of the Grand Instructor?

"Upon every elevated hill there must come to be streams"

structor will scatter their graven images, viewing them as something disgusting. **(Read Isaiah 30:22.)** Then, those responsive ones will enjoy wonderful blessings. These are described by Isaiah, as recorded in Isaiah 30:23-26, a delightful restoration prophecy that has its initial fulfillment when a Jewish remnant returns from captivity in 537 B.C.E. Today, this prophecy helps us to see the marvelous blessings that the Messiah brings about in the spiritual paradise now and the literal Paradise to come.

20 *"He will certainly give the rain for your seed with which you sow the ground, and as the produce of the ground bread, which must become fat and oily. Your livestock will graze in that day in a spacious pasture. And the cattle and the full-grown asses cultivating the ground will eat fodder seasoned with sorrel, which was winnowed with the shovel and with the fork."* (Isaiah 30:23, 24) "Fat and oily" bread—food rich in nourishment—will be man's daily staple. The land will produce so abundantly that even the animals will benefit. Livestock will be fed "fodder seasoned with sorrel"—tasty fodder reserved for rare occasions. This food has even been "winnowed"—a treatment normally

reserved for grain intended for human consumption. What delightful details Isaiah presents here to illustrate the richness of Jehovah's blessings on faithful mankind!

21 *"Upon every high mountain and upon every elevated hill there must come to be streams." (Isaiah 30:25a)** Isaiah presents an apt word picture emphasizing the completeness of Jehovah's blessings. No shortage of water—a precious commodity that will flow not only in the lowlands but on every mountain, even "upon every high mountain and upon every elevated hill." Yes, hunger will be a thing of the past. (Psalm 72:16) Further, the prophet's

---

* Isaiah 30:25b reads: "In the day of the big slaughter when the towers fall." In the initial fulfillment, this may refer to the fall of Babylon, which opened the way for Israel to enjoy the blessings foretold at Isaiah 30:18-26. (See paragraph 19.) It may also refer to the destruction at Armageddon, which will make possible the grandest fulfillment of these blessings in the new world.

---

21. Describe the completeness of the blessings to come.

Jehovah will come "with his anger and with heavy clouds"

attention shifts to things even higher than the mountains. *"The light of the full moon must become as the light of the glowing sun; and the very light of the glowing sun will become seven times as much, like the light of seven days, in the day that Jehovah binds up the breakdown of his people and heals even the severe wound resulting from the stroke by him."* (Isaiah 30:26) What a thrilling climax to this brilliant prophecy! The glory of God will shine forth in all its splendor. The blessings in store for God's faithful worshipers will exceed vastly—sevenfold—anything that they have experienced before.

Judgment and Joy

22 The tone of Isaiah's message changes again. *"Look!"* he says, as if to get his listeners' attention. *"The name of Jehovah is coming from far away, burning with his anger and with heavy clouds. As for his lips, they have become full of denunciation, and his tongue is like a devouring fire."* (Isaiah 30:27) Thus far, Jehovah has stayed away, allowing the enemies of his people to follow their own course. Now he draws closer—like a steadily approaching thunderstorm—to execute judgment. *"His spirit is like a flooding torrent that reaches clear to the neck, to swing the nations to and fro with a sieve of worthlessness; and a bridle that causes one to wander about will be in the jaws of the peoples."* (Isaiah 30:28) Enemies of God's people will be encircled by "a flooding torrent," violently shaken "to and fro with a sieve," and reined in with "a bridle." They will be destroyed.

23 Again Isaiah's tone changes as he describes the happy condition of faithful worshipers who will one day return

---

22. In contrast with the blessings to come for the faithful, what does Jehovah have in store for the wicked?
23. What causes "rejoicing of heart" for Christians today?

to their land. *"You people will come to have a song like that in the night that one sanctifies oneself for a festival, and rejoicing of heart like that of one walking with a flute to enter into the mountain of Jehovah, to the Rock of Israel."* (*Isaiah 30:29*) True Christians today experience a similar "rejoicing of heart" as they contemplate the judgment of Satan's world; the protection extended to them by Jehovah, the "Rock of salvation;" and the Kingdom blessings to come.—Psalm 95:1.

24 After this expression of gladness, Isaiah returns to the theme of judgment and identifies the object of God's wrath. *"Jehovah will certainly make the dignity of his voice to be heard and will make the descending of his arm to be seen, in the raging of anger and the flame of a devouring fire and cloudburst and rainstorm and hailstones. For because of the voice of Jehovah Assyria will be struck with terror; he will strike it even with a staff."* (*Isaiah 30:30, 31*) With this graphic description, Isaiah emphasizes the reality of God's judgment of Assyria. In effect, Assyria stands before God and trembles at the sight of his 'descending arm' of judgment.

25 The prophet continues: *"Every swing of his rod of chastisement that Jehovah will cause to settle down upon Assyria will certainly prove to be with tambourines and with harps; and with battles of brandishing he will actually fight against them. For his Topheth is set in order from recent times; it is also prepared for the king himself. He has made its pile deep. Fire and wood are in abundance. The breath of Jehovah, like a torrent of sulphur, is burning against it."* (*Isaiah 30:32, 33*) Topheth, in the Valley of Hinnom, is used here as a figurative place burning with fire. By showing that Assyria will end up there, Isa-

---

24, 25. How does Isaiah's prophecy emphasize the reality of Assyria's coming judgment?

iah stresses the sudden and complete destruction that is to come upon that nation.—Compare 2 Kings 23:10.

26 Although this judgment message is directed against Assyria, the significance of Isaiah's prophecy goes further. (Romans 15:4) Jehovah will again, as it were, come from afar to flood, shake, and bridle all those who oppress his people. (Ezekiel 38:18-23; 2 Peter 3:7; Revelation 19:11-21) May that day come quickly! Meanwhile, Christians eagerly await the day of deliverance. They derive strength from reflecting upon the vivid words recorded in Isaiah chapter 30. These words encourage God's servants to treasure the privilege of prayer, apply themselves to Bible study, and meditate upon the Kingdom blessings to come. (Psalm 42:1, 2; Proverbs 2:1-6; Romans 12:12) Thus Isaiah's words help all of us to keep in expectation of Jehovah.

---

26. (a) Jehovah's proclamations against Assyria have what modern-day application? (b) How do Christians today keep in expectation of Jehovah?

CHAPTER TWENTY-FOUR

No Help From This World

Isaiah 31:1-9

JERUSALEM'S inhabitants are terrified—and with good reason! Assyria, the mightiest empire of the day, has attacked "all the fortified cities of Judah and proceeded to seize them." Now, Assyria's military machine is threatening the capital city of Judah. (2 Kings 18:13, 17) What will King Hezekiah and the rest of Jerusalem's inhabitants do?

2 Since the other cities of his land have already fallen, Hezekiah knows that Jerusalem is no match for Assyria's powerful military force. Moreover, the Assyrians have an unparalleled reputation for cruelty and violence. That nation's army is so fear-inspiring that opponents sometimes flee without even a fight! In view of Jerusalem's dire circumstances, where can her inhabitants turn for help? Is there any escape from the Assyrian army? And how did God's people get into such a situation? To answer these questions, we have to look back and see how Jehovah dealt with his covenant nation in earlier years.

Apostasy in Israel

3 From the time that Israel left Egypt until the death of David's son Solomon—a period of just over 500 years—the

---

1, 2. (a) Why are Jerusalem's inhabitants terrified? (b) In view of Jerusalem's predicament, what questions are fitting?

3, 4. (a) When and how was the nation of Israel divided into two kingdoms? (b) What bad start did Jeroboam give the northern ten-tribe kingdom?

12 tribes of Israel were united as one nation. After the death of Solomon, Jeroboam led the ten northern tribes in rebellion against the house of David, and from then on the nation was divided into two kingdoms. This was in the year 997 B.C.E.

4 Jeroboam was the first king of the northern kingdom of Israel, and he led his subjects on the path of apostasy by replacing the Aaronic priesthood and the lawful worship of Jehovah with an illegitimate priesthood and a system of calf worship. (1 Kings 12:25-33) This was abhorrent to Jehovah. (Jeremiah 32:30, 35) For this and other reasons, he allowed Assyria to subjugate Israel. (2 Kings 15: 29) King Hoshea tried to break the Assyrian yoke by conspiring with Egypt, but the scheme failed.—2 Kings 17:4.

Israel Turns to a False Refuge

5 Jehovah wants to bring the Israelites back to their senses.* So he sends the prophet Isaiah with the following warning: *"Woe to those going down to Egypt for assistance, those who rely on mere horses, and who put their trust in war chariots, because they are numerous, and in steeds, because they are very mighty, but who have not looked to the Holy One of Israel and have not searched for Jehovah himself." (Isaiah 31:1)* How tragic! Israel places greater trust in horses and in war chariots than in the living God, Jehovah. To Israel's fleshly way of thinking, Egypt's horses are numerous and mighty. Surely Egypt will be a valuable ally against the Assyrian army! However, the Israelites will soon find that their fleshly alliance with Egypt is futile.

---

* Likely, the first three verses of Isaiah chapter 31 are directed mainly to Israel. The final six verses seem to apply to Judah.

---

5. To whom does Israel turn for help?

6 Through the Law covenant, the inhabitants of both Israel and Judah are in a dedicated relationship with Jehovah. (Exodus 24:3-8; 1 Chronicles 16:15-17) By turning to Egypt for help, Israel reveals a lack of faith in Jehovah and a disregard for the laws that are part of that holy covenant. Why? Because included in the terms of the covenant is Jehovah's promise to protect his people if they render exclusive devotion to him. (Leviticus 26:3-8) True to that promise, Jehovah has repeatedly proved to be a "fortress in the time of distress." (Psalm 37:39; 2 Chronicles 14:2, 9-12; 17:3-5, 10) Moreover, through Moses, the mediator of the Law covenant, Jehovah told future kings of Israel not to increase horses for themselves. (Deuteronomy 17:16) Obedience to this regulation would show that these kings look to "the Holy One of Israel" for protection. Sadly, the rulers of Israel do not have that kind of faith.

7 There is a lesson in this for Christians today. Israel looked to visible support from Egypt rather than to the far more powerful support that Jehovah provides. Likewise today, Christians may be tempted to place their confidence in fleshly sources of security—bank accounts, social position, connections in the world—rather than in Jehovah. Granted, Christian family heads take seriously their responsibility to provide materially for their families. (1 Timothy 5:8) But they do not put their faith in material things. And they guard against "every sort of covetousness." (Luke 12:13-21) The only "secure height in times of distress" is Jehovah God.—Psalm 9:9; 54:7.

8 Isaiah, in effect, mocks the Israelite leaders who craft-

6. Why does Israel's turning to Egypt betray a blatant lack of faith in Jehovah?
7. What can Christians today learn from Israel's lack of faith?
8, 9. (a) Although Israel's plans may seem strategically sound, what will be the outcome, and why? (b) What is the difference between human promises and Jehovah's promises?

ed the treaty with Egypt, saying: ***"He is also wise and will bring in what is calamitous, and he has not called back his own words; and he will certainly rise up against the house of evildoers and against the assistance of those practicing what is hurtful." (Isaiah 31:2)*** Israel's leaders may think that they are wise. But is not the Creator of the universe supremely wise? By all appearances Israel's scheme to seek help from Egypt is strategically sound. Nevertheless, forming such a political alliance constitutes spiritual

Those who put their trust in material things will be disappointed

adultery in Jehovah's sight. (Ezekiel 23:1-10) As a result, Isaiah says that Jehovah will "bring in what is calamitous."

⁹ Human promises are notoriously unreliable, and human protection is uncertain. Jehovah, on the other hand, does not need to 'call back his own words.' He will without fail do what he promises. His word does not return to him without results.—Isaiah 55:10, 11; 14:24.

¹⁰ Will the Egyptians prove to be a reliable protection for Israel? No. Isaiah tells Israel: *"The Egyptians, though, are earthling men, and not God; and their horses are flesh, and not spirit. And Jehovah himself will stretch out his hand, and he that is offering help will have to stumble, and he that is being helped will have to fall, and at the same time they will all of them come to an end."* (*Isaiah 31:3*) Both the helper (Egypt) and the helped (Israel) will stumble, fall, and come to their end when Jehovah stretches out his hand to execute his judgment by means of Assyria.

Samaria's Fall

¹¹ In his mercy Jehovah repeatedly sends prophets to encourage Israel to repent and return to pure worship. (2 Kings 17:13) Despite this, Israel adds to its sin of calf worship by engaging in divination, immoral Baal worship, and the use of sacred poles and high places. The Israelites even make "their sons and their daughters pass through the fire," sacrificing the fruit of their own flesh to demon gods. (2 Kings 17:14-17; Psalm 106:36-39; Amos 2:8) To bring an end to Israel's wickedness, Jehovah decrees: "Samaria and her king will certainly be silenced, like a snapped-off twig on the surface of waters." (Hosea 10:

---

10. What will happen to both Egypt and Israel?
11. What record of sin has Israel amassed, and what is the end result?

1, 7) In 742 B.C.E., Assyrian forces attack Samaria, the capital city of Israel. After a three-year siege, Samaria falls, and in 740 B.C.E., the ten-tribe kingdom ceases to exist.

12 In our day Jehovah has commissioned a worldwide preaching work to warn "mankind that they should all everywhere repent." (Acts 17:30; Matthew 24:14) Those who reject God's means of salvation will become like "a snapped-off twig," destroyed like the apostate nation of Israel. On the other hand, those hoping in Jehovah "will possess the earth, and they will reside forever upon it." (Psalm 37:29) How wise, then, to avoid the mistakes of the ancient kingdom of Israel! Let us put our whole confidence in Jehovah for salvation.

Jehovah's Saving Power

13 Situated a few miles from Israel's southern border is Jerusalem, the capital city of Judah. The inhabitants of Jerusalem are only too aware of what has happened to Samaria. Now they find themselves threatened by the same terrifying enemy that brought about the end of their northern neighbor. Will they learn from what befell Samaria?

14 Isaiah's next words are comforting to Jerusalem's residents. He assures them that Jehovah still loves his covenant people, saying: *"This is what Jehovah has said to me: 'Just as the lion growls, even the maned young lion, over its prey, when there is called out against it a full number of shepherds, and in spite of their voice he will not be terrified and in spite of their commotion he will not stoop; in*

---

12. What work has Jehovah commissioned today, and what happens to those who disregard the warning?
13, 14. What comforting words does Jehovah have for Zion?

the same way Jehovah of armies will come down to wage war over Mount Zion and over her hill.'" **(Isaiah 31:4)** Like a young lion standing over its prey, Jehovah will jealously protect his holy city, Zion. No boasting, no threatening words, nor any other commotion by Assyrian troops will turn Jehovah from his purpose.

*Like a lion guarding
its prey, Jehovah will protect his holy city*

15 Notice, now, the tender and compassionate way that Jehovah will deal with the inhabitants of Jerusalem: *"Like birds flying, Jehovah of armies will in the same way defend Jerusalem. Defending her, he will also certainly deliver her. Sparing her, he must also cause her to escape."* (Isaiah 31:5) A mother bird is ever vigilant to defend her young. With outstretched wings she hovers above her brood, and with watchful eyes she searches for any sign of danger. If a predator comes near, she quickly swoops down to defend her chicks. In a similar way, Jehovah will tenderly care for the inhabitants of Jerusalem because of the invading Assyrians.

"Return, You People"

16 Jehovah now reminds his people that they have sinned and encourages them to abandon their erring ways: *"Return, you people, to the One against whom the sons of Israel have gone deep in their revolt."* (Isaiah 31:6) The ten-tribe kingdom of Israel has not been alone in her rebellion. The people of Judah, also "sons of Israel," have gone "deep in their revolt." This will be especially evident when, shortly after Isaiah concludes his prophetic message, Hezekiah's son Manasseh becomes king. According to the Bible record, "Manasseh kept seducing Judah and the inhabitants of Jerusalem to do worse than the nations that Jehovah had annihilated." (2 Chronicles 33:9) Imagine that! Jehovah annihilates pagan nations because they are disgusting in their filth, yet the inhabitants of Judah, in a covenant relationship with Jehovah, are even worse than the people of those nations.

---

15. How does Jehovah deal tenderly and compassionately with the inhabitants of Jerusalem?
16. (a) What loving appeal does Jehovah make to his people? (b) When does the revolt of the people of Judah become especially evident? Explain.

17 At the dawn of the 21st century, conditions are similar in many respects to those in Judah in the days of Manasseh. The world is increasingly polarized by religious, racial, and ethnic hatreds. Horrific acts of murder, torture,

17. In what way are conditions today comparable to those in Judah under Manasseh?

The world is polarized by religious, racial, and ethnic hatreds

rape, and so-called ethnic cleansing have victimized millions. Without a doubt, people and nations—especially the nations of Christendom—have gone "deep in their revolt." We can be certain, however, that Jehovah will not allow wickedness to continue indefinitely. Why? Because of what took place in Isaiah's day.

Jerusalem Delivered

18 Assyrian kings gave credit to their gods for victory on the battlefield. The book *Ancient Near Eastern Texts* contains writings of Ashurbanipal, an Assyrian monarch who claimed that he was guided "by Ashur, Bel, Nebo, the great gods, [his] lords, who (always) march at [his] side, [when he] defeated the battle (-experienced) soldiers . . . in a great open battle." In Isaiah's day, Rabshakeh, who represents King Sennacherib of Assyria, shows a similar belief in the involvement of gods in human warfare when he addresses King Hezekiah. He warns the Jewish king against relying on Jehovah for salvation and points out that the gods of other nations have been ineffective in protecting their people against the mighty Assyrian war machine.—2 Kings 18:33-35.

19 How does King Hezekiah react? The Bible account says: "As soon as King Hezekiah heard, he immediately ripped his garments apart and covered himself with sackcloth and came into the house of Jehovah." (2 Kings 19:1) Hezekiah recognizes that there is only One who can help him in this frightening situation. He humbles himself and looks to Jehovah for direction.

20 Jehovah gives the sought-for direction. Through the prophet Isaiah, he says: *"In that day they will reject each*

---

18. What warning does Rabshakeh give to Hezekiah?
19. How does Hezekiah react to Rabshakeh's taunts?
20. How will Jehovah act in behalf of the inhabitants of Judah, and what should they learn from this?

one his worthless gods of silver and his valueless gods of gold, that your hands have made for yourselves as a sin." (*Isaiah 31:7*) When Jehovah fights for his people, Sennacherib's gods will be exposed for what they are—worthless. This is a lesson that the inhabitants of Judah should take to heart. Despite the faithfulness of King Hezekiah, the land of Judah, like Israel, has been filled with idols. (Isaiah 2:5-8) For the inhabitants of Judah, rebuilding their relationship with Jehovah will require repenting of their sins and rejecting "each one his worthless gods." —See Exodus 34:14.

21 Isaiah now prophetically describes Jehovah's executional acts against Judah's fearsome enemy: *"The Assyrian must fall by the sword, not that of a man; and a sword, not that of earthling man, will devour him. And he must flee because of the sword, and his own young men will come to be for forced labor itself."* (*Isaiah 31:8*) When the showdown comes, Jerusalem's inhabitants do not even have to draw their swords from their sheaths. The cream of Assyria's troops are devoured, not by the swords of men, but by the sword of Jehovah. As for Assyrian King Sennacherib, "he must flee because of the sword." After the death of 185,000 of his warriors at the hand of Jehovah's angel, he returns home. Later, while bowing to his god Nisroch, he is assassinated by his own sons.—2 Kings 19:35-37.

22 No one, including Hezekiah, could foresee how Jehovah would deliver Jerusalem from the Assyrian army. Nevertheless, Hezekiah's way of dealing with the crisis

---

21. How does Isaiah prophetically describe Jehovah's executional acts against the Assyrian?
22. What can Christians today learn from the events involving Hezekiah and the Assyrian army?

Hezekiah went to the house of Jehovah for help

provides an excellent example for those who face trials today. (2 Corinthians 4:16-18) In view of the terrifying reputation of the Assyrians threatening Jerusalem, Hezekiah understandably was afraid. (2 Kings 19:3) Still, he had faith in Jehovah, and he sought His guidance, not man's. What a blessing for Jerusalem that he did! God-fearing Christians today may also experience intense emotion when under stress. In many situations, fear is understandable. Yet, if we 'throw all our anxiety upon Jehovah,' he will care for us. (1 Peter 5:7) He will help us overcome our fear and will strengthen us to cope with the situation that is causing stress.

23 In the end, it is Sennacherib, not Hezekiah, who is left with fearful emotions. To whom can he turn? Isaiah foretells: *"'His own crag will pass away out of sheer fright, and because of the signal his princes must be terrified,' is the utterance of Jehovah, whose light is in Zion and whose furnace is in Jerusalem." (Isaiah 31:9)* Sennacherib's gods —his "crag," the refuge in which he has trusted—fail him. They "pass away out of sheer fright," as it were. Moreover, even Sennacherib's princes are of little help. They too are struck with terror.

24 This part of Isaiah's prophecy provides a clear message for any would-be opposer of God. There is no weapon, no power, no device that can frustrate Jehovah's purposes. (Isaiah 41:11, 12) At the same time, those who claim to serve God yet turn away from him to seek security in fleshly things will meet with disappointment. Any who "have not looked to the Holy One of Israel" will see Jehovah "bring in what is calamitous." (Isaiah 31:1, 2) Truly, the only real and lasting refuge is Jehovah God.—Psalm 37:5.

---

23. In what way is Sennacherib, not Hezekiah, left with fearful emotions?
24. What clear message can be learned from what happened to the Assyrian?

CHAPTER TWENTY-FIVE

The King and His Princes

Isaiah 32:1-20

TOWARD the end of the 1940's, a remarkable collection of scrolls was found in caves located near the Dead Sea, in Palestine. They became known as the Dead Sea Scrolls and are believed to have been written sometime between 200 B.C.E. and 70 C.E. Best known among them is a scroll of Isaiah written in Hebrew on durable leather. This scroll is almost complete, and its text differs very little from that of manuscripts of the Masoretic text dated about 1,000 years later. Thus, the scroll demonstrates the accurate transmission of the Bible text.

2 A noteworthy detail about the Dead Sea Scroll of Isaiah is that the portion making up what is today known as Isaiah chapter 32 is marked with an "X" scrawled in the margin by a scribe. We do not know why the scribe made such a mark, but we do know that there is something special about this portion of the Holy Bible.

Ruling for Righteousness and Justice

3 Isaiah chapter 32 opens with a thrilling prophecy that is finding remarkable fulfillment in our day: *"Look! A king will reign for righteousness itself; and as respects princes, they will rule as princes for justice itself."* (*Isaiah 32:1*) Yes, "Look!" This exclamation calls to mind a similar

---

1, 2. What can be said about the text of the Dead Sea Scroll of Isaiah?
3. What administration is prophesied in the books of Isaiah and Revelation?

exclamation found in the last prophetic book of the Bible: "The One seated on the throne said: *'Look!* I am making all things new.'" (Revelation 21:5) The Bible books of Isaiah and Revelation, written some 900 years apart, both present a glowing description of a new administration—"a new heaven," composed of the King, Christ Jesus, enthroned in the heavens in 1914, and 144,000 corulers "bought from among mankind"—together with "a new earth," a global, united human society.* (Revelation 14:1-4; 21:1-4; Isaiah 65:17-25) This entire arrangement is made possible by Christ's ransom sacrifice.

4 After seeing in vision the final sealing of these 144,000 corulers, the apostle John reports: "I saw, and, *look!* a great crowd, which no man was able to number, out of all nations and tribes and peoples and tongues, standing before the throne and before the Lamb." Here is the nucleus of the new earth—a great crowd now numbering into the millions, who have been gathered to the side of the few, mostly elderly remaining ones of the 144,000. This great crowd will survive the fast-approaching great tribulation and in the Paradise earth will be joined by resurrected faithful ones and billions of others who will be given the opportunity to exercise faith. All who do so will be blessed with everlasting life.—Revelation 7:4, 9-17.

5 However, as long as the present hate-filled world exists, members of the great crowd need protection. In large

------

* The "king" in Isaiah 32:1 may have had a preliminary reference to King Hezekiah. However, the main fulfillment of Isaiah chapter 32 is in relation to the King, Christ Jesus.

------

4. What nucleus of the new earth is now present?
5-7. What role do the foretold "princes" play in God's flock?

*In the Dead Sea Scrolls, Isaiah chapter 32
is marked with an "X"*

measure this is provided by the "princes" who "rule . . . for justice itself." What a grand arrangement! These "princes" are described further in the glowing words of Isaiah's prophecy: *"Each one must prove to be like a hiding place from the wind and a place of concealment from the rainstorm, like streams of water in a waterless country, like the shadow of a heavy crag in an exhausted land."—Isaiah 32:2.*

6 Right now in this time of worldwide distress, there is a need for "princes," yes, elders who will "pay attention to . . . all the flock," caring for Jehovah's sheep and administering justice in harmony with Jehovah's righteous principles. (Acts 20:28) Such "princes" must meet the qualifications set out in 1 Timothy 3:2-7 and Titus 1:6-9.

7 In his great prophecy describing the distressful "conclusion of the system of things," Jesus said: "See that you are not terrified." (Matthew 24:3-8) Why are Jesus' followers not terrified by today's dangerous world conditions? One reason is that the "princes"—whether they be anointed or "other sheep"—are loyally protecting the flock. (John 10:16) They fearlessly care for their brothers and sisters, even in the face of such horrors as ethnic wars and genocide. In a spiritually exhausted world, they see to it that depressed souls are refreshed by the upbuilding truths of God's Word, the Bible.

8 During the past 50 years, the "princes" have come clearly into view. "Princes" who are of the other sheep are being trained as a developing "chieftain" class so that after the great tribulation, qualified ones from among them will

---

8. How is Jehovah training and using the "princes" who are of the other sheep?

Each 'prince' is like a hiding place from the wind, shelter from the rain, water in the desert, and shade from the sun

be ready for appointment to serve in an administrative capacity in the "new earth." (Ezekiel 44:2, 3; 2 Peter 3:13) By providing spiritual guidance and refreshment as they take the lead in Kingdom service, they are proving themselves to be "like the shadow of a heavy crag," bringing relief to the flock in its realm of worship.*

9 In these perilous last days of Satan's wicked world, dedicated Christians sorely need such protection. (2 Timothy 3:1-5, 13) Strong winds of false doctrine and twisted propaganda are blowing. Storms are raging in the form of wars between and within nations as well as direct assaults against faithful worshipers of Jehovah God. In a world parched by spiritual drought, Christians badly need the streams of water of pure, unadulterated truth in order to quench their spiritual thirst. Happily, Jehovah has promised that his reigning King, through his anointed brothers and supportive "princes" of the other sheep, will provide encouragement and guidance to despondent and discouraged ones in this time of need. Jehovah will thus see to it that what is righteous and just will prevail.

Paying Attention With Eyes, Ears, and Hearts

10 How have the great crowd responded to Jehovah's theocratic arrangement? The prophecy continues: *"The eyes of those seeing will not be pasted together, and the very ears of those hearing will pay attention." (Isaiah 32:3)* Over the years, Jehovah has provided for the instruction and bringing to maturity of his precious servants. The Theocratic Ministry School and other meetings oper-

---

* See *The Watchtower*, March 1, 1999, pages 13-18, published by the Watchtower Bible and Tract Society of New York, Inc.

---

9. What conditions show the need for "princes" today?
10. What provisions has Jehovah made so that his people can 'see' and 'hear' spiritual things?

ating in the congregations of Jehovah's Witnesses world-wide; the district, national, and international conventions; as well as the specialized training of the "princes" to treat the flock with loving care have all contributed to the building up of a united, global brotherhood of millions. Wherever these shepherds are on earth, their ears are wide open to adjustments in understanding of the advancing word of truth. With Bible-trained consciences, they are ever ready to hear and to obey.—Psalm 25:10.

11 The prophecy then cautions: *"The heart itself of those who are overhasty will consider knowledge, and even the tongue of the stammerers will be quick in speaking clear things." (Isaiah 32:4)* Let no one be overhasty in drawing conclusions about what is right and what is wrong. The Bible says: "Have you beheld a man hasty with his words? There is more hope for someone stupid than for him." (Proverbs 29:20; Ecclesiastes 5:2) Before 1919, even Jehovah's people were tainted with Babylonish ideas. But starting in that year, Jehovah has given them a clearer understanding of his purposes. They have found the truths he has revealed to be, not overhasty, but well thought out, and they are now speaking with the certainty of belief, not stammering with uncertainty.

"The Senseless One"

12 Isaiah's prophecy next draws a contrast: *"The senseless one will no longer be called generous; and as for the unprincipled man, he will not be said to be noble; because the senseless one himself will speak mere senselessness." (Isaiah 32:5, 6a)* Who is "the senseless one"? As if for emphasis, King David twice supplies the answer: "The senseless

---

11. Why are God's people now speaking with confidence, not stammering with uncertainty?
12. Who are 'the senseless ones' today, and in what way do they lack generosity?

one has said in his heart: 'There is no Jehovah.' They have acted ruinously, they have acted detestably in their dealing. There is no one doing good." (Psalm 14:1; 53:1) Of course, confirmed atheists say that there is no Jehovah. In effect, so do "intellectuals" and others who act as if there were no God, believing that they are accountable to no one. The truth is not in such ones. There is no generosity in their hearts. They have no gospel of love. In contrast with genuine Christians, they are slow to provide for needy ones in distress or fail to do so entirely.

13 Many such senseless ones come to hate those who champion God's truth. *"His very heart will work at what is hurtful, to work at apostasy and to speak against Jehovah what is wayward." (Isaiah 32:6b)* How true this is of modern-day apostates! In a number of countries in Europe and Asia, apostates have joined forces with other opponents of truth, speaking outright lies to the authorities, with a view to having Jehovah's Witnesses banned or restricted. They manifest the spirit of the "evil slave," of whom Jesus prophesied: "If ever that evil slave should say in his heart, 'My master is delaying,' and should start to beat his fellow slaves and should eat and drink with the confirmed drunkards, the master of that slave will come on a day that he does not expect and in an hour that he does not know, and will punish him with the greatest severity and will assign him his part with the hypocrites. There is where his weeping and the gnashing of his teeth will be."—Matthew 24:48-51.

14 In the meantime, the apostate causes *"the soul of the hungry one to go empty, and he causes even the thirsty one to go without drink itself." (Isaiah 32:6c)* Enemies of truth

13, 14. (a) How do modern-day apostates work what is hurtful? (b) Of what do apostates try to deprive the hungry and the thirsty, but what will be the final outcome?

try to deprive truth-hungry people of spiritual food, and they try to keep thirsty ones from drinking the refreshing waters of the Kingdom message. But the final outcome will be what Jehovah declares to his people through another of his prophets: "They will be certain to fight against you, but they will not prevail against you, for 'I am with you,' is the utterance of Jehovah, 'to deliver you.'"—Jeremiah 1:19; Isaiah 54:17.

15 From the middle years of the 20th century, immorality has openly run riot in the lands of Christendom. Why? The prophecy foretold one reason: *"As for the unprincipled man, his instruments are bad; he himself has given counsel for acts of loose conduct, to wreck the afflicted ones with false sayings, even when someone poor speaks what is right."* (Isaiah 32:7) In fulfillment of these words, many of the clergy in particular have adopted a permissive attitude toward premarital sex, cohabitation of the unmarried, homosexuality—indeed, "fornication and uncleanness of every sort." (Ephesians 5:3) Thus, they "wreck" their flocks with their false sayings.

16 In contrast, how refreshing is the fulfillment of the prophet's next words! *"As regards the generous one, it is for generous things that he has given counsel; and in favor of generous things he himself will rise up."* (Isaiah 32:8) Jesus himself encouraged generosity when he said: "Practice giving, and people will give to you. They will pour into your laps a fine measure, pressed down, shaken together and overflowing. For with the measure that you are measuring out, they will measure out to you in return." (Luke 6:38) The apostle Paul too pointed to the blessings that come to generous ones when he said: "Bear in mind the

---

15. Today, who particularly are "unprincipled," what "false sayings" have they promoted, and with what result?
16. What makes genuine Christians happy?

*A Christian finds great
happiness in sharing the good news with others*

words of the Lord Jesus, when he himself said, 'There is more happiness in giving than there is in receiving.' " (Acts 20:35) Genuine Christians are made happy, not by gaining material wealth or social prominence, but by being generous—in the same way that their God, Jehovah, is generous. (Matthew 5:44, 45) Their greatest happiness is found in doing God's will, in generously giving of themselves in order to make known to others "the glorious good news of the happy God."—1 Timothy 1:11.

17 Isaiah's prophecy continues: *"You women who are at ease, rise up, listen to my voice! You careless daughters, give ear to my saying! Within a year and some days you careless ones will be agitated, because the grape picking will have come to an end but no fruit gathering will come*

---

17. Who today are like the "careless daughters" referred to by Isaiah?

in. Tremble, you women who are at ease! Be agitated, you careless ones!" (Isaiah 32:9-11a) The attitude of these women may remind us of those today who claim to serve God but who are not zealous in his service. Such ones are found in the religions of "Babylon the Great, the mother of the harlots." (Revelation 17:5) For example, members of Christendom's religions are very much as Isaiah describes these "women." They are "at ease," complacent as to the judgment and agitation that will soon engulf them.

18 The call goes forth, then, to false religion: *"Undress and make yourselves naked, and gird sackcloth upon the loins. Beat yourselves upon the breasts in lamentation over the desirable fields, over the fruit-bearing vine. Upon the ground of my people merely thorns, spiny bushes come up, for they are upon all the houses of exultation, yes, the highly elated town." (Isaiah 32:11b-13)* The expression "Undress and make yourselves naked" does not appear to mean total disrobing. The ancient custom was to wear an outer garment over an undergarment. The outer garment was often a means of identification. (2 Kings 10:22, 23; Revelation 7:13, 14) The prophecy is thus commanding members of false religions to remove their outer garments —their pretended identity as servants of God—and to put on instead garments of sackcloth, symbols of mourning over their imminent judgment. (Revelation 17:16) No godly fruitfulness is to be found among the religious organizations of Christendom, which claims to be God's "highly elated town," or among the rest of the members of the world empire of false religion. Their domain of operation brings forth "merely thorns, spiny bushes" of neglect and abandonment.

19 This picture of gloom extends to all parts of apostate "Jerusalem": *"The dwelling tower itself has been forsaken,*

---

18. Who is instructed to "gird sackcloth upon the loins," and why?
19. What condition of apostate "Jerusalem" is exposed by Isaiah?

*the very hubbub of the city has been abandoned; Ophel
and the watchtower themselves have become bare fields,
for time indefinite the exultation of zebras, the pasture of
droves." (Isaiah 32:14)* Yes, even Ophel is included. Ophel
is an elevated part of Jerusalem that provides a strong defensive position. To say that Ophel becomes a bare field
bespeaks complete desolation for the city. Isaiah's words
show that apostate "Jerusalem"—Christendom—is not
watchful of doing God's will. It is barren spiritually, far removed from truth and justice—beastlike in the extreme.

A Glorious Contrast!

20 Isaiah next presents a heartwarming hope for those
who do Jehovah's will. Any desolation of God's own people will last only *"until upon us the spirit is poured out from
on high, and the wilderness will have become an orchard,
and the orchard itself is accounted as a real forest." (Isaiah 32:15)* Happily, since 1919, Jehovah's spirit has been
poured out in abundance upon his people, restoring, as it
were, a fruit-bearing orchard of anointed Witnesses, to be
followed by an expanding forest of other sheep. Prosperity
and growth are the keynotes of his organization on earth
today. In the restored spiritual paradise, "the glory of Jehovah, the splendor of our God," is reflected by his people
as they proclaim his incoming Kingdom worldwide.—Isaiah 35:1, 2.

21 Listen, now, to Jehovah's glorious promise: *"In the wilderness justice will certainly reside, and in the orchard righteousness itself will dwell. And the work of the true righteousness must become peace; and the service of the
true righteousness, quietness and security to time indefinite." (Isaiah 32:16, 17)* How well this describes the spiri-

---

20. What is the effect of God's spirit being poured out upon his people?
21. Where is righteousness, quietness, and security found today?

tual condition of Jehovah's people today! In contrast with the majority of mankind, who are divided by hatred, violence, and abject spiritual poverty, true Christians are globally united, even though they are "out of all nations and tribes and peoples and tongues." They live, work, and serve in harmony with God's righteousness, doing so in confidence of enjoying, at last, true peace and security to time indefinite.—Revelation 7:9, 17.

22 In the spiritual paradise, *Isaiah 32:18* is already being fulfilled. It says: *"My people must dwell in a peaceful abiding place and in residences of full confidence and in undisturbed resting-places."* But for the imitation Christians, *"it will certainly hail when the forest goes down and the city becomes low in an abased state."* (*Isaiah 32:19*) Yes, like a tempestuous hailstorm, Jehovah's judgment is poised to strike the counterfeit city of false religion, debasing its "forest" of supporters, obliterating these for all time!

23 This portion of the prophecy concludes: *"Happy are you people who are sowing seed alongside all waters, sending forth the feet of the bull and of the ass."* (*Isaiah 32:20*) The bull and the ass were beasts of burden used by God's ancient people in plowing fields and sowing seed. Today, Jehovah's people use printing equipment, electronic tools, modern buildings and transport and, above all, a united, theocratic organization to print and distribute billions of Bible publications. Willing workers use these instruments to sow seeds of Kingdom truth throughout the earth, literally "alongside all waters." Millions of God-fearing men and women have already been harvested, and other multitudes are joining them. (Revelation 14:15, 16) All of them are indeed to be counted "happy"!

---

22. What is the difference between the condition of God's people and that of those in false religion?
23. What global work is nearing completion, and how are those sharing in it to be counted?

CHAPTER TWENTY-SIX

"No Resident Will Say: 'I Am Sick'"

Isaiah 33:1-24

"ALL creation keeps on groaning together and being in pain together until now." So said the apostle Paul. (Romans 8:22) Despite advances in medical science, sickness and death continue to plague the human race. How wonderful, then, the promise that climaxes this part of Isaiah's prophecy is! Imagine the time when "no resident will say: 'I am sick.'" (Isaiah 33:24) When and how will this promise be fulfilled?

2 Isaiah is writing at a time when God's covenant people are sick spiritually. (Isaiah 1:5, 6) They have plunged so deeply into apostasy and immorality that they need severe discipline from Jehovah God. Assyria serves as Jehovah's "rod" to administer that discipline. (Isaiah 7:17; 10:5, 15) First, the northern ten-tribe kingdom of Israel falls to the Assyrians in the year 740 B.C.E. (2 Kings 17:1-18; 18:9-11) A few years later, King Sennacherib of Assyria launches an all-out attack on the southern kingdom of Judah. (2 Kings 18:13; Isaiah 36:1) As the Assyrian juggernaut sweeps through the land, Judah's complete annihilation seems inevitable.

3 But Assyria, going beyond its mandate to discipline

---

1. Why are the words of Isaiah 33:24 comforting?
2, 3. (a) In what way is the nation of Israel sick? (b) How does Assyria serve as God's "rod" of discipline?

God's people, is now pursuing its own greedy ambition for world conquest. (Isaiah 10:7-11) Will Jehovah allow its brutal mistreatment of his people to go unpunished? Will there be a healing of the nation's spiritual illness? In Isaiah chapter 33, we read Jehovah's answers to these questions.

Despoiling the Despoiler

4 The prophecy begins: *"Woe to you who are despoiling, without you yourself being despoiled, and to you who are dealing treacherously, without others having dealt treacherously with you! As soon as you have finished as a despoiler, you will be despoiled. As soon as you have done with dealing treacherously, they will deal treacherously with you."* (*Isaiah 33:1*) Isaiah directly addresses the despoiler, Assyria. At the peak of its power, that aggressive nation seems unbeatable. It has 'despoiled without being despoiled,' ravaging the cities of Judah, even stripping the house of Jehovah of its wealth—and doing so with seeming impunity! (2 Kings 18:14-16; 2 Chronicles 28:21) Now, though, the tables will be turned. "You will be despoiled," Isaiah boldly declares. How comforting this prophecy is to faithful ones!

5 During that frightening period of time, loyal worshipers of Jehovah will need to turn to him for help. Isaiah thus prays: *"O Jehovah, show us favor. In you we have hoped. Become our arm* [of *strength and support*] *every morning, yes, our salvation in the time of distress. At the sound of turmoil peoples have fled. At your arising nations have been dispersed."* (*Isaiah 33:2, 3*) Appropriately, Isaiah prays that Jehovah deliver His people as He has done

---

4, 5. (a) What reversal will Assyria experience? (b) What prayer does Isaiah offer on behalf of Jehovah's people?

many times in the past. (Psalm 44:3; 68:1) And no sooner does Isaiah offer this prayer than he foretells Jehovah's answer to it!

6 *"The spoil of you people [the Assyrians] will actually be gathered like the cockroaches when gathering in, like the onrush of locust swarms that is rushing against one." (Isaiah 33:4)* Judah is familiar with devastating insect invasions. This time, though, it is Judah's enemies that will be devastated. Assyria will suffer a humiliating defeat, and its soldiers will be forced to flee, leaving behind a great spoil for the inhabitants of Judah to collect! It is only fitting that Assyria, known for its cruelty, will experience being despoiled.—Isaiah 37:36.

The Modern-Day Assyrian

7 How does Isaiah's prophecy apply in our day? The spiritually sick nation of Israel can be compared to unfaithful Christendom. Just as Jehovah used Assyria as a "rod" to punish Israel, so he will use a "rod" to punish Christendom—as well as the rest of the world empire of false religion, "Babylon the Great." (Isaiah 10:5; Revelation 18:2-8) That "rod" will be member nations of the United Nations—an organization pictured in Revelation as a seven-headed, ten-horned, scarlet-colored wild beast.—Revelation 17:3, 15-17.

8 When the modern-day Assyrian rampages throughout

---

6. What will happen to Assyria, and why is this fitting?
7. (a) Who today can be compared to the spiritually sick nation of Israel? (b) Who will serve as Jehovah's "rod" to destroy Christendom?
8. (a) Who today can be compared to Sennacherib? (b) Who will the modern-day Sennacherib be emboldened to attack, and with what outcome?

Isaiah prays confidently to Jehovah

the realm of false religion, it will appear to be unstoppable. With an attitude like that of Sennacherib, Satan the Devil will be emboldened to strike out—not only against apostate organizations deserving of punishment but also against true Christians. Alongside the remaining ones of Jehovah's anointed spiritual sons, millions who have come out of Satan's world, which includes Babylon the Great, take their stand for Jehovah's Kingdom. Angered at the refusal of true Christians to pay him homage, "the god of this system of things," Satan, will launch an all-out attack against them. (2 Corinthians 4:4; Ezekiel 38:10-16) As terrifying as this attack will no doubt be, Jehovah's people will not need to cower in fear. (Isaiah 10:24, 25) They have assurance from God that he will be their "salvation in the time of distress." He will intervene, bringing devastation upon Satan and his crowd. (Ezekiel 38:18-23) Just as in ancient times, those trying to despoil God's people will themselves be despoiled! (Compare Proverbs 13:22b.) Jehovah's name will be sanctified, and survivors will be rewarded for having sought *"wisdom and knowledge [and] the fear of Jehovah."—Read Isaiah 33:5, 6.*

A Warning to Faithless Ones

9 What, though, will be the fate of faithless ones in Judah? Isaiah paints a grim picture of their impending doom at the hands of Assyria. *(Read Isaiah 33:7.)* Judah's military *"heroes"* cry out in fear at the Assyrian advance. *"Messengers of peace,"* diplomats sent to negotiate peace with the warlike Assyrians, face mockery and humiliation. They will weep bitterly over their failure. (Compare Jeremiah 8:15.) The brutal Assyrian will not pity them. *(Read Isaiah 33:8, 9.)* He will ruthlessly ignore covenants he has

9. (a) What will Judah's "heroes" and "messengers of peace" do? (b) How will the Assyrian respond to peace initiatives from Judah?

made with the inhabitants of Judah. (2 Kings 18:14-16) The Assyrian will *'contemn the cities'* of Judah, viewing them with contempt and scorn, having no regard for human life. The situation will be so devastating that the land itself will, as it were, mourn. Lebanon, Sharon, Bashan, and Carmel will likewise mourn over the desolation.

10 Similar circumstances will no doubt develop in the near future as the nations begin their assault on religion. As in Hezekiah's day, physical resistance to these destructive forces will be futile. Christendom's "heroes"—its politicians, financiers, and other people of influence—will be unable to come to her aid. Political and financial 'covenants,' or agreements, designed to protect Christendom's interests will be violated. (Isaiah 28:15-18) Frantic attempts to stave off destruction by diplomacy will fail. Commercial activities will come to a halt, as Christendom's properties and investments are confiscated or destroyed. Any who still have friendly feelings toward Christendom will do little more than stand at a safe distance and mourn her passing. (Revelation 18:9-19) Will true Christianity be swept away with the false? No, for Jehovah himself gives this assurance: *"'Now I will rise up,' says Jehovah, 'now I will exalt myself; now I will lift myself up.'"* (Isaiah 33:10) Finally, Jehovah will intervene in behalf of faithful ones, like Hezekiah, and halt the Assyrian's advance.—Psalm 12:5.

11 The unfaithful cannot count on such protection. Jehovah says: *"You people conceive dried grass; you will give birth to stubble. Your own spirit, as a fire, will eat you*

---

10. (a) How will Christendom's "heroes" prove to be ineffective? (b) Who will protect genuine Christians during Christendom's day of distress?
11, 12. (a) When and how do the words of Isaiah 33:11-14 find fulfillment? (b) Jehovah's words give what warning for today?

*up. And peoples must become as the burnings of lime.
As thorns cut away, they will be set ablaze even with fire.
Hear, you men who are far away, what I must do! And
know, you who are nearby, my mightiness. In Zion the
sinners have come to be in dread; shivering has grabbed
hold of the apostates: 'Who of us can reside for any
time with a devouring fire? Who of us can reside for any
time with long-lasting conflagrations?'"* (Isaiah 33:11-14)
These words evidently apply to the time when Judah faces
a new enemy, Babylon. After the death of Hezekiah, Judah reverts to her wicked ways. Over the next few decades,
conditions in Judah deteriorate to the point where the entire nation has to suffer the fire of God's anger.—Deuteronomy 32:22.

12 Wicked plans and schemes hatched by disobedient
ones to avert God's judgment prove to be of no more sub-
stance than stubble. In fact, the proud, rebellious spirit of
the nation will actually trigger the events leading to its destruction. (Jeremiah 52:3-11) Wicked ones will "become
as the burnings of lime"—utterly destroyed! As they contemplate this impending doom, the rebellious inhabitants
of Judah experience a sickening dread. Jehovah's words to
unfaithful Judah illustrate the situation of Christendom's
members today. If they do not heed God's warning, a grim
future awaits them.

"Walking in Continual Righteousness"

13 By way of contrast, Jehovah next says: *"There is one
who is walking in continual righteousness and speaking what is upright, who is rejecting the unjust gain from
frauds, who is shaking his hands clear from taking hold on
a bribe, who is stopping up his ear from listening to blood-*

---

13. What promise is made to one "walking in continual righteousness," and how was it fulfilled in Jeremiah's case?

shed, and who is closing his eyes so as not to see what is bad. He is the one that will reside on the heights themselves; his secure height will be craggy places difficult to approach. His own bread will certainly be given him; his water supply will be unfailing." (Isaiah 33:15, 16) As the apostle Peter later expresses it, "Jehovah knows how to deliver people of godly devotion out of trial, but to reserve unrighteous people for the day of judgment to be cut off." (2 Peter 2:9) Jeremiah experienced such deliverance. During the Babylonian siege, people had to "eat bread by weight and in anxious care." (Ezekiel 4:16) Some women even ate the flesh of their own children. (Lamentations 2:20) Yet, Jehovah saw to it that Jeremiah was kept safe.

14 Christians today must likewise 'walk in continual righteousness,' daily observing Jehovah's standards. (Psalm 15:1-5) They must 'speak what is upright' and reject lying and untruth. (Proverbs 3:32) Fraud and bribery may be common in many lands, but they are repugnant to one "walking in continual righteousness." Christians must also keep "an honest conscience" in business dealings, studiously avoiding shady or fraudulent schemes. (Hebrews 13:18; 1 Timothy 6:9, 10) And one who has 'stopped up his ear from listening to bloodshed and closed his eyes so as not to see what is bad' will be selective in his choice of music and entertainment. (Psalm 119:37) During his day of judgment, Jehovah will protect and sustain his worshipers, who live by such standards.—Zephaniah 2:3.

Beholding Their King

15 Isaiah next gives this glowing glimpse of the future: *"A king in his handsomeness is what your eyes will behold;*

---

14. How can Christians today keep "walking in continual righteousness"?
15. What promise will sustain faithful Jewish exiles?

*they will see a land far away. Your own heart will com-
ment in low tones on a frightful thing: 'Where is the secretary? Where is the one that does the paying out? Where is
the one counting the towers?' No insolent people will
you see, a people too deep in language to listen to, of a
stammering tongue without your understanding."* **(Isaiah
33:17-19)** The promise of the future Messianic King and
his Kingdom will sustain faithful Jews during the long decades of exile in Babylon, even though they can see that
Kingdom only from afar. (Hebrews 11:13) When Messiah's rule finally becomes a reality, the Babylonian tyran-
ny will be a distant memory. Survivors of the attack of the
Assyrian will happily ask: "Where are the tyrant's officers,
who taxed us, charged us, took our tribute?"—Isaiah 33:
18, *Moffatt.*

16 Although Isaiah's words guarantee a restoration from
Babylonian captivity, individual Jewish exiles will have to
await the resurrection to enjoy the complete fulfillment of
this part of the prophecy. What about God's servants today? Since 1914, Jehovah's people have been able to "behold," or discern, the Messianic King, Jesus Christ, in all
his spiritual beauty. (Psalm 45:2; 118:22-26) As a result,
they have experienced deliverance from the oppression
and control of Satan's wicked system. Under Zion, the seat
of God's Kingdom, they enjoy true spiritual security.

17 Isaiah continues: *"Behold Zion, the town of our festal occasions! Your own eyes will see Jerusalem an undisturbed abiding place, a tent that no one will pack up. Never will its tent pins be pulled out, and none of its ropes will*

16. Since when have God's people been able to "behold" the Messianic King, and with what result?
17. (a) What promises are made regarding Zion? (b) How are Jehovah's promises regarding Zion fulfilled on the Messianic Kingdom
and on its supporters on earth?

be torn in two. But there the Majestic One, Jehovah, will be for us a place of rivers, of wide canals. On it no galley fleet will go, and no majestic ship will pass over it." *(Isaiah 33:20, 21)* Isaiah assures us that God's Messianic Kingdom cannot be uprooted or destroyed. Moreover, such protection clearly extends to faithful Kingdom supporters on earth today. Even if many individuals are put to severe tests, subjects of God's Kingdom are assured that no effort to destroy them as a congregation can possibly succeed. (Isaiah 54:17) Jehovah will protect his people in the way that a moat or canal protects a city. Any enemy coming up against them—even one as powerful as a "galley fleet" or a "majestic ship"—will face destruction!

18 Why, though, can lovers of God's Kingdom feel so confident of divine protection? Explains Isaiah: *"Jehovah is our Judge, Jehovah is our Statute-giver, Jehovah is our King; he himself will save us."* *(Isaiah 33:22)* Jehovah accepts the responsibility of protecting and directing his people, who recognize his position as Supreme Sovereign. These willingly submit to his rule through his Messianic King, recognizing that Jehovah has the authority not only to make laws but also to enforce them. However, because Jehovah is a lover of righteousness and justice, his rule, through his Son, is not a burden to his worshipers. Rather, they 'benefit themselves' by submitting to his authority. (Isaiah 48:17) He will never abandon his loyal ones. —Psalm 37:28.

19 Isaiah tells enemies of Jehovah's faithful people: *"Your ropes must hang loose; their mast they will not hold firmly erect; they have not spread a sail. At that time even spoil*

---

18. What responsibility does Jehovah accept?
19. How does Isaiah describe the ineffectiveness of enemies of Jehovah's faithful people?

in abundance will have to be divided up; the lame ones themselves will actually take a big plunder." (Isaiah 33:23) Any approaching enemy will prove to be as ineffective and helpless against Jehovah as a warship with loose rigging, a wobbling mast, and no sail. The destruction of God's enemies will result in so much spoil that even disabled ones will share in taking plunder. We can therefore be confident that through the King Jesus Christ, Jehovah will triumph over his enemies in the coming "great tribulation." —Revelation 7:14.

A Healing

20 This section of Isaiah's prophecy concludes with a heartwarming promise: *"No resident will say: 'I am sick.' The people that are dwelling in the land will be those pardoned for their error." (Isaiah 33:24)* The sickness that Isaiah speaks of is primarily spiritual, for it is connected with sin, or "error." In the first application of these words, Jehovah promises that after their release from Babylonian captivity, the nation will be healed spiritually. (Isaiah 35:5, 6; Jeremiah 33:6; compare Psalm 103:1-5.) Having been forgiven for their former sins, the returning Jews will reestablish pure worship in Jerusalem.

21 However, Isaiah's prophecy has a modern fulfillment. Jehovah's people today have also enjoyed a spiritual healing. They have been liberated from such false teachings as the immortality of the soul, the Trinity, and hellfire. They receive moral guidance, freeing them from immoral

20. God's people will experience what kind of healing, and when?
21. In what ways do Jehovah's worshipers today experience spiritual healing?

Thanks to the ransom sacrifice,
Jehovah's people have a clean standing before him

practices and helping them to make good decisions. And thanks to the ransom sacrifice of Jesus Christ, they have a clean standing before God and enjoy a clean conscience. (Colossians 1:13, 14; 1 Peter 2:24; 1 John 4:10) This spiritual healing has physical benefits. For example, avoiding immoral sex and the use of tobacco products protects Christians against sexually transmitted diseases and certain forms of cancer.—1 Corinthians 6:18; 2 Corinthians 7:1.

22 Moreover, there will be a grander fulfillment of the words of Isaiah 33:24 after Armageddon, in God's new world. Under the rulership of the Messianic Kingdom, humans will experience a great *physical* healing along with their spiritual healing. (Revelation 21:3, 4) Shortly after the destruction of Satan's system of things, miracles like those that Jesus performed while on earth will no doubt take place on a global scale. The blind will see, the deaf will hear, the lame will walk! (Isaiah 35:5, 6) This will allow all survivors of the great tribulation to share in the grand work of bringing the earth to a paradisaic condition.

23 Later, when the resurrection begins, those coming back to life will no doubt be raised with good health. But as the value of the ransom sacrifice is applied to an increasing extent, more physical benefits will ensue, until mankind is lifted to perfection. Then, righteous ones will "come to life" in the fullest sense. (Revelation 20:5, 6) At that time, in both a spiritual and a physical way, "No resident will say: 'I am sick.'" What an exciting promise! May all true worshipers today resolve to be among those who will experience its fulfillment!

22, 23. (a) What grand fulfillment will Isaiah 33:24 have in the future? (b) What is the resolve of true worshipers today?

In the new world, there will be a great physical healing

CHAPTER TWENTY-SEVEN

Jehovah Pours Out Indignation Upon the Nations

Isaiah 34:1-17

JEHOVAH GOD is patient not only with his faithful servants but also, when his purpose warrants it, with his enemies. (1 Peter 3:19, 20; 2 Peter 3:15) Jehovah's adversaries may not appreciate his patience and may view it as an inability or an unwillingness to act. Still, as the 34th chapter of Isaiah shows, in the end Jehovah always demands an accounting from his enemies. (Zephaniah 3:8) For a while, God permitted Edom and other nations to oppose his people without hindrance. But Jehovah had his own due time for retribution. (Deuteronomy 32:35) Similarly, in his appointed time, Jehovah will express his vengeance upon all elements of the present wicked world that defy his sovereignty.

2 The primary purpose of God's executing vengeance is to demonstrate his sovereignty and glorify his name. (Psalm 83:13-18) His retribution also vindicates his servants as being truly his representatives and delivers them from undesirable circumstances. Moreover, Jehovah's vengeance is always in full harmony with his justice.—Psalm 58:10, 11.

Pay Attention, You Nations

3 Before focusing attention on retribution against Edom,

1, 2. (a) Regarding Jehovah's vengeance, of what can we be certain? (b) What does God accomplish by executing vengeance?
3. What invitation does Jehovah through Isaiah extend to the nations?

Jehovah through Isaiah extends a solemn invitation to all nations: *"Come up close, you nations, to hear; and you national groups, pay attention. Let the earth and that which fills it listen, the productive land and all its produce." (Isaiah 34:1)* The prophet has repeatedly spoken against ungodly nations. Now he is about to summarize the divine denunciations against them. Do these warnings have any meaning for our day?

4 Yes. The Sovereign of the universe has a controversy with all segments of this ungodly system of things. That is why the "national groups" and "the earth" are called upon to hear the Bible-based message that Jehovah has caused to be proclaimed worldwide. In language reminiscent of Psalm 24:1, Isaiah says that all the earth will be covered with this message—a prophecy that has come true in our time, when Jehovah's Witnesses preach "to the most distant part of the earth." (Acts 1:8) The nations, however, have not listened. They have not taken seriously the warning about their forthcoming demise. This, of course, will not prevent Jehovah from fulfilling his word.

5 The prophecy now describes the dark outlook for ungodly nations—a complete contrast to the bright hope of God's people that is described later. (Isaiah 35:1-10) The prophet states: *"Jehovah has indignation against all the nations, and rage against all their army. He must devote them to destruction; he must give them to the slaughter. And their slain ones will be thrown out; and as for their carcasses, their stink will ascend; and the mountains must melt because of their blood."—Isaiah 34:2, 3.*

---

4. (a) What are the nations called upon to do, as recorded at Isaiah 34:1? (b) Does Jehovah's expression of judgment on the nations prove that he is a cruel God? (See box on page 363.)
5, 6. (a) For what are the nations called to account by God? (b) How is it true that "the mountains must melt because of their blood"?

6 Attention is drawn to the bloodguilt of the nations. Today the nations of Christendom have the most bloodguilt of all. In two world wars and in many smaller conflicts, they have soaked the earth with human blood. Who should rightly demand justice for all this bloodguilt? None other than the Creator, the great Life-Giver. (Psalm 36:9) Jehovah's law has set the standard: "You must give soul for soul." (Exodus 21:23-25; Genesis 9:4-6) True to this law, he will cause the blood of the nations to flow —to their death. The stench of their unburied, dead bodies will fill the air—a truly shameful death! (Jeremiah 25: 33) The blood asked back in repayment will be enough to melt, or dissolve, as it were, the mountains. (Zephaniah 1: 17) With the complete destruction of their military forces, the worldly nations will see the fall of their governments, which in Bible prophecy are sometimes pictured as mountains.—Daniel 2:35, 44, 45; Revelation 17:9.

7 Again employing vivid imagery, Isaiah goes on to say: *"All those of the army of the heavens must rot away. And the heavens must be rolled up, just like a book scroll; and their army will all shrivel away, just as the leafage shrivels off the vine and like a shriveled fig off the fig tree." (Isaiah 34:4)* The expression "all those of the army of the heavens" does not mean the literal stars and planets. Verses 5 and 6 speak of a sword of execution being drenched with blood in those "heavens." Hence, this must be a symbol of something in the human realm. (1 Corinthians 15: 50) Because of their loftiness as superior authorities, the governments of mankind are likened to heavens ruling over earthly human society. (Romans 13:1-4) So "the army of the heavens" represents the combined armies of these governments of mankind.

---

7. What are "the heavens," and what is "the army of the heavens"?

Christendom has soaked the earth with blood

"The heavens must be rolled up, just like a book scroll"

8 This "army" will "rot away," molder, like something perishable. (Psalm 102:26; Isaiah 51:6) To the naked eye, the literal heavens above us appear curved, like an ancient book scroll, the writing of which was generally on the inner side. When the material written on the inner side of a scroll has passed before the eyes of the reader, the finished scroll is rolled up and put away. Similarly, "the heavens must be rolled up, just like a book scroll," in that human

8. How do the symbolic heavens prove to be "just like a book scroll," and what happens to their 'armies'?

governments must come to their end. Reaching the final page of their history, they must be brought to their finish at Armageddon. Their impressive-looking 'armies' will fall just as withered leaves fall off a grapevine or "a shriveled fig" drops off a fig tree. Their time will be past.—Compare Revelation 6:12-14.

A Day of Retribution

9 Now the prophecy singles out a nation that exists in Isaiah's day—Edom. The Edomites are descendants of Esau (Edom), who sold his birthright to his twin brother, Jacob, for bread and lentil stew. (Genesis 25:24-34) Because Jacob supplanted him in the birthright, Esau became filled with hatred for his brother. Later the nation of Edom and the nation of Israel became enemies, even though they descended from twin brothers. For this hostility against God's people, Edom has incurred the wrath of Jehovah, who now says: *"In the heavens my sword will certainly be drenched. Look! Upon Edom it will descend, and upon the people devoted by me to destruction in justice. Jehovah has a sword; it must be filled with blood; it must be made greasy with the fat, with the blood of young rams and he-goats, with the fat of the kidneys of rams. For Jehovah has a sacrifice in Bozrah, and a great slaughtering in the land of Edom."—Isaiah 34:5, 6.*

10 Edom occupies a high, mountainous region. (Jeremiah 49:16; Obadiah 8, 9, 19, 21) Nevertheless, even these natural fortifications will be of no help when Jehovah

---

9. (a) What is the origin of Edom, and what relationship developed between Israel and Edom? (b) What does Jehovah decree concerning Edom?
10. (a) Whom does Jehovah bring down when he wields his sword "in the heavens"? (b) What attitude does Edom display when Judah is attacked by Babylon?

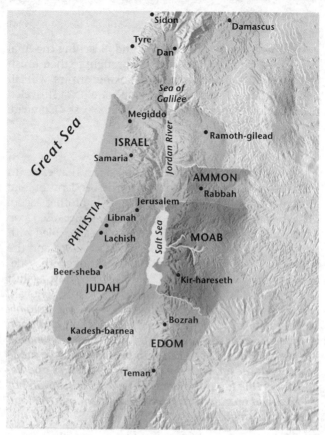

wields his sword of judgment "in the heavens," abasing Edom's rulers from their elevated position. Edom is heavily militarized, and its armed forces march through high mountain ranges to safeguard the country. But powerful Edom furnishes no assistance when Judah is attacked by the armies of Babylon. Rather, Edom is overjoyed to see the tumbling of the kingdom of Judah and urges her conquerors on. (Psalm 137:7) Edom even chases down Jews

An Angry God?

Expressions such as those found at Isaiah 34:2-7 have moved many to think that Jehovah, as described in the Hebrew Scriptures, is a cruel, wrathful God. Is that so?

No. While God does at times express his anger, such anger is always justified. It is always based on principle, not on uncontrolled emotion. Moreover, it is always dictated by the Creator's right to receive exclusive devotion and his constancy in upholding truth. Divine anger is governed both by God's love of righteousness and by his love for those practicing righteousness. Jehovah sees all the issues involved in a matter and has complete, unlimited knowledge of a situation. (Hebrews 4: 13) He reads the heart; he notes the degree of ignorance, negligence, or willful sin; and he acts with impartiality.—Deuteronomy 10:17, 18; 1 Samuel 16:7; Acts 10:34, 35.

However, Jehovah God is "slow to anger and abundant in loving-kindness." (Exodus 34:6) Those who fear him and strive to work righteousness receive mercy, for the Almighty recognizes man's inherited imperfection and shows mercy to him on this account. Today God does this on the basis of Jesus' sacrifice. (Psalm 103: 13, 14) At the proper time, Jehovah's anger is removed from those who acknowledge their sin, repent, and truly serve him. (Isaiah 12:1) Fundamentally, Jehovah is not an angry God but a happy God, not unapproachable but welcoming, peaceable, and calm toward those who properly approach him. (1 Timothy 1:11) This is in sharp contrast to the merciless, cruel characteristics ascribed to the false gods of the pagans and portrayed in images of those gods.

running for their lives and hands them over to the Babylonians. (Obadiah 11-14) The Edomites plan to take over the abandoned country of the Israelites, and they speak boastfully against Jehovah.—Ezekiel 35:10-15.

11 Does Jehovah overlook this unbrotherly conduct on the part of the Edomites? No. Rather, he foretells of Edom: *"The wild bulls must come down with them, and young bulls with the powerful ones; and their land must be drenched with blood, and their very dust will be made greasy with the fat."* *(Isaiah 34:7)* Jehovah speaks of the greater ones and the lesser ones in the nation as symbolic wild bulls and young bulls, as young rams and he-goats. The land of this bloodguilty nation must be drenched with the people's own blood by means of the executional "sword" of Jehovah.

12 God purposes to punish Edom for what has maliciously been done to His earthly organization, called Zion. Says the prophecy: *"Jehovah has a day of vengeance, a year of retributions for the legal case over Zion."* *(Isaiah 34:8)* Not long after the destruction of Jerusalem in 607 B.C.E., Jehovah begins to express his righteous vengeance upon the Edomites by means of the king of Babylon, Nebuchadnezzar. (Jeremiah 25:15-17, 21) When Babylon's armies move against Edom, nothing can save the Edomites! It is "a year of retributions" upon that mountainous land. Jehovah

---

11. How will Jehovah repay the Edomites for their treacherous conduct?
12. (a) Whom does Jehovah use to bring punishment upon Edom? (b) What does the prophet Obadiah foretell regarding Edom?

foretells through the prophet Obadiah: "Because of the violence to your brother Jacob, shame will cover you, and you will have to be cut off to time indefinite. . . . In the way that you have done, it will be done to you. Your sort of treatment will return upon your own head."—Obadiah 10, 15; Ezekiel 25:12-14.

Christendom's Bleak Future

13 In modern times, there exists an organization with a record like that of Edom. What organization? Well, who in modern times has taken the lead in reviling and persecuting Jehovah's servants? Has it not been Christendom, through its clergy class? Yes! Christendom has elevated herself to mountainlike heights in the affairs of this world. She claims a lofty position in mankind's system of things, and her religions form the dominant part of Babylon the Great. But Jehovah has decreed "a year of retributions" against this modern-day Edom for outrageous misconduct toward His people, His Witnesses.

14 Therefore, as we consider the rest of this part of Isaiah's prophecy, we think not only of ancient Edom but

13. Who today is like Edom, and why?
14, 15. (a) What will happen both to the land of Edom and to Christendom? (b) What do the references to burning pitch and indefinitely lasting smoke mean, and what do they not mean?

also of Christendom: ***"Her torrents must be changed into pitch, and her dust into sulphur; and her land must become as burning pitch. By night or by day it will not be extinguished; to time indefinite its smoke will keep ascending."*** *(Isaiah 34:9, 10a)* The land of Edom becomes so parched that it is as if the dust were sulfur and the torrent valleys were filled, not with water, but with pitch. Then these highly combustible substances are set afire!—Compare Revelation 17:16.

15 Some have viewed the mention of fire, pitch, and sulfur as evidence of the existence of a burning hell. But Edom is not hurled into some mythical hellfire to burn forever. Rather, it is destroyed, disappearing from the world scene as if totally consumed with fire and sulfur. As the prophecy goes on to show, the final result is, not everlasting torment, but "emptiness . . . wasteness . . . nothing." (Isaiah 34:11, 12) The smoke 'ascending to time indefinite' vividly illustrates this. When a house burns down, smoke keeps coming from the ashes for some time after the flames have died down, providing onlookers with evidence that there has been a conflagration. Since Christians today are learning lessons from the destruction of Edom, the smoke of Edom's burning is still, in a sense, ascending.

16 Isaiah's prophecy continues, foretelling that Edom's human population will be replaced by wild animals, implying a coming desolation: ***"From generation to generation she will be parched; forever and ever no one will be passing across her. And the pelican and the porcupine must take possession of her, and long-eared owls and ravens themselves will reside in her; and he must stretch out***

16, 17. What will Edom become, and how long will it continue in such a state?

over her the measuring line of emptiness and the stones of wasteness. Her nobles—there are none there whom they will call to the kingship itself, and her very princes will all become nothing. On her dwelling towers thorns must come up, nettles and thorny weeds in her fortified places; and she must become an abiding place of jackals, the courtyard for the ostriches. And haunters of waterless regions must meet up with howling animals, and even the goat-shaped demon will call to its companion. Yes, there the nightjar will certainly take its ease and find for itself a resting-place. There the arrow snake has made its nest and lays eggs."—Isaiah 34:10b-15. *

17 Yes, Edom will become an empty land. It will become a wasteland with only wild beasts, birds, and snakes in it. This parched state of the land will continue, as verse 10 says, "forever and ever." There will be no restoration. —Obadiah 18.

Sure Fulfillment of Jehovah's Word

18 What a hopeless future this foreshadows for that modern-day equivalent of Edom, Christendom! She has proved herself to be a bitter enemy of Jehovah God, whose Witnesses she viciously persecutes. And there is no doubt that Jehovah will fulfill his word. Whenever anyone compares the prophecy with the fulfillment, the two will be found to coincide—just as surely as the creatures that inhabit the desolated Edom each 'have their own mate.'

---

* By Malachi's time, this prophecy had been fulfilled. (Malachi 1:3) Malachi reports that Edomites hoped to repossess their desolated land. (Malachi 1:4) However, this was not Jehovah's will, and later another people, the Nabataeans, took possession of what had been the land of Edom.

18, 19. What is "the book of Jehovah," and what is reserved for Christendom in this "book"?

Isaiah addresses future students of Bible prophecy, saying: ***"Search for yourselves in the book of Jehovah and read out loud: not one has been missing of them; they actually do not fail to have each one her mate, for it is the mouth of Jehovah that has given the command, and it is his spirit that has collected them together. And it is He that has cast for them the lot, and his own hand has apportioned the place to them by the measuring line. To time indefinite they will take possession of it; for generation after generation they will reside in it."—Isaiah 34:16, 17.***

19 The impending destruction of Christendom has been foretold in "the book of Jehovah." This "book of Jehovah" details the accounts that Jehovah will settle with those who are his implacable enemies and who are unrepentant oppressors of his people. What was written concerning ancient Edom came true, and this strengthens our confidence that the prophecy as applying to Christendom, the modern-day parallel of Edom, will likewise come true. "The measuring line," Jehovah's rule of action, guarantees that this spiritually moribund organization will become a desolate wasteland.

20 Christendom does all she can to pacify her political friends, but to no avail! According to Revelation chapters 17 and 18, Almighty God, Jehovah, will put it into their hearts to act against all of Babylon the Great, including Christendom. This will rid the whole earth of fake Christianity. Christendom's situation will become like the bleak condition described in Isaiah chapter 34. She will not even be on hand during the all-decisive "war of the great day of God the Almighty"! (Revelation 16:14) Like ancient Edom, Christendom will be totally cleared from the surface of the earth, "forever and ever."

20. Like ancient Edom, Christendom will experience what?

CHAPTER TWENTY-EIGHT

Paradise Restored!

Isaiah 35:1-10

"THE nostalgia for paradise is among the powerful nostalgias that seem to haunt human beings. It may be the most powerful and persistent of all. A certain longing for paradise is evidenced at every level of religious life." So says *The Encyclopedia of Religion.* Such nostalgia is only natural, since the Bible tells us that human life began in Paradise—a beautiful garden free of disease and death. (Genesis 2:8-15) It is not surprising that many of the world's religions hold out the hope of future life in a paradise of one kind or another.

2 In many parts of the Bible, we can read of the true hope of the future Paradise. (Isaiah 51:3) For example, the part of Isaiah's prophecy recorded in chapter 35 describes the transformation of wilderness regions into gardenlike parks and fruitful fields. The blind gain sight, the mute can speak, and the deaf can hear. In this promised Paradise, there is no grief or sighing, which implies that even death is no more. What a wonderful promise! How should these words be understood? Do they hold out hope for us today? A consideration of this chapter of Isaiah will provide the answers to these questions.

A Desolate Land Rejoices

3 Isaiah's inspired prophecy of Paradise restored begins

---

1. Why do many religions hold out the hope of life in a paradise?
2. Where can we find the true hope of future Paradise?
3. According to Isaiah's prophecy, what transformation will the land undergo?

with these words: *"The wilderness and the waterless region will exult, and the desert plain will be joyful and blossom as the saffron. Without fail it will blossom, and it will really be joyful with joyousness and with glad crying out. The glory of Lebanon itself must be given to it, the splendor of Carmel and of Sharon. There will be those who will see the glory of Jehovah, the splendor of our God."—Isaiah 35:1, 2.*

4 Isaiah writes these words about the year 732 B.C.E. Some 125 years later, the Babylonians destroy Jerusalem and the people of Judah are sent into exile. Their homeland is left uninhabited, desolated. (2 Kings 25:8-11, 21-26) In this way Jehovah's warning that the people of Israel would go into exile if they proved unfaithful is fulfilled. (Deuteronomy 28:15, 36, 37; 1 Kings 9:6-8) When the Hebrew nation becomes captive in a foreign land, their well-irrigated fields and orchards are left unattended for 70 years and become like a wilderness.—Isaiah 64:10; Jeremiah 4:23-27; 9:10-12.

5 However, Isaiah's prophecy foretells that the land will not lie desolate forever. It will be restored to a veritable paradise. "The glory of Lebanon" and "the splendor of Carmel and of Sharon" will be given to it.* How? Upon their return from exile, the Jews are again able to cultivate and irrigate their fields, and their land returns to the rich fruitfulness that it had before. For this, credit can go only to

---

* The Scriptures describe ancient Lebanon as a fruitful land with luxuriant forests and majestic cedars, comparable to the Garden of Eden. (Psalm 29:5; 72:16; Ezekiel 28:11-13) Sharon was known for its streams and oak forests; Carmel was famous for its vineyards, orchards, and flower-carpeted slopes.

---

4. When and how does the Jews' homeland take on the appearance of a wilderness?
5. (a) How are paradiselike conditions restored to the land? (b) In what sense do people "see the glory of Jehovah"?

Jehovah. It is by his will and with his support and blessing that the Jews get to enjoy such paradiselike conditions. People are able to see "the glory of Jehovah, the splendor of [their] God" when they acknowledge Jehovah's hand in the amazing transformation of their land.

6 Nevertheless, in the restored land of Israel, there is a more important fulfillment of Isaiah's words. In a spiritual sense, Israel has been in a dry, desertlike state for many years. While the exiles were in Babylon, pure worship was severely restricted. There was no temple, no altar, and no organized priesthood. Daily sacrifices were suspended. Now, Isaiah prophesies a reversal. Under the leadership of such men as Zerubbabel, Ezra, and Nehemiah, representatives from all 12 tribes of Israel return to Jerusalem, rebuild the temple, and worship Jehovah freely. (Ezra 2:1, 2) This is indeed a spiritual paradise!

Aglow With the Spirit

7 The words of Isaiah chapter 35 have a ring of joy. The prophet is proclaiming a bright future for the repentant nation. Indeed, he speaks with conviction and optimism. Two centuries later, at the threshold of their restoration, exiled Jews need the same conviction and optimism. Through Isaiah, Jehovah prophetically exhorts them: *"Strengthen the weak hands, you people, and make the knees that are wobbling firm. Say to those who are anxious at heart: 'Be strong. Do not be afraid. Look! Your own God will come with vengeance itself, God even with a repayment. He himself will come and save you people.'"* —Isaiah 35:3, 4.

8 The end of the long exile is a time for action. King Cy-

---

6. What important fulfillment of Isaiah's words is seen?
7, 8. Why do the Jewish exiles need a positive attitude, and how do Isaiah's words provide encouragement?

rus of Persia, the instrument of Jehovah's vengeance against Babylon, has proclaimed that Jehovah's worship is to be restored in Jerusalem. (2 Chronicles 36:22, 23) Thousands of Hebrew families need to get organized in order to make the hazardous trip from Babylon to Jerusalem. When they arrive there, they will have to erect adequate living facilities and prepare for the monumental task of rebuilding the temple and the city. For some Jews in Babylon, all of this may seem daunting. However, it is no time to be weak or apprehensive. The Jews are to strengthen one another and have confidence in Jehovah. He assures them that they will be saved.

9 Those released from captivity in Babylon will have good reason to rejoice, for a grand future awaits them

---

9. What grand promise is held out to returning Jews?

upon their return to Jerusalem. Isaiah foretells: *"At that time the eyes of the blind ones will be opened, and the very ears of the deaf ones will be unstopped. At that time the lame one will climb up just as a stag does, and the tongue of the speechless one will cry out in gladness."—Isaiah 35:5, 6a.*

10 Jehovah evidently has in mind the spiritual condition of his people. They have been punished with 70 years of exile for their earlier apostasy. Still, in administering his discipline, Jehovah did not strike his people with blindness, deafness, lameness, and muteness. Hence, restoring the nation of Israel does not require the healing of physical disabilities. Jehovah restores that which was lost, namely, spiritual health.

11 Repentant Jews are healed in that they regain their spiritual senses—their spiritual vision and their ability to hear, obey, and speak Jehovah's word. They become aware of their need to stay close to Jehovah. By their fine conduct, they "cry out" in joyful praise of their God. The formerly "lame one" becomes eager and energetic in his worship of Jehovah. Figuratively, he will "climb up just as a stag does."

Jehovah Refreshes His People

12 It is difficult to imagine a paradise without water. The original Paradise in Eden had an abundance of water. (Genesis 2:10-14) The land given to Israel was also "a land of torrent valleys of water, springs and watery deeps issuing forth." (Deuteronomy 8:7) Appropriately, then, Isaiah makes this refreshing promise: *"In the wilderness wa-*

10, 11. For returning Jews, why must Isaiah's words have a spiritual meaning, and what do they imply?
12. To what extent will Jehovah bless the land with water?

ters will have burst out, and torrents in the desert plain. And the heat-parched ground will have become as a reedy pool, and the thirsty ground as springs of water. In the abiding place of jackals, a resting-place for them, there will be green grass with reeds and papyrus plants." (*Isaiah 35: 6b, 7*) When the Israelites again care for the land, the desolate areas where jackals once roamed will be covered with verdant, luxuriant vegetation. Dry and dusty ground will be transformed into "a swampy place" where papyrus and other aquatic reeds can grow.—Job 8:11.

13 More important, though, is the spiritual water of truth, which the repatriated Jews will enjoy in abundance. Jehovah will provide knowledge, encouragement, and comfort through his Word. Moreover, faithful older men and princes will be "like streams of water in a waterless country." (Isaiah 32:1, 2) Those who promote pure

---

13. What abundant spiritual water will be available to the restored nation?

Desert places become well-watered places of reeds and papyrus plants

worship, such as Ezra, Haggai, Jeshua, Nehemiah, Zechariah, Zerubbabel, will indeed be living testimony to the fulfillment of Isaiah's prophecy.—Ezra 5:1, 2; 7:6, 10; Nehemiah 12:47.

"The Way of Holiness"

14 Before the exiled Jews can enjoy such physical and spiritual paradisaic conditions, however, they will have to make the long and hazardous journey from Babylon to Jerusalem. Taking a direct route would mean crossing some 500 miles of arid, inhospitable terrain. A less-challenging route would involve traveling 1,000 miles. Either journey would mean spending months exposed to the elements and in danger of meeting both wild beasts and beastlike men. Still, those who believe Isaiah's prophecy are not overly concerned. Why?

15 Through Isaiah, Jehovah promises: *"There will certainly come to be a highway there, even a way; and the Way of Holiness it will be called. The unclean one will not pass over it. And it will be for the one walking on the way, and no foolish ones will wander about on it. No lion will prove to be there, and the rapacious sort of wild beasts will not come up on it. None will be found there; and the repurchased ones must walk there."* (Isaiah 35:8, 9) Jehovah has reclaimed his people! They are his "repurchased ones," and he guarantees them safe conduct on their way home. Is there a literal paved, elevated, and fenced-in road from Babylon to Jerusalem? No, but Jehovah's protection of his people on their journey is so sure that it is as if they were on such a highway.—Compare Psalm 91:1-16.

---

14. Describe travel between Babylon and Jerusalem.
15, 16. (a) What protection does Jehovah provide for faithful Jews on their journey home? (b) In what other sense does Jehovah provide a safe highway for the Jews?

16 The Jews are also protected from spiritual dangers. The figurative highway is "the Way of Holiness." Those who disrespect sacred things or are spiritually unclean are not qualified to travel on it. They are not wanted in the restored land. Approved ones are rightly motivated. They are not returning to Judah and Jerusalem in a spirit of national pride or in pursuit of personal interests. Spiritually-minded Jews realize that the principal reason for their return is to reestablish the pure worship of Jehovah in that land.—Ezra 1:1-3.

Jehovah's People Rejoice

17 Chapter 35 of Isaiah's prophecy ends on a joyful note: *"The very ones redeemed by Jehovah will return and certainly come to Zion with a joyful cry; and rejoicing to time indefinite will be upon their head. To exultation and rejoicing they will attain, and grief and sighing must flee away."* (Isaiah 35:10) The captive Jews who have looked to this prophecy for comfort and hope during their exile may have wondered how its various details would be fulfilled. Likely they have not understood many aspects of the prophecy. Still, it has been crystal clear that they would "return and certainly come to Zion."

18 Hence, in the year 537 B.C.E., some 50,000 men (including more than 7,000 slaves and temple singers) along with women and children make the four-month journey back to Jerusalem, with full confidence in Jehovah. (Ezra 2:64, 65) Just a few months later, Jehovah's altar is rebuilt, setting the stage for a full reconstruction of the temple. The 200-year-old prophecy of Isaiah is fulfilled. The

17. How has the prophecy of Isaiah comforted faithful Jews during their long exile?
18. In what way is grief and sighing in Babylon replaced by exultation and rejoicing in the restored land?

Jesus healed the sick, both spiritually and physically

nation's grief and sighing while in Babylon is replaced by exultation and rejoicing in the restored land. Jehovah has fulfilled his promise. Paradise—both literal and spiritual—has been restored!

The Birth of a New Nation

19 Of course, in the sixth century B.C.E., the fulfillment of Isaiah chapter 35 is limited. The paradisaic conditions enjoyed by the repatriated Jews do not last. In time, false religious teachings and nationalism contaminate pure worship. Spiritually, the Jews again experience grief and sighing. Jehovah eventually rejects them as his people. (Matthew 21:43) Because of renewed disobedience, their rejoicing is not permanent. All of this points to a further, greater fulfillment of Isaiah chapter 35.

20 In Jehovah's due time, another Israel, a spiritual one, came into existence. (Galatians 6:16) Jesus set the stage

---

19. Why must it be said that Isaiah's prophecy has only a limited fulfillment in the sixth century B.C.E.?
20. What new Israel came into existence in the first century C.E.?

for the birth of this new Israel during his earthly ministry. He restored pure worship, and with his teachings, waters of truth began to flow once again. He healed the sick, both physically and spiritually. A joyful cry went forth as the good news of God's Kingdom was proclaimed. Seven weeks after his death and resurrection, the glorified Jesus established the Christian congregation, a spiritual Israel made up of Jews and others redeemed by Jesus' shed blood, begotten as God's spiritual sons and brothers of Jesus, and anointed by holy spirit.—Acts 2:1-4; Romans 8:16, 17; 1 Peter 1:18, 19.

21 When writing to the members of spiritual Israel, the apostle Paul referred to the words of Isaiah 35:3 by saying: "Straighten up the hands that hang down and the enfeebled knees." (Hebrews 12:12) Evidently, then, in the first century C.E., there was a fulfillment of the words of Isaiah chapter 35. In a literal sense, Jesus and his disciples miraculously gave sight to blind ones and hearing to deaf ones. They enabled 'lame ones' to walk and speechless ones to regain their speech. (Matthew 9:32; 11:5; Luke 10:9) More important, righthearted ones escaped from false religion and came to enjoy a spiritual paradise within the Christian congregation. (Isaiah 52:11; 2 Corinthians 6:17) As in the case of the Jews returning from Babylon, these escapees found that a positive, courageous spirit was essential.—Romans 12:11.

22 What of our day? Does the prophecy of Isaiah have another fulfillment, a more complete one involving the Christian congregation today? Yes. After the death of the

----

21. Regarding the first-century Christian congregation, what events may be viewed as a fulfillment of certain features of Isaiah's prophecy?
22. How did sincere, truth-seeking Christians in modern times come into Babylonish captivity?

apostles, the number of true anointed Christians greatly diminished, and false Christians, "weeds," flourished on the world scene. (Matthew 13:36-43; Acts 20:30; 2 Peter 2: 1-3) Even when during the 19th century, sincere individuals began to separate themselves from Christendom and seek pure worship, their understanding remained tainted with unscriptural teachings. In 1914, Jesus was enthroned as Messianic King, but soon thereafter, the situation looked bleak for these sincere truth seekers. In fulfillment of prophecy, the nations 'made war with them and conquered them,' and the attempts of these sincere Christians to preach the good news were stifled. In effect, they went into Babylonish captivity.—Revelation 11:7, 8.

23 In 1919, however, things changed. Jehovah brought his people out of captivity. They began to reject the false teachings that had earlier corrupted their worship. As a result, they enjoyed a healing. They came to be in a spiritual paradise, which even today continues to spread throughout the earth. In a spiritual sense, the blind are learning to see and the deaf, to hear—becoming fully alert to the operation of God's holy spirit, constantly aware of the need to stay close to Jehovah. (1 Thessalonians 5:6; 2 Timothy 4:5) No longer mute, true Christians are eager to "cry out," declaring Bible truths to others. (Romans 1:15) Those who were spiritually weak, or "lame," now display zeal and joy. Figuratively, they are able to "climb up just as a stag does."

24 These restored Christians walk on "the Way of Holiness." This "Way," which leads out of Babylon the Great into a spiritual paradise, is open to all spiritually clean worshipers. (1 Peter 1:13-16) They can count on Jehovah for protection and be confident that Satan will not succeed in

23, 24. In what ways have Isaiah's words been fulfilled among God's people since 1919?

his animalistic attacks to eliminate true worship. (1 Peter 5:8) Disobedient ones and any who behave like rapacious wild beasts are not allowed to corrupt those on God's highway of holiness. (1 Corinthians 5:11) Within this protected environment, Jehovah's redeemed ones—anointed and "other sheep"—find joy in serving the only true God. —John 10:16.

25 What of the future? Will Isaiah's prophecy ever be fulfilled in a physical way? Yes. The miraculous healings by Jesus and his apostles in the first century demonstrated Jehovah's desire and ability to perform such healings on a large scale in the future. The inspired Psalms speak of everlasting life in peaceful conditions on earth. (Psalm 37:9, 11, 29) Jesus promised life in Paradise. (Luke 23:43) Down to its very last book, the Bible provides hope for a literal paradise. At that time, the blind, the deaf, the lame, and the speechless will be healed physically and permanently. Grief and sighing will flee away. Rejoicing will indeed be to time indefinite, even forever.—Revelation 7:9, 16, 17; 21:3, 4.

26 While true Christians await the restoration of the physical earthly Paradise, even now they enjoy the blessings of the spiritual paradise. They face trials and tribulations with optimism. With unwavering confidence in Jehovah, they encourage one another, heeding the admonition: "Strengthen the weak hands, you people, and make the knees that are wobbling firm. Say to those who are anxious at heart: 'Be strong. Do not be afraid.'" They have complete trust in the prophetic assurance: "Look! Your own God will come with vengeance itself, God even with a repayment. He himself will come and save you people."—Isaiah 35:3, 4.

25. Will there be a physical fulfillment of Isaiah chapter 35? Explain.
26. How do Isaiah's words strengthen Christians today?

CHAPTER TWENTY-NINE

A King's Faith Is Rewarded

Isaiah 36:1–39:8

HEZEKIAH was 25 years old when he became king of Judah. What kind of ruler would he be? Would he follow in the footsteps of his father, King Ahaz, and induce his subjects to follow after false gods? Or would he lead the people in the worship of Jehovah, as did his forefather King David?—2 Kings 16:2.

2 Soon after Hezekiah came to the throne, it became clear that he intended "to do what was right in Jehovah's eyes." (2 Kings 18:2, 3) In his first year, he ordered Jehovah's temple repaired and temple services resumed. (2 Chronicles 29:3, 7, 11) Then he organized a grand Passover celebration to which the entire nation was invited —including the ten northern tribes of Israel. What an unforgettable feast that was! There had been none like it since the days of King Solomon.—2 Chronicles 30: 1, 25, 26.

3 At the conclusion of the Passover celebration, those in attendance were moved to cut down the sacred poles, break up the sacred pillars, pull down the high places and the altars of their false gods, after which they returned to their cities, determined to serve the true God.

1, 2. How did Hezekiah prove to be a better king than Ahaz?

3. (a) What action was taken by the inhabitants of Israel and Judah who attended the Passover arranged by Hezekiah? (b) What do Christians today learn from the decisive action taken by those who attended that Passover?

King Hezekiah trusts in Jehovah when he faces the might of Assyria

(2 Chronicles 31:1) What a contrast that was to their former religious attitude! True Christians today can learn from this the importance of 'not forsaking the gathering of themselves together.' Such gatherings, whether in local congregations or on a larger scale at assemblies and conventions, play a vital role in their receiving encouragement and being moved by the brotherhood as well as by God's spirit to "incite to love and fine works."—Hebrews 10:23-25.

Faith Put to the Test

4 Serious trials lie ahead for Jerusalem. Hezekiah has broken an alliance that his faithless father, Ahaz, concluded with the Assyrians. He has even subdued the Philistines, who are allies of Assyria. (2 Kings 18:7, 8) This has angered the king of Assyria. Hence, we read: *"It came about in the fourteenth year of King Hezekiah that Sennacherib the king of Assyria came up against all the fortified cities of*

4, 5. (a) How has Hezekiah demonstrated his independence from Assyria? (b) What military action has Sennacherib taken against Judah, and what steps does Hezekiah take to avoid an immediate assault on Jerusalem? (c) How does Hezekiah prepare to defend Jerusalem from the Assyrians?

Judah and proceeded to seize them." (Isaiah 36:1) Perhaps hoping to protect Jerusalem from an immediate assault by the relentless Assyrian army, Hezekiah agrees to pay Sennacherib an enormous tribute of 300 silver talents and 30 gold talents.*—2 Kings 18:14.

5 Since there is not enough gold and silver in the royal treasury to pay the tribute, Hezekiah retrieves what precious metals he can from the temple. He also cuts down the temple doors, which have been overlaid with gold, and sends them to Sennacherib. This satisfies the Assyrian, but only for a while. (2 Kings 18:15, 16) Evidently, Hezekiah realizes that the Assyrians will not leave Jerusalem alone for long. Therefore, preparations have to be made. The people block up water sources that could supply water to invading Assyrians. Hezekiah also strengthens the fortifications of Jerusalem and builds an arsenal of weapons, including "missiles in abundance and shields."—2 Chronicles 32:4, 5.

6 However, Hezekiah puts his trust, not in clever war strategies or in fortifications, but in Jehovah of armies. He admonishes his military chiefs: "Be courageous and strong. Do not be afraid nor be terrified because of the king of Assyria and on account of all the crowd that is with him; for with us there are more than there are with him. With him there is an arm of flesh, but with us there is Jehovah our God to help us and to fight our battles." Responsively, the people begin "to brace themselves upon the words of Hezekiah the king of Judah." (2 Chronicles 32:7, 8) Visualize the exciting events that follow as chapters 36 to 39 of Isaiah's prophecy are reviewed.

---

* Worth more than $9.5 million (U.S.) at current values.

---

6. In whom does Hezekiah put his trust?

Rabshakeh Presents His Case

7 Sennacherib dispatches Rabshakeh (a military title, not a personal name) along with two other dignitaries to Jerusalem to demand the city's surrender. (2 Kings 18:17) These are met outside the city wall by three of Hezekiah's representatives, Eliakim the overseer of Hezekiah's household, Shebna the secretary, and Joah the son of Asaph the recorder.—*Isaiah 36:2, 3.*

8 Rabshakeh's aim is simple—convince Jerusalem to surrender without a fight. Speaking in Hebrew, he first cries out: *"What is this confidence in which you have trusted? . . . In whom have you put trust, that you have rebelled against me?"* (Isaiah 36:4, 5) Then Rabshakeh taunts the frightened Jews, reminding them that they are completely isolated. To whom can they turn for support? To that *"crushed reed,"* Egypt? (Isaiah 36:6) At this time, Egypt does resemble a crushed reed; in fact, that former world power has been temporarily conquered by Ethiopia, and Egypt's present Pharaoh, King Tirhakah, is not an Egyptian but an Ethiopian. And he is about to be defeated by Assyria. (2 Kings 19:8, 9) Since Egypt cannot save itself, it will be of little help to Judah.

9 Rabshakeh now argues that Jehovah will not fight for His people because He is displeased with them. Rabshakeh says: *"In case you should say to me, 'It is Jehovah our God in whom we have trusted,' is he not the one whose high places and whose altars Hezekiah has removed?"* (Isaiah 36:7) Of course, far from rejecting Jehovah by tearing down the high places and the altars in the land, the Jews have actually returned to Jehovah.

------

7. Who is Rabshakeh, and why is he sent to Jerusalem?
8. How does Rabshakeh try to break Jerusalem's resistance?
9. What evidently leads Rabshakeh to conclude that Jehovah would forsake His people, but what are the facts?

10 Next Rabshakeh reminds the Jews that militarily they are hopelessly outclassed. He issues this arrogant challenge: *"Let me give you two thousand horses to see whether you are able, on your part, to put riders upon them."* (*Isaiah 36:8*) In reality, though, does it matter whether Judah's trained cavalry are many or few? No, for Judah's salvation does not depend upon superior military strength. Proverbs 21:31 explains matters this way: "The horse is something prepared for the day of battle, but salvation belongs to Jehovah." Then Rabshakeh claims that Jehovah's blessing is with the Assyrians, not the Jews. Otherwise, he argues, the Assyrians could never have penetrated so far into Judah's territory.—*Isaiah 36:9, 10.*

11 Hezekiah's representatives are concerned about the effect that Rabshakeh's arguments will have on the men who can hear him from the top of the city wall. These Jewish officials request: *"Speak, please, to your servants in the Syrian language, for we are listening; and do not speak to us in the Jews' language in the ears of the people that are on the wall."* (*Isaiah 36:11*) But Rabshakeh has no intention of speaking in the Syrian language. He wants to sow seeds of doubt and fear in the Jews so that they will surrender and Jerusalem can be conquered without a fight! (*Isaiah 36:12*) Hence the Assyrian speaks again in "the Jews' language." He warns the inhabitants of Jerusalem: *"Do not let Hezekiah deceive you people, for he is not able to deliver you."* Following this, he tries to tempt those listening by painting a picture of life as it could be for the Jews under Assyrian rule: *"Make a capitulation to me and*

---

10. Why does it not matter whether Judah's defenders are many or few?
11, 12. (a) Why does Rabshakeh insist on speaking in "the Jews' language," and how does he try to tempt the listening Jews? (b) What effect might Rabshakeh's words have on the Jews?

come out to me and eat each one from his own vine and each one from his own fig tree and drink each one the water of his own cistern, until I come and actually take you to a land like your own land, a land of grain and new wine, a land of bread and vineyards."—Isaiah 36:13-17.

12 There will be no harvest for the Jews this year—the Assyrian invasion has prevented them from planting crops. The prospect of eating succulent grapes and of drinking cool water must be very appealing to the men listening on the wall. But Rabshakeh has not yet finished trying to weaken the Jews.

13 From his arsenal of arguments, Rabshakeh draws another verbal weapon. He warns the Jews against believing Hezekiah should he say: *"Jehovah himself will deliver us."* Rabshakeh reminds the Jews that the gods of Samaria were unable to prevent the ten tribes from being overcome by the Assyrians. And what of the gods of the other nations Assyria has conquered? *"Where are the gods of Hamath and Arpad?"* he demands. *"Where are the gods of Sepharvaim? And have they delivered Samaria out of my hand?"* —Isaiah 36:18-20.

14 Of course, Rabshakeh, a worshiper of false gods, does not understand that there is a big difference between apostate Samaria and Jerusalem under Hezekiah. Samaria's false gods had no power to save the ten-tribe kingdom. (2 Kings 17:7, 17, 18) On the other hand, Jerusalem under Hezekiah has turned its back on false gods and has returned to serving Jehovah. However, the three Judean representatives do not try to explain this to Rabshakeh. *"They continued to keep silent and did not answer him a word, for the commandment of the king was, saying: 'You must*

13, 14. Despite Rabshakeh's arguments, why is what happened to Samaria irrelevant to Judah's situation?

*The king sends emissaries
to Isaiah to hear Jehovah's counsel*

not answer him.'" (Isaiah 36:21) Eliakim, Shebna, and Joah return to Hezekiah and make an official report of the words of Rabshakeh.—Isaiah 36:22.

Hezekiah Makes a Decision

15 King Hezekiah now has a decision to make. Will Jerusalem surrender to the Assyrians? join forces with Egypt? or stand her ground and fight? Hezekiah is under great pressure. He goes to Jehovah's temple, while dispatching Eliakim and Shebna, along with the older men of the priests, to inquire of Jehovah through the prophet Isaiah. (Isaiah 37:1, 2) Dressed in sackcloth, the king's emissaries

---

15. (a) What decision now faces Hezekiah? (b) How does Jehovah reassure his people?

*Hezekiah prays that Jehovah's
name be magnified by Assyria's defeat*

approach Isaiah, saying: *"This day is a day of distress and
of rebuke and of scornful insolence . . . Perhaps Jehovah
your God will hear the words of Rabshakeh, whom the
king of Assyria his lord sent to taunt the living God, and he
will actually call him to account for the words that Jehovah your God has heard."* (Isaiah 37:3-5) Yes, the Assyrians are challenging the living God! Will Jehovah give attention to their taunts? Through Isaiah, Jehovah reassures
the Jews: *"Do not be afraid because of the words that you
have heard with which the attendants of the king of Assyria spoke abusively of me. Here I am putting a spirit in him,
and he must hear a report and return to his own land; and
I shall certainly cause him to fall by the sword in his own
land."—Isaiah 37:6, 7.*

16 Meanwhile, Rabshakeh is called away to be at Sennacherib's side while the king wages war at Libnah. Sennacherib will deal with Jerusalem later. *(Isaiah 37:8)* Still, Rabshakeh's departure brings no letup of pressure on Hezekiah. Sennacherib sends threatening letters describing what the inhabitants of Jerusalem can expect if they refuse to surrender: *"You yourself have heard what the kings of Assyria did to all the lands by devoting them to destruction, and will you yourself be delivered? Have the gods of the nations that my forefathers brought to ruin delivered them? . . . Where is the king of Hamath and the king of Arpad and the king of the city of Sepharvaim—of Hena and of Ivvah?" (Isaiah 37:9-13)* Basically, the Assyrian is saying that it is senseless to resist—resistance will only bring more trouble!

17 Deeply concerned about the consequences of the decision he must make, Hezekiah spreads Sennacherib's letters out before Jehovah in the temple. *(Isaiah 37:14)* In heartfelt prayer he implores Jehovah to give ear to the Assyrian's threats, concluding his prayer with the words: *"And now, O Jehovah our God, save us out of his hand, that all the kingdoms of the earth may know that you, O Jehovah, are God alone." (Isaiah 37:15-20)* From this it is clear that Hezekiah is primarily concerned, not with his own deliverance, but with the reproach that will be heaped upon Jehovah's name if Assyria defeats Jerusalem.

18 Jehovah's answer to Hezekiah's prayer comes through Isaiah. Jerusalem must not surrender to Assyria; she must stand her ground. Speaking as to Sennacherib, Isaiah boldly states Jehovah's message to the Assyrian: *"The virgin daughter of Zion has despised you, she has held*

---

16. What letters are sent by Sennacherib?
17, 18. (a) What is Hezekiah's motive in asking Jehovah for protection? (b) How does Jehovah through Isaiah answer the Assyrian?

you in derision. Behind you the daughter of Jerusalem has wagged her head [mockingly]." *(Isaiah 37:21, 22)* Jehovah then adds, in effect: 'Who are you to taunt the Holy One of Israel? I know your deeds. You have great ambitions; you make great boasts. You have trusted in your military power and have conquered much land. But you are not invincible. I will frustrate your plans. I will conquer you. Then I will do to you as you have done to others. I will put a hook in your nose and lead you back to Assyria!' —Isaiah 37:23-29.

"This Will Be the Sign for You"

19 What guarantee does Hezekiah have that Isaiah's prophecy will be fulfilled? Jehovah answers: *"This will be the sign for you: There will be an eating this year of the growth from spilled kernels, and in the second year grain that shoots up of itself; but in the third year sow seed, you people, and reap, and plant vineyards and eat their fruitage." (Isaiah 37:30)* Jehovah will provide food for the trapped Jews. Although unable to plant seed because of the Assyrian occupation, they will be able to eat from the gleanings of the preceding year's harvest. The following year, a sabbath year, they must let their fields lie fallow, despite their desperate situation. (Exodus 23:11) Jehovah promises that if the people obey his voice, enough grain will sprout in the fields to sustain them. Then, in the following year, men will sow seed in the usual way and enjoy the fruitage of their labor.

20 Jehovah now compares his people to a plant that cannot easily be uprooted: *"Those who escape of the house of Judah . . . will certainly take root downward and produce*

---

19. What sign does Jehovah give Hezekiah, and what does it mean?
20. In what way will those who escape the Assyrian attack "take root downward and produce fruitage upward"?

fruitage upward." (*Isaiah 37:31, 32*) Yes, those who trust in Jehovah have nothing to fear. They and their offspring will remain firmly established in the land.

21 What of the Assyrian's threats against Jerusalem? Jehovah answers: "*He will not come into this city, nor will he shoot an arrow there, nor confront it with a shield, nor cast up a siege rampart against it. By the way by which he came he will return, and into this city he will not*

21, 22. (a) What is prophesied concerning Sennacherib? (b) How and when are Jehovah's words about Sennacherib fulfilled?

Jehovah's angel strikes down 185,000 Assyrians

come." **(Isaiah 37:33, 34)** There will be no battle between Assyria and Jerusalem after all. Surprisingly, it will be the Assyrians, not the Jews, who are defeated without a fight.

22 True to his word, Jehovah sends an angel who strikes down the cream of Sennacherib's troops—185,000 men. This apparently happens at Libnah, and Sennacherib himself wakes up to find the leaders, chiefs, and mighty men of his army dead. Shamefaced, he returns to Nineveh, but despite his resounding defeat, he stubbornly remains devoted to his false god Nisroch. Some years later, while worshiping in the temple of Nisroch, Sennacherib is assassinated by two of his sons. Once again, lifeless Nisroch proves powerless to save.—*Isaiah 37:35-38*.

Hezekiah's Faith Is Further Strengthened

23 About the time that Sennacherib first comes up against Judah, Hezekiah falls gravely ill. Isaiah tells him that he is going to die. **(Isaiah 38:1)** The 39-year-old king is devastated. His concern is not only for his own well-being but also for the future of the people. Jerusalem and Judah are in danger of being invaded by the Assyrians. If Hezekiah dies, who will lead the fight? At that time, Hezekiah has no son to assume the rulership. In fervent prayer Hezekiah begs Jehovah to show him mercy.—*Isaiah 38: 2, 3*.

24 Isaiah has not yet left the palace courtyards when Jehovah sends him back to the stricken king's bedside with another message: *"I have heard your prayer. I have seen your tears. Here I am adding onto your days fifteen years;*

---

23. What crisis does Hezekiah face when Sennacherib first comes up against Judah, and what are the implications of this crisis?
24, 25. (a) How does Jehovah graciously answer Hezekiah's prayer? (b) What miracle does Jehovah perform, as described at Isaiah 38: 7, 8?

and out of the palm of the king of Assyria I shall deliver you and this city, and I will defend this city." (Isaiah 38:4-6; 2 Kings 20:4, 5) Jehovah will confirm his promise with an unusual sign: *"Here I am making the shadow of the steps that had gone down on the steps of the stairs of Ahaz by the sun retrace backward ten steps."—Isaiah 38:7, 8a.*

25 According to the Jewish historian Josephus, there was a staircase inside the royal palace, probably with a column near it. When the sun's rays hit the column, they cast a shadow on the stairs. One could measure the time of day by observing the progress of the shadow on the steps. Now Jehovah will perform a miracle. After the shadow drifts down the steps in the usual way, it will retrace its path backward ten steps. Who ever heard of such a thing? The Bible states: *"And the sun gradually went back ten steps on the steps of the stairs that it had gone down." (Isaiah 38: 8b)* Shortly thereafter, Hezekiah recovers from his illness. News of this spreads as far as Babylon. When the king of Babylon hears it, he sends messengers to Jerusalem to obtain the facts.

26 About three years after Hezekiah's miraculous recovery, his first son, Manasseh, is born. When Manasseh grows up, he does not show appreciation for God's compassion, without which he would not have been born! Instead, during most of his lifetime, Manasseh does on a large scale what is bad in Jehovah's eyes.—2 Chronicles 32: 24; 33:1-6.

A Lapse in Judgment

27 Like his forefather David, Hezekiah is a man of faith. He treasures God's Word. According to Proverbs 25:1, he arranged for the compiling of the material now found in Proverbs chapters 25 to 29. Some believe that he also

26. What is one result of the lengthening of Hezekiah's life?
27. In what ways does Hezekiah show appreciation for Jehovah?

composed the 119th Psalm. The moving song of gratitude that Hezekiah composes after recovering from his illness shows him to be a man of deep feeling. He concludes that the most important thing in life is to be able to praise Jehovah at His temple *"all the days of our life." (Isaiah 38:9-20)* May all of us feel the same way about pure worship!

28 Although faithful, Hezekiah is imperfect. He makes a serious error in judgment sometime after Jehovah heals him. Isaiah explains: *"At that time Merodachbaladan the son of Baladan the king of Babylon sent letters and a gift to Hezekiah, after he heard that he had been sick but was strong again. So Hezekiah began to rejoice over them and proceeded to show them his treasure-house, the silver and the gold and the balsam oil and the good oil and all his armory and all that was to be found in his treasures. There proved to be nothing that Hezekiah did not show them in his own house and in all his dominion."—Isaiah 39:1, 2.**

29 Even after the stinging defeat by Jehovah's angel, Assyria continues to pose a threat to many nations, including Babylon. Hezekiah may have wanted to impress the king of Babylon as a possible future ally. However, Jehovah does not want the inhabitants of Judah to consort with their enemies; he wants them to trust in him! Through

---

* After Sennacherib's defeat, surrounding nations brought gifts of gold, silver, and other precious things to Hezekiah. At 2 Chronicles 32:22, 23, 27, we read that "Hezekiah came to have riches and glory to a very great amount" and that "he came to be exalted in the eyes of all the nations." These gifts may have allowed him to replenish his treasure-house, which he had emptied when paying tribute to the Assyrians.

---

28. What error in judgment does Hezekiah make sometime after being miraculously healed?
29. (a) What may be the motive of Hezekiah when he shows his wealth to the Babylonian delegation? (b) What will be the consequences of Hezekiah's error in judgment?

the prophet Isaiah, Jehovah discloses the future to Hezekiah: ***"Days are coming, and all that is in your own house and that your forefathers have stored up down to this day will actually be carried to Babylon. Nothing will be left . . . And some of your own sons that will come forth from you, to whom you will become father, will themselves be taken and actually become court officials in the palace of the king of Babylon."*** *(Isaiah 39:3-7)* Yes, the very nation that Hezekiah sought to impress will eventually plunder Jerusalem's treasures and reduce her citizens to slavery. Hezekiah's showing his treasure to the Babylonians only serves to whet their greedy appetite.

30 Apparently referring to the incident in which Hezekiah showed his treasure to the Babylonians, 2 Chronicles 32:26 states: "Hezekiah humbled himself for the haughtiness of his heart, he and the inhabitants of Jerusalem, and Jehovah's indignation did not come upon them in the days of Hezekiah."

31 Despite his imperfection, Hezekiah was a man of faith. He knew that his God, Jehovah, is a real person who has feelings. When under pressure, Hezekiah prayed fervently to Jehovah, and Jehovah answered him. Jehovah God granted him peace for the rest of his days, and for that, Hezekiah was grateful. *(Isaiah 39:8)* Jehovah should be just as real to us today. When problems arise, may we, like Hezekiah, look to Jehovah for wisdom and the way out, "for he gives generously to all and without reproaching." (James 1:5) If we continue to endure and to exercise faith in Jehovah, we can be sure that he will become "the rewarder of those earnestly seeking him," both now and in the future.—Hebrews 11:6.

---

30. How did Hezekiah show a good attitude?
31. How did things turn out for Hezekiah, and what does this teach us?

CHAPTER THIRTY

"Comfort My People"

JEHOVAH is 'the God who supplies comfort.' One way that he comforts us is through the promises he has had recorded in his Word. (Romans 15:4, 5) For example, when faced with the death of someone dear to you, what could be more comforting than the prospect of that loved one's being resurrected in God's new world? (John 5:28, 29) And what about Jehovah's promise that he will soon end wickedness and transform this earth into a paradise? Is it not comforting to have the prospect of surviving into that coming Paradise and never dying?—Psalm 37:9-11, 29; Revelation 21:3-5.

2 Can we really trust the promises of God? Indeed, we can! The Maker of those promises is completely reliable. He has both the capability and the will to carry out his word. (Isaiah 55:10, 11) This was powerfully demonstrated in connection with Jehovah's statement through the prophet Isaiah that he would restore true worship in Jerusalem. Let us consider that prophecy, as it appears in Isaiah chapter 40, for doing so can strengthen our faith in Jehovah, the Fulfiller of promises.

A Comforting Promise

3 In the eighth century B.C.E., the prophet Isaiah records

---

1. What is one way that Jehovah comforts us?
2. Why can we trust the promises of God?
3, 4. (a) Isaiah records what words of comfort that God's people will need at a later time? (b) Why will the inhabitants of Judah and Jerusalem be taken into exile to Babylon, and how long will their servitude last?

words of comfort that Jehovah's people will need at a later time. Immediately after telling King Hezekiah of the approaching destruction of Jerusalem and the deportation of the Jewish people to Babylon, Isaiah sets forth Jehovah's words that promise restoration: *"'Comfort, comfort my people,' says the God of you men. 'Speak to the heart of Jerusalem and call out to her that her military service has been fulfilled, that her error has been paid off. For from the hand of Jehovah she has received a full amount for all her sins.'"—Isaiah 40:1, 2.*

4 "Comfort," the opening word of Isaiah chapter 40, well describes the message of light and hope contained in the rest of the book of Isaiah. For turning apostate the inhabitants of Judah and Jerusalem will be taken into exile to Babylon in 607 B.C.E. But those Jewish captives will not serve the Babylonians forever. No, their servitude will last only until their error is "paid off." How long will that be? According to Jeremiah the prophet, 70 years. (Jeremiah 25: 11, 12) After that, Jehovah will lead a repentant remnant from Babylon back to Jerusalem. In the 70th year of Judah's desolation, what a comfort it will be for the captives to realize that the time for their promised deliverance is at hand!—Daniel 9:1, 2.

5 The journey from Babylon to Jerusalem is 500 to 1,000 miles, depending upon the route taken. Will the long trip impede the fulfillment of God's promise? By no means! Isaiah writes: *"Listen! Someone is calling out in the wilderness: 'Clear up the way of Jehovah, you people! Make the highway for our God through the desert plain straight. Let every valley be raised up, and every mountain*

5, 6. (a) Why will the long journey from Babylon to Jerusalem not impede the fulfillment of God's promise? (b) The restoration of the Jews to their homeland will have what effect on other nations?

*and hill be made low. And the knobby ground must be-
come level land, and the rugged ground a valley plain. And
the glory of Jehovah will certainly be revealed, and all flesh
must see it together, for the very mouth of Jehovah has
spoken it.'"—Isaiah 40:3-5.*

6 Before embarking on a journey, Eastern rulers would
often send out men to prepare the way by removing big
stones and even building causeways and leveling hills. In
the case of the returning Jews, it will be as if God himself
is in the forefront, clearing away any obstacles. After all,
these are Jehovah's name people, and fulfilling his promise to restore them to their homeland will cause his glory
to be manifest before all the nations. Like it or not, those
nations will be forced to see that Jehovah is the Fulfiller of
his promises.

7 The restoration in the sixth century B.C.E. was not the
only fulfillment of this prophecy. There was also a fulfillment in the first century C.E. John the Baptizer was the
voice of someone "crying out in the wilderness," in fulfillment of Isaiah 40:3. (Luke 3:1-6) Under inspiration, John
applied Isaiah's words to himself. (John 1:19-23) Starting
in 29 C.E., John began preparing the way for Jesus Christ.*
John's advance proclamation aroused people to look for
the promised Messiah so that they, in turn, might listen
to him and follow him. (Luke 1:13-17, 76) Through Jesus,

---

* Isaiah foretells the preparing of the way before *Jehovah.* (Isaiah
40:3) However, the Gospels apply that prophecy to what John the
Baptizer did in preparing the way for *Jesus Christ.* The inspired writers of the Christian Greek Scriptures made such application because
Jesus *represented* his Father and came in his Father's name.—John 5:
43; 8:29.

7, 8. (a) The words of Isaiah 40:3 had what fulfillment in the first
century C.E.? (b) Isaiah's prophecy had what larger fulfillment in
1919?

Jehovah would lead repentant ones into the freedom that only God's Kingdom can provide—liberation from bondage to sin and death. (John 1:29; 8:32) Isaiah's words had a larger fulfillment in the deliverance of the remnant of spiritual Israel from Babylon the Great in 1919 and in their restoration to true worship.

8 What, though, about those who are in line to benefit from the initial fulfillment of the promise—the Jewish captives in Babylon? Can they really trust Jehovah's promise to return them to their beloved homeland? Indeed, they can! With vivid words and illustrations taken from everyday life, Isaiah now gives compelling reasons why they can have complete confidence that Jehovah will prove true to his word.

A God Whose Word Lasts Forever

9 First, the word of the One who promises restoration lasts forever. Isaiah writes: *"Listen! Someone is saying: 'Call out!' And one said: 'What shall I call out?' 'All flesh is green grass, and all their loving-kindness is like the blossom of the field. The green grass has dried up, the blossom has withered, because the very spirit of Jehovah has blown upon it. Surely the people are green grass. The green grass has dried up, the blossom has withered; but as for the word of our God, it will last to time indefinite.' "—Isaiah 40:6-8.*

10 The Israelites well know that grass does not last forever. During the dry season, the sun's intense heat changes it from green to a parched brown. In some respects, man's life is like grass—so temporary in nature. (Psalm 103:15, 16; James 1:10, 11) Isaiah contrasts the transitoriness of man's

---

9, 10. How does Isaiah contrast the transitoriness of man's life with the permanence of God's "word"?

life with the permanence of God's "word," or stated purpose. Yes, "the word of our God" endures forever. When God speaks, nothing can annul his words or prevent them from being fulfilled.—Joshua 23:14.

11 Today we have Jehovah's statement of purpose in written form in the Bible. The Bible has faced bitter opposition over the centuries, and fearless translators and others have risked their lives to preserve it. Yet, their efforts alone do not explain why it has survived. All credit for its survival must go to Jehovah, "the living and enduring God" and the Preserver of his Word. (1 Peter 1:23-25) Think about this: Since Jehovah has preserved his written Word, can we not trust him to fulfill the promises it contains?

A Strong God Who Tenderly Cares for His Sheep

12 Isaiah gives a second reason why the promise of restoration can be trusted. The One who makes the promise is a strong God who tenderly cares for his people. Isaiah continues: *"Make your way up even onto a high mountain, you woman bringing good news for Zion. Raise your voice even with power, you woman bringing good news for Jerusalem. Raise it. Do not be afraid. Say to the cities of Judah: 'Here is your God.' Look! The Sovereign Lord Jehovah himself will come even as a strong one ["even with strength," footnote], and his arm will be ruling for him. Look! His reward is with him, and the wage he pays is before him. Like a shepherd he will shepherd his own drove. With his arm*

---

11. Why can we trust Jehovah to fulfill the promises contained in his written Word?
12, 13. (a) Why can the promise of restoration be trusted? (b) What good news is there for the Jewish exiles, and why can they have confidence?

John the Baptizer was a voice "crying out in the wilderness"

he will collect together the lambs; and in his bosom he will carry them. Those giving suck he will conduct with care."
—Isaiah 40:9-11.

13 In Bible times it was the custom for women to celebrate victories, crying out or singing the good news of battles won or of coming relief. (1 Samuel 18:6, 7; Psalm 68: 11) Isaiah prophetically indicates that there is good news for the Jewish exiles, news that can be fearlessly shouted,

Jehovah, a Loving Shepherd

Isaiah compares Jehovah to a loving shepherd who carries his lambs in his bosom. (Isaiah 40:10, 11) Isaiah evidently bases this warm illustration on the real-life practices of shepherds. A modern-day observer who watched shepherds on the slopes of Mount Hermon in the Middle East reports: "Each shepherd watched his flock closely to see how they fared. When he found a new-born lamb he put it in the folds of his . . . great coat, since it would be too feeble to follow the mother. When his bosom was full, he put lambs on his shoulders, holding them by the feet, or in a bag or basket on the back of a donkey, until the little ones were able to follow the mothers." Is it not comforting to know that we serve a God who has such tender concern for his people?

even from the mountaintops—Jehovah will lead his people back to their beloved Jerusalem! They can have confidence, for Jehovah will come "even with strength." Nothing, therefore, can prevent him from fulfilling his promise.

14 There is, however, a gentle side to this strong God. Isaiah warmly describes how Jehovah will lead his people back to their homeland. Jehovah is like a loving shepherd who collects his lambs together and carries them in his "bosom." The word "bosom" here evidently refers to the upper folds of the garment. This is where shepherds sometimes carry newborn lambs that cannot keep pace with the flock. (2 Samuel 12:3) Such a touching scene from pastoral life no doubt reassures Jehovah's exiled people of his loving concern for them. Surely such a strong yet tender God can be trusted to fulfill what he has promised them!

15 Isaiah's words are filled with prophetic meaning for our day. In 1914, Jehovah came "even with strength" and established his Kingdom in the heavens. The 'arm that is ruling for him' is his Son, Jesus Christ, whom Jehovah has installed upon his heavenly throne. In 1919, Jehovah delivered his anointed servants on earth from bondage to Babylon the Great and set about completely restoring the pure worship of the living and true God. This is good news that must be fearlessly proclaimed, as if by shouting from the mountaintops so that the proclamation carries far and wide. Let us, then, lift up our voices and boldly let others know that Jehovah God has restored his pure worship on this earth!

---

14. (a) How does Isaiah illustrate the tender way in which Jehovah will lead his people? (b) What example illustrates how shepherds tenderly care for their sheep? (See box on page 405.)
15. (a) When did Jehovah come "even with strength," and who is the 'arm that is ruling for him'? (b) What good news must be fearlessly proclaimed?

16 The words of Isaiah 40:10, 11 have further practical value for us today. It is comforting to note the tender manner in which Jehovah leads his people. Just as a shepherd understands the needs of individual sheep—including the little lambs that cannot keep up with the rest—Jehovah understands the limitations of each one of his faithful servants. In addition, Jehovah, as a tender Shepherd, sets a pattern for Christian shepherds. Elders must treat the flock with tenderness, imitating the loving concern shown by Jehovah himself. They must be ever mindful of the way that Jehovah feels about each member of the flock, "which he purchased with the blood of his own Son."—Acts 20:28.

All-Powerful, All-Wise

17 The Jewish exiles can have confidence in the promise of restoration because God is all-powerful and all-wise. Says Isaiah: *"Who has measured the waters in the mere hollow of his hand, and taken the proportions of the heavens themselves with a mere span and included in a measure the dust of the earth, or weighed with an indicator the mountains, and the hills in the scales? Who has taken the proportions of the spirit of Jehovah, and who as his man of counsel can make him know anything? With whom did he consult together that one might make him understand, or who teaches him in the path of justice, or teaches him knowledge, or makes him know the very way of real understanding?"*—Isaiah 40:12-14.

18 These are awe-inspiring questions for the Jewish exiles to ponder. Can mere humans turn back the tide of the

---

16. In what manner does Jehovah lead his people today, and what pattern does this set?
17, 18. (a) Why can the Jewish exiles have confidence in the promise of restoration? (b) What awe-inspiring questions does Isaiah raise?

mighty seas? Of course not! Yet, to Jehovah, the seas that cover the earth are like a drop of water in the palm of his hand.* Can puny men measure the vast, starry heavens or weigh earth's mountains and hills? No. Yet, Jehovah measures the heavens as easily as a man might measure an object with a span—the distance between the end of the thumb and the end of the little finger when the hand is spread out. God can, in effect, weigh mountains and hills in a pair of scales. Can even the wisest humans advise God what to do under present circumstances or tell him what to do in the future? Certainly not!

19 What about the mighty nations of the earth—can they resist God as he fulfills his word of promise? Isaiah answers by describing the nations as follows: *"Look! The nations are as a drop from a bucket; and as the film of dust on the scales they have been accounted. Look! He lifts the islands themselves as mere fine dust. Even Lebanon is not sufficient for keeping a fire burning, and its wild animals are not sufficient for a burnt offering. All the nations are as something nonexistent in front of him; as nothing and an unreality they have been accounted to him."—Isaiah 40:15-17.*

20 To Jehovah, entire nations are as a drop of water falling from a bucket. They are no more than the fine dust that accumulates on a scale, without effect.# Suppose that

---

* It has been calculated that "the mass of the oceans is approximately 1.35 quintillion (1.35×10^{18}) metric tons, or about 1/4400 of the total mass of the Earth."—*Encarta 97 Encyclopedia.*

The Expositor's Bible Commentary notes: "Near Eastern marketplace commerce would take no account of the minute water drop in the measuring bucket or a little dust on the scales when meat or fruit was weighed."

19, 20. To emphasize the greatness of Jehovah, Isaiah uses what graphic word pictures?

someone were to construct a huge altar and use as firewood for the altar all the trees that covered the mountains of Lebanon. Then suppose that he were to offer as sacrifices all the animals that roamed on those mountains. Even such an offering would not be worthy of Jehovah. As if the imagery used thus far were not sufficient, Isaiah resorts to an even stronger statement—*all* the nations are as "less than nothing" in Jehovah's eyes.—Isaiah 40:17, *New Revised Standard Version.*

21 To emphasize further that Jehovah is beyond compare, Isaiah proceeds to show the folly of those who make idols out of gold, silver, or wood. How foolish to think that any such idol could be a fitting representation of the *"One who is dwelling above the circle of the earth"* and who holds sway over its inhabitants!—*Read Isaiah 40:18-24.*

22 All these vivid descriptions lead us to one conclusion —nothing can prevent the all-powerful, all-wise, and incomparable Jehovah from fulfilling his promise. How Isaiah's words must have comforted and strengthened the Jewish exiles in Babylon who longed to return to their homeland! Today we too can have confidence that Jehovah's promises for our future will become a reality.

"Who Has Created These Things?"

23 There is yet another reason why the Jewish exiles can take heart. The One who promises deliverance is the Creator of all things and the Source of all dynamic energy. To stress his astounding capacity, Jehovah calls attention to

---

21, 22. (a) How does Isaiah emphasize that Jehovah is incomparable? (b) Isaiah's vivid descriptions lead us to what conclusion? (c) The prophet Isaiah records what scientifically sound statement? (See box on page 412.)
23. For what reason can the Jewish exiles take heart, and what does Jehovah now stress about himself?

his ability manifest in creation: *" 'To whom can you people like me so that I should be made his equal?' says the Holy One. 'Raise your eyes high up and see. Who has created these things? It is the One who is bringing forth the army of them even by number, all of whom he calls even by name. Due to the abundance of dynamic energy, he also being vigorous in power, not one of them is missing.' "*—Isaiah 40:25, 26.

24 The Holy One of Israel is speaking for himself. To show that he is without equal, Jehovah directs attention to the stars of the heavens. Like a military commander able to marshal his troops, Jehovah is in command of the stars. If he were to muster them, 'not one of them would be missing.' Though the number of the stars is great, he calls each one by name, either an individual name or a namelike designation. Like obedient soldiers, they keep their place and observe proper order, for their Leader has an abundance of "dynamic energy" and is "vigorous in power." Therefore, the Jewish exiles have reason for confidence. The Creator, who commands the stars, has the power to support his servants.

25 Who of us can resist the divine invitation recorded at Isaiah 40:26: "Raise your eyes high up and see"? The discoveries of modern-day astronomers have shown that the starry heavens are even more awe-inspiring than they appeared to be in Isaiah's day. Astronomers who peer into the heavens with their powerful telescopes estimate that the observable universe contains as many as 125 billion galaxies. Why, just one of these—the Milky Way gal-

---

24. Speaking for himself, how does Jehovah show that he is without equal?

25. How may we respond to the divine invitation recorded at Isaiah 40:26, and with what effect?

axy—contains, according to some estimates, over 100 billion stars! Such knowledge should awaken in our hearts reverence for our Creator and complete trust in his word of promise.

26 Knowing that the years in captivity will dampen the spirits of the Jewish exiles, Jehovah inspires Isaiah to record in advance these words of reassurance: *"For what reason do you say, O Jacob, and do you speak out, O Israel, 'My way has been concealed from Jehovah, and justice to me eludes my God himself'? Have you not come to know or have you not heard? Jehovah, the Creator of the extremities of the earth, is a God to time indefinite. He does*

26, 27. How are the feelings of the exiles in Babylon described, and what things should they know?

What Is the Shape of the Earth?

In ancient times humans in general believed that the earth was flat. As early as the sixth century B.C.E., however, Greek philosopher Pythagoras theorized that the earth must be a sphere. Even so, two centuries before Pythagoras formulated his theory, the prophet Isaiah stated with extraordinary clarity and certainty: "There is One who is dwelling above the *circle* of the earth." (Isaiah 40:22) The Hebrew word *chugh* here translated "circle" may be rendered "sphere." Interestingly, only a spherical object appears as a circle from every angle.* Far ahead of his time, then, the prophet Isaiah recorded a statement that is scientifically sound and free from ancient myths.

* Technically speaking, the earth is an oblate spheroid. It is slightly flattened at the poles.

not tire out or grow weary. There is no searching out of his understanding."—Isaiah 40:27, 28.

27 Isaiah records Jehovah's words describing the feelings of the exiles in Babylon, hundreds of miles from their homeland. Some think that their "way"—the hard course of their life—is unseen or unknown by their God. They think that Jehovah is indifferent to the injustices they suffer. They are reminded of things that they should know, if not from personal experience, then at least from information that has been handed down. Jehovah is able and willing to deliver his people. He is the eternal God and the Creator of the *entire* earth. Hence, he still possesses the power he displayed in creation, and not even mighty Babylon is beyond his reach. Such a God cannot grow tired and fail his people. They ought not to expect to be able fully to grasp Jehovah's doings, for his understanding—or insight, discernment, and perception—is beyond their comprehension.

28 Through Isaiah, Jehovah continues with encouragement for the despondent exiles: *"He is giving to the tired one power; and to the one without dynamic energy he makes full might abound. Boys will both tire out and grow weary, and young men themselves will without fail stumble, but those who are hoping in Jehovah will regain power. They will mount up with wings like eagles. They will run and not grow weary; they will walk and not tire out."—Isaiah 40:29-31.*

29 When speaking of the need to give to the tired one

---

* At Isaiah 40:28, the expression "time indefinite" means "forever," for Jehovah is "the King of eternity."—1 Timothy 1:17.

28, 29. (a) How does Jehovah remind his people that he will come to the aid of weary ones? (b) What illustration is used to show how Jehovah empowers his servants?

power, Jehovah may have in mind the arduous journey that the exiles will have to make in order to return home. Jehovah reminds his people that it is characteristic of him to come to the aid of weary ones who look to him for support. Even the most vibrant of humans—"boys" and "young men"—may be worn down by fatigue and stumble from exhaustion. Yet, Jehovah promises to give power —unwearied power to run and to walk—to those who are trusting in him. The seemingly effortless flight of the eagle, a powerful bird that can soar for hours at a time, is used to illustrate how Jehovah empowers his servants.* With prospects of such divine support, the Jewish exiles have no cause for despair.

30 These closing verses of Isaiah chapter 40 contain words of comfort for true Christians living in the last days of this wicked system. With so many pressures and problems that tend to dishearten, it is reassuring to know that the hardships we endure and the injustices we suffer do not go unnoticed by our God. We can be sure that the Creator of all things, the One whose "understanding is beyond recounting," will correct all injustices in his own time and way. (Psalm 147:5, 6) Meanwhile, we need not endure in our own strength. Jehovah, whose resources are inexhaustible, can impart power—even "power beyond what is normal"—to his servants in times of trial.—2 Corinthians 4:7.

31 Think of those Jewish captives in Babylon in the sixth century B.C.E. Hundreds of miles away, their beloved Jerusalem lay desolate, its temple in ruins. For them, Isaiah's prophecy contained a comforting promise of light and hope—Jehovah would restore them to their homeland! In 537 B.C.E., Jehovah led his people home, proving that he is the Fulfiller of promises. We too can have absolute confidence in Jehovah. His Kingdom promises, which are so beautifully expressed in Isaiah's prophecy, will become a reality. That is indeed good news—a message of light for all mankind!

---

* The eagle stays aloft with a minimum expenditure of energy. It does so by making skillful use of thermals, or columns of rising warm air.

---

30. How can true Christians today draw comfort from the closing verses of Isaiah chapter 40?
31. What promise of light did Isaiah's prophecy contain for the Jewish captives in Babylon, and in what can we have absolute confidence?

Would you welcome more information?
Write Watch Tower at appropriate address below.

ALASKA 99507: 2552 East 48th Ave., Anchorage. **ANGOLA:** Caixa Postal 6877, Luanda. **ARGENTINA:** Casilla de Correo 83 (Suc. 27B), 1427 Buenos Aires. **AUSTRALIA:** Box 280, Ingleburn, NSW 2565. **AUSTRIA (also Bulgaria, Macedonia, Yugoslavia):** Postfach 67, A-1134 Vienna. **BAHAMAS:** Box N-1247, Nassau, N.P. **BARBADOS:** Fontabelle Rd., Bridgetown. **BELGIUM:** rue d'Argile-Potaardestraat 60, B-1950 Kraainem. **BELIZE:** Box 257, Belize City. **BENIN, REP. OF:** 06 B.P. 1131, Akpakpa pk3, Cotonou. **BOLIVIA:** Casilla 6397, Santa Cruz. **BRAZIL:** Caixa Postal 92, 18270-970 Tatuí, SP. **BRITAIN:** The Ridgeway, London NW7 1RN. **CAMEROON:** B.P. 889, Douala. **CANADA:** Box 4100, Halton Hills (Georgetown), Ontario L7G 4Y4. **CENTRAL AFRICAN REPUBLIC:** B.P. 662, Bangui. **CHILE:** Casilla 267, Puente Alto. **COLOMBIA:** Apartado Aéreo 85058, Santa Fe de Bogotá 8, D.C. **CONGO, DEMOCRATIC REPUBLIC OF:** B.P. 634, Limete, Kinshasa. **COSTA RICA:** Apartado 187-3006, Barreal, Heredia. **CÔTE D'IVOIRE (IVORY COAST), WEST AFRICA:** 06 B P 393, Abidjan 06. **CROATIA:** p.p. 6058, HR-10090 Zagreb. **CURAÇAO, NETHERLANDS ANTILLES:** P.O. Box 4708, Willemstad. **CYPRUS:** P.O. Box 11033, CY-2550 Dali. **CZECH REPUBLIC:** P.O. Box 90, 198 21 Prague 9. **DENMARK:** Stenhusvej 28, DK-4300 Holbæk. **DOMINICAN REPUBLIC:** Apartado 1742, Santo Domingo. **ECUADOR:** Casilla 09-01-1334, Guayaquil. **EL SALVADOR:** Apartado Postal 401, San Salvador. **ESTONIA:** Postbox 1075, 10302 Tallinn. **ETHIOPIA:** P.O. Box 5522, Addis Ababa. **FIJI:** Box 23, Suva. **FINLAND (also Latvia, Lithuania):** Postbox 68, FIN-01301 Vantaa 30. **FRANCE:** B.P. 625, F-27406 Louviers cedex. **GERMANY:** Niederselters, Am Steinfels, D-65618 Selters. **GHANA:** P. O. Box GP 760, Accra. **GREECE:** 77 Kifisias Ave., GR-151 24, Marousi, Athens. **GUADELOUPE:** Monmain, 97180 Sainte Anne. **GUATEMALA:** Apartado postal 711, 01901 Guatemala. **GUYANA:** 50 Brickdam, Georgetown 16. **GUYANE FRANÇAISE (FRENCH GUIANA):** CD 2, Route du Tigre, 97300 Cayenne. **HAITI:** Post Box 185, Port-au-Prince. **HAWAII 96819:** 2055 Kam IV Rd., Honolulu. **HONDURAS:** Apartado 147, Tegucigalpa. **HONG KONG:** 4 Kent Road, Kowloon Tong. **HUNGARY:** Cserkút u. 13, H-1162 Budapest. **INDIA:** Post Bag 10, Lonavla, Pune Dis., Mah. 410 401. **IRELAND:** Newcastle, Greystones, Co. Wicklow. **ITALY (also Albania, Israel):** Via della Bufalotta 1281, I-00138 Rome RM. **JAMAICA:** P. O. Box 103, Old Harbour, St. Catherine. **JAPAN:** 1271 Nakashinden, Ebina City, Kanagawa Pref., 243-0496. **KENYA:** Box 47788, Nairobi. **KOREA, REPUBLIC OF:** Box 33 Pyungtaek P. O., Kyunggido, 450-600. **LIBERIA:** P. O. Box 10-0380, 1000 Monrovia 10. **LUXEMBOURG:** B. P. 2186, L-1021 Luxembourg, G. D. **MADAGASCAR:** B.P. 116, 105 Ivato. **MALAWI:** Box 30749, Lilongwe 3. **MALAYSIA:** Peti Surat No. 580, 75760 Melaka. **MARTINIQUE:** 20, rue de la Cour Campêche, 97200 Fort de France. **MAURITIUS:** Rue Baissac, Petit Verger, Pointe aux Sables. **MEXICO:** Apartado Postal 896, 06002 Mexico, D. F. **MOZAMBIQUE:** Caixa Postal 2600, Maputo. **MYANMAR:** P.O. Box 62, Yangon. **NETHERLANDS:** Noordbargerstraat 77, NL-7812 AA Emmen. **NEW CALEDONIA:** BP 1741, 98810 Mont Dore. **NEW ZEALAND:** P.O. Box 142, Manurewa. **NICARAGUA:** Apartado 3587, Managua. **NIGERIA:** P.M.B. 1090, Benin City, Edo State. **NORWAY:** Gaupeveien 24, N-1914 Ytre Enebakk. **PANAMA:** Apartado 6-2671, Zona 6A, El Dorado. **PAPUA NEW GUINEA:** Box 636, Boroko, NCD 111. **PARAGUAY:** Casilla de Correo 482, 1209 Asunción. **PERU:** Apartado 18-1055, Lima 18. **PHILIPPINES, REP. OF:** P. O. Box 2044, 1060 Manila. **POLAND:** Skr. Poczt. 13, PL-05-830 Nadarzyn. **PORTUGAL:** Apartado 91, P-2766-955 Estoril. **PUERTO RICO 00970:** P.O. Box 3980, Guaynabo. **ROMANIA (also Moldova):** Căsuţa Poştală nr. 132, O.P. 39 Bucureşti. **RUSSIA (also Georgia, Kazakhstan):** Srednyaya 6, Solnechnoye, 189649 St. Petersburg. **SLOVAKIA:** P.O. Box 17, 810 00 Bratislava 1. **SLOVENIA:** Poljanska cesta 77 A, p.p. 2019, SI-1001 Ljubljana. **SOLOMON ISLANDS:** P.O. Box 166, Honiara. **SOUTH AFRICA:** Private Bag X2067, Krugersdorp, 1740. **SPAIN:** Apartado postal 132, 28850 Torrejón de Ardoz (Madrid). **SRI LANKA, REP. OF:** 711 Station Road, Wattala 11300. **SURINAME:** P.O. Box 2914, Paramaribo. **SWEDEN:** Box 5, SE-732 21 Arboga. **SWITZERLAND:** P.O. Box 225, CH-3602 Thun. **TAHITI:** B.P. 7715, 98719 Taravao. **TAIWAN:** No. 3-12, 10 Lin, Shetze, Hsinwu, Taoyuan, 327. **THAILAND:** 69/1 Soi Phasuk, Sukhumwit Rd., Soi 2, Bangkok 10110. **TOGO:** B.P. 4460, Lome. **TRINIDAD AND TOBAGO, REP. OF:** Lower Rapsey Street & Laxmi Lane, Curepe. **UKRAINE:** P.O. Box 246, 79000 Lviv. **UNITED STATES OF AMERICA:** 25 Columbia Heights, Brooklyn, NY 11201-2483. **URUGUAY:** Francisco Bauzá 3372, Casilla de Correo 16006, 11600 Montevideo. **VENEZUELA:** Apartado 20.364, Caracas, DF 1020A. **ZAMBIA:** Box 33459, Lusaka 10101. **ZIMBABWE:** P. Bag A-6113, Avondale.

Contact your local office for addresses in the following countries: Antigua, Guam, Iceland, Pakistan, Samoa, Senegal, Sierra Leone.